BERKELEY: THE CENTRAL ARGUMENTS

Berkeley: The Central Arguments

A. C. Grayling

Duckworth

First published in 1986 by
Gerald Duckworth & Co. Ltd.
The Old Piano Factory
43 Gloucester Crescent, London NW1

© 1986 by A.C. Grayling

All rights reserved. No part of this publication may be reproduced, stored in a retrieval system, or transmitted, in any form or by any means, electronic, mechanical, photocopying, recording or otherwise, without the prior permission of the publishers.

ISBN 0 7156 2065 7

British Library Cataloguing in Publication Data

Grayling, A.C.
  Berkeley : the central arguments
  1. Berkeley, George
  I. Title
  192   B1348

ISBN 0-7156-2065-7

Photoset in North Wales by
Derek Doyle & Associates, Mold, Clywd.
Printed in Great Britain by
Ebenezer Baylis & Son Limited, Worcester

Contents

Preface	vii
Note on references	xi

Chapter One: Context, Aims, Interpretation	1
1. Context	2
2. Aims	12
3. Interpretation: method, meaning and empiricism	22
Chapter Two: *Esse est Percipi*: Against Matter	47
1. The New Principle	47
2. Ideas and things	50
3. Existence	81
4. Perceivability	95
5. Continuity	117
6. Berkeley's realism	129
7. Matter	138
Chapter Three: *Esse est Percipere*: The Nature of Substance	154
1. Finite spirit	158
2. The mind-idea relation	168
3. Mind and time	174
4. Infinite spirit	183
Chapter Four: Concluding Comments: Metaphysics and Realism	204
Bibliography	211
Index	215

fratri et amico
John Grayling

Preface

My aim in this book is to treat Berkeley's central arguments as having live philosophical interest and to show that some of them are less indefensible than has generally been supposed. This involves not just evaluation of Berkeley's views, but correct interpretation of the way he puts them; on both counts certain revisions to the current understanding of his thought are offered.

Berkeley's central arguments are to be found in the first seven sections of his *A Treatise Concerning the Principles of Human Knowledge* (1710). They are presented there in condensed and summary form, and their fuller demonstration, together with some of their consequences, are set out in the rest of the *Principles* and in the *Three Dialogues Between Hylas and Philonous* (1713). Aspects of them are discussed in the earlier *Essay Towards a New Theory of Vision* (1709) and are further illuminated by some of what Berkeley has to say in his later works. For our understanding of these arguments Berkeley's private philosophical notebooks, given the title *Philosophical Commentaries* by Luce in his *editio diplomatica* of 1944, are of extraordinary interest and value – provided, it has immediately to be said, that they are treated with a judicious caution. In them Berkeley carried out the preparatory work for his first two major publications, the *New Theory of Vision* and the *Principles*. In exploring Berkeley's arguments I range widely among all his texts, but the *Principles*, *Three Dialogues* and notebooks receive, because they invite, most attention.

In focussing upon the central arguments I have had to leave aside detailed discussion of Berkeley's theory of vision, his philosophies of mathematics and science, and his views on morals, except where they bear directly on the central concerns. We do not yet have a thorough study of Berkeley's philosophies of mathematics and science, which is regrettable because they are important and interesting; one hopes that this want will soon be supplied.

The aim of this study, set out in the opening paragraph above, requires comment. First, to treat Berkeley's arguments as having live philosophical interest is not to claim that they can be detached from their historical context and investigated without reference to it. Nor is it, still less, to seek to think in a general way about Berkeleyan themes in accordance with the spirit rather than the letter of Berkeley's work. My interest here is *Berkeley*, and Berkeley's *arguments*, and accordingly I shall throughout pay close attention to his texts, which in turn means that the texts have to be located in their historical context if they are properly to be understood. In this I agree with Ayers, who justly deprecates the treatment of past philosophers in a way so far unhistorical as to 'constitute an assumption that the first task of the commentator is to isolate from a philosopher's work what is consonant with currently respectable themes, as if the only way of bringing the dead to life is to patch them up, by a kind of cosmetic surgery, as fit participants in some modern debate' (Ayers 1 p38). At the same time, however, Berkeley and the other major figures of our philosophical tradition *are* participants in the modern debate; they largely shaped it, and in many ways their problems remain ours – a point too familiar, indeed, to require stressing. It is accordingly right that in exploring and evaluating their views we should bring to bear what has since been learned. Provided that doing so does not come to a mere reading-in of what is 'currently respectable', there is everything to be gained in the direction of understanding the views of past thinkers by putting to use the philosophical equipment we now possess; this, with the above strictures in mind, I do here.

Secondly, to aim to show that Berkeley's views are, in some important respects, more defensible than has in general been allowed is not to signal an adherence to Berkeleyanism. The theory which admits of that label is extraordinarily tightly-knit and consistent, which is in fact its greatest weakness, for it rests on metaphysical commitments without which its internal consistency and plausibility cannot be sustained. But these metaphysical commitments are themselves questionable, and indeed I shall show that Berkeley does not manage to substantiate one major aspect of them; from which it follows that *Berkeleyanism* – which is to say, Berkeley's version of immaterialism – does not survive. But neither does this mean that a version of phenomenalism is left over as a result, for I shall show that subtracting the relevant part of the metaphysical basis of Berkeley's views from the rest of them does not issue in what could with propriety count as a thesis of that kind. There are however two things to note about these comments: one is that they do not prejudge the issue of whether or not some form of immaterialism is made more plausible by Berkeley's arguments, despite the failure of his own distinctive version of it; and the other is that they are not intended to derogate from the substantial achievements Berkeley made in the course of working out his views, from which, as I hope it will emerge, there are lessons to be learned of relevance to contemporary concerns in philosophy.

The discussion proceeds as follows. In Chapter One I address three preliminaries. These are: Berkeley's aims, the philosophical background to them, and his methods. This last is a crucial issue because a correct understanding of Berkeley's assumptions and argumentative technique illuminates the content of much of his case, and indeed makes it more plausible. The philosophical background is sketched very briefly; there is not the space to do otherwise, and I am sharply aware that summaries, especially quick summaries, of complex philosophical views are both dissatisfying and potentially distorting, so that Section 1 of Chapter One below represents an unavoidably inadequate compromise between economy and completeness. I have elected to emphasise points in the views of Descartes, Malebranche, and Bayle, and in those also of Locke and the corpuscularians, which are directly relevant to an understanding of Berkeley. These points should, in view of their brevity, perhaps be treated as reminders rather than expositions of the views in question.

In Chapter Two I discuss the *esse est percipi* thesis and the correlative attack on the notion of material substance. Berkeley's argument here is seamless, with intimate relations of dependence among its parts, and my articulation into numbered sections of this as with other chapters is a matter of expository convenience only.

The arguments of Chapter Two in turn depend on those of Chapter Three, which concerns the *esse est percipere* thesis. This is Berkeley's view of the nature of spirit or mind, which is to say, *substance*. It is here that the crucial metaphysical commitments underpinning the arguments of Chapter Two are addressed, and on which, therefore, the overall success of Berkeley's version of immaterialism depends.

Finally, in Chapter Four, I discuss some of the consequences for metaphysics of the respects in which Berkeley's views succeed.

My approach throughout is to seek to understand Berkeley's central arguments correctly, and to ask whether, on the basis of the austere constraints which he places on the concepts of sense and possibility – and which I agree are the right ones – those arguments are plausible. A significant part of this enterprise consists in placing the correct interpretation on what Berkeley *says*, a matter on which I often enough find myself unconvinced by the commentators; here the textual evidence is central, and accordingly full use is made of quotation to substantiate interpretational claims. In discussing the commentators I have chosen to focus a good deal of attention on the best known and most widely read of them, namely Luce, Warnock, Tipton, Bennett and Pitcher (see bibliography). It is with no disrespect to the last two of these that I find myself disagreeing frequently with their reading of and responses to Berkeley; if anything, this is a reflection of the philosophical interest their discussions of Berkeley contain.

A certain familiarity with Berkeley's principal texts – especially the *Principles* and *Three Dialogues* – is naturally assumed throughout, because the aim here is less expository than it is interpretative and evaluatory; but with the needs of students in mind also, I have not assumed more than that.

The traditional liberties of the Preface tempt me to indulge a remark on the fact that, in the interests of several kinds of economy, I have entirely dispensed with footnotes or notes of any kind in what follows. It turns out that doing so is surprisingly hard work, since the asides, clarifications, qualifications and connection-drawings for which notes standardly provide a home have either to be foregone or worked into the main body of the discussion. It has the additional drawback of littering the text with bracketed references, which sometimes have to occur in the middle of sentences. For this last inconvenience, in particular, apologies are due.

I am grateful to the Librarian at Magdalen College, Oxford, for giving me permission to consult the College's copy of Taylor's translation of Malebranche in its edition of 1700; and to Sue Ward for her remarkable achievements with the typescript under so many pressures. Among the colleagues and students to whom thanks are owed, a special acknowledgement is due to those of my students at New College, Oxford, and King's College, London, whose open minds and fresh responses made discussion of Berkeley, just as I was writing about him, a highly relevant and profitable pleasure.

Berkeley was born on 12 March 1685. This book was written in the three hundredth anniversary year of his birth, and I offer it as one among the observances of that anniversary, to mark the enduring interest and importance of his views, the subtlety and ingeniousness of their content, and the excellence of their expression, all of which merit celebration.

London
August 1985   A.C.G.

References

All references to Berkeley are to the Luce-Jessop edition (9 vols, 1948-57) except for those to the *Philosophical Commentaries*, for which I have used Luce's *editio diplomatica* of 1944, with Luce's suggested improvements in *Hermathena* 1971. See below for the abbreviations I employ. Apart from the Three Dialogues Berkeley's work is written in numbered sections, and references are accordingly effected by citation of the relevant section number in the standard way. Thus section 34 of the Principles is given as 'P34'. In citing the *Three Dialogues* I give the page numbers of Volume II of the Luce-Jessop edition, but as a further aid I state which dialogue is in question, thus: 2D215 refers to the second dialogue, p215. In citations I abbreviate the titles of Berkeley's works as follows:

P	*The Principles of Human Knowledge*
D	*Three Dialogues Between Hylas and Philonous*
C	*Philosophical Commentaries*
V	*An Essay Towards a New Theory of Vision*
VV	*The New Theory of Vision ... Vindicated*
DeM	*De Motu*
A	*Alciphron*
S	*Siris*

When I refer to the works as a whole, except in the case of the last two, I do so simply by using the letters P, D, C, and so on.

The best one-volume edition of Berkeley is the Everyman volume edited by Ayers. It gives the Luce-Jessop pagination of D and also contains C in full.

References to Locke, Hume, and Kant are made in the standard way. Thus Locke's *Essay* is cited by Book, Chapter, and Section number, e.g. IV. iv. 3; Hume's *Treatise* by Book, Part, and Section number, e.g. I. II. VI; and Kant's first *Critique* by the AB numbers, e.g. A94/B126. All other references are effected by citation, in brackets in the text, of author's name and page number; there is a bibliography at the end to which these abbreviated references themselves refer. In the case of authors who have more than one work cited, each work is chronologically numbered; thus (Luce 3 p10) refers to the third work listed under Luce in the bibliography, p10.

CHAPTER ONE
Context, Aims, Interpretation

In this chapter I deal with three preliminaries. They concern Berkeley's aims, the philosophical background to them, and the method Berkeley employed in trying to realise them. These are important matters, discussion of which provides the framework required for a proper understanding and assessment of Berkeley's arguments.

Berkeley had two related aims, which were to defend 'common sense' by refuting scepticism and to defend religion by refuting atheism. These objectives had equal importance for him, but in his major works the first takes priority. I discuss the reasons for this, and the nature of the aims themselves, in the second section of this chapter. First, however, in order to understand why Berkeley thought it important to refute scepticism and atheism, it is necessary to look at the philosophical background to his work, with the intention of identifying the positive and negative influences which set Berkeley's problem for him and shaped the nature of his response. Two connected sources of influence are chiefly at issue: one is the Cartesian debate and in particular the contributions to it of Malebranche and Bayle; the other is the rise of natural science in the form of the corpuscularian theory of Newton, Boyle and others, to which Locke gave philosophical expression in his *Essay*. I sketch these influences *briefly* in the first section below, reserving more particular discussion of certain topics to the appropriate places in the sequel.

In the third and final section of this chapter I look at Berkeley's philosophical method. Failure to grasp the character of his method has resulted in misunderstandings, often serious misunderstandings, on the part of Berkeley's commentators, and in this section I endeavour to show why and to supply the appropriate corrective. A good deal of what Berkeley was concerned to argue becomes both clearer and more plausible once the nature of his approach to philosophical problems is understood, and I shall often have occasion in later chapters to refer to the discussion here.

I. Context, Aims, Interpretation

1. Context

Until quite recently Berkeley has been interpreted as reacting chiefly if not wholly to Locke, and in consequence his work is treated in many studies as a disagreeing commentary on Locke's *Essay*. A prime example of this way with Berkeley is afforded by Bennett, and to a lesser extent Tipton (see bibliography). Although it is true that Locke had a large influence on Berkeley, it distorts one's view of Berkeley's work to neglect what was otherwise happening in philosophy at that period. There is, first, the pervasive influence of Descartes, whose views in a number of respects constitute the terms of reference for seventeenth-century preoccupations, a fact evidenced by the effect of his thought on philosophers as opposed in intellectual temperament as Locke and Spinoza. Among the main outcomes of the debate initiated by Descartes were two of particular significance to an understanding of Berkeley. One was the work of Malebranche, widely discussed and energetically championed or criticised in its own time, but since then relegated to the status of an historical curiosity. The other was the revival of interest in epistemological scepticism generated by the *Meditations* and reported, with some relish, in Bayle's *Dictionary*. Largely as a result of the proper editing and study of C it is now established that Malebranche and Bayle had a formative impact on Berkeley's thought, and accordingly their influence has to be taken into account along with that of Locke. In brief, the relevant aspects of what Descartes, Malebranche and Bayle had to say are as follows.

Descartes held that there are two kinds of created substance, apart from the uncreated substance, God, and these are thinking substance or mind, and extended substance or matter. The physical world is a complex mechanism, describable wholly in terms of mechanical principles. The *essence* of matter is extension, in which inhere the intrinsic properties of number, motion or rest, and figure. By contrast, the properties of material things which later came to be called 'secondary qualities', namely colour, odour, taste, smell and sound, are not 'in' things themselves but exist only in relation to perceivers. God ultimately sustains the world and keeps in being those necessary laws which govern all that happens in it. Moreover, Descartes held, God is wholly good, and therefore is not a deceiver, which provides a guarantee of truth for whatever we can clearly and distinctly perceive to be true; from which it follows that we can attain to certainty.

1. Context

Descartes' proof of the existence of matter turns on this last thesis. He argued first that our sensory experience comes to us from an independent external source, which is demonstrated by the fact that we are not free to choose what sensations we have. These give rise in us to clear and distinct ideas of external, spatial, material things which affect us in various ways and cause us to have experiences of colour and the other secondary qualities. Since we have a clear idea of these things as independent both of God and ourselves, and since God is no deceiver, it follows that extended substance, that is matter or body, exists (*Principles of Philosophy* II.i).

A problem which, familiarly, infects this view, and which Descartes was unable to solve, concerns the question of how mind and matter interact. The difficulty this posed constitutes the chief point of departure for Malebranche, whose attempts to find a way round it issued in the philosophical theory which had so decisive an influence on Berkeley.

The first volume of Malebranche's *De La Recherche de la Vérité* was published in 1674. The entire work appeared in English translations in 1694-5, one by Thomas Taylor of Magdalen College, Oxford, the other by Richard Salt. A second edition of Taylor's translation, which Luce identifies as the version used by Berkeley, followed in 1700 (cf Luce 1 p4). The Sixth Book of the *Search*, as it came to be known to its English-language readers, is a study of method, and it made a particular impression on Berkeley, a fact evidenced by his use of it – to the extent of his directly echoing its phraseology – in the early Latin essays *Arithmetica* and *Miscellanea Mathematica* of 1707 (cf. Luce 1 pp15ff).

Malebranche's philosophical views constitute a departure from the then prevailing Cartesian outlook in two important respects. One of these is Malebranche's denial that the existence of the external world can be proved, at any rate conclusively, on the evidence either of sense or of reason; the other is his claim that certain knowledge of any kind can only be attained by unmediated acquaintance with ideas in God's mind. In support of the first claim Malebranche argued from versions of the familiar sceptical arguments concerning perceptual relativities, dreams and hallucinations, and from the feebleness of human reason, to the conclusion that our belief in the existence of the material world must rest on belief either in the revelation of Genesis I which states that God created heaven and earth (cf.Popkin 2 p3), or perhaps in the credal commitments associated with the doctrine of transubstantiation (as Luce follows Hamilton in suggesting, Luce 1 p61). So far as the testimony of the senses and the deliverances of human reason go, Malebranche argued, we have only a balance of probability in favour of there being an external world, together with a 'natural propension' to think so. In support of the second claim Malebranche again appealed to the finitude and impotence of the human mind, which he took to show the inadequacy of the Cartesian doctrine that what is clearly and distinctly perceived is true because God, being good, is not a deceiver. His reasons were that the objects of knowledge, which in his view are the eternal and immutable essences of things, cannot be part of a finite mind, and anyway finite minds, being powerless, cannot on their own come to have clear and distinct ideas of things, for such power is to be found in the divinity alone. Therefore, he argued, the Cartesian account of knowing must lead to scepticism, for it has it that ideas are modifications of the mind, and eternal essences cannot be modifications of *finite* minds; and moreover since finite minds can never do more than *think* that their ideas conform to things, they therefore cannot be *certain* that such a correspondence holds. Hence when finite minds have clear and distinct ideas it must be because they are in direct contact with the only power capable of apprehending a conformity between ideas and things, namely the mind of God. This is what he meant by his dictum 'we see all things in God'.

In Malebranche's view, there are three substances: God, who contains all power and all essences and is the cause of everything; finite minds, which through God can come to have knowledge of things; and material substance, which is inert, unknown and unknowable with respect to finite minds, and not required for explanation of natural phenomena, but whose existence is revealed to finite minds through God's will. This catalogue of what there is in the universe is not in itself an unfamiliar one; what is different in it is the ordering of the relations between its elements and the peculiarly redundant character it ascribes to material substance. Malebranche's reason for this ordering was, as the foregoing shows, that he found himself troubled by the sceptical propensities of Cartesian epistemology; his anxieties about the validity of empirical knowledge had their source in the interest, revived among Descartes' followers by the *Meditations*, in the sceptical arguments of antiquity, and his anxieties about the powers – or rather, lack of them – of finite minds resulted from dissatisfied reflection on the Cartesian conceptions of truth and the nature of cognition. In both cases Malebranche saw Pyrrhonism as the inevitable outcome. A central feature of his attempt to block that outcome is the denial of a distinction between

1. Context

ideas and things; a consequence of it is the at best ambivalent position of material substance as something 'indemonstrable, unknowable and unimportant' (Popkin 2 p5). Both of these points are crucially significant for an understanding of Berkeley.

Malebranche's arguments about, more particularly, the existence of body or matter are given a fuller treatment in an appendix to the *Search* which he styled an '*éclaircissement*' and which was known to his English-language readers, Berkeley included, as 'the Illustration' (see Luce 1 p58, 3 p64). In Taylor's translation the Illustration is entitled 'That 'tis very difficult to Prove the Existence of Bodies; what we ought to esteem of the proofs which are brought of their existence'. Here Malebranche discusses, for example, the subjectivity of sensible qualities like colour and odour; the variability of perceived objects, exemplified by the fact that the moon's appearance differs depending on whether it is viewed through a glass or with the naked eye; and the fact that we sometimes appear to have sense-experience of things when, as in dreams, there are no things there. From these considerations he concludes that sensory evidence cannot establish the existence of body independently of perception. Since he also gave grounds for taking it that reason likewise cannot establish this, we are left, in his view, with faith as our only resource. Berkeley comments on these arguments directly at C800: 'Malebranche in his Illustration differs widely from me He doubts of the existence of Bodies I doubt not in the least of this' (and see C686a).

The influence of Malebranche is recorded in a number of other places in C and at several important points in Berkeley's published writings, cf. P148 and 2D214 where he is expressly concerned to distance his own view from Malebranche's conception of 'seeing all things in God', not just because his views are indeed different from Malebranche's in *crucial* respects, but because a number of Berkeley's early readers saw him, to his dismay, as a Malebranchist (cf. Bracken *passim*, McCracken pp205-6). What is chiefly significant for present purposes is the fact, grasped by Berkeley as these of his comments show, that Malebranche saw scepticism as the outcome of the Cartesian philosophy, which he agreed it was essential to resist; what Berkeley disagreed with was the detail of Malebranche's attempt to block that outcome. (For a full discussion of the numerous differences and points of contact between the views of Malebranche and Berkeley see McCracken Ch.6 *passim*.)

The sceptical tendencies implicit in Cartesianism were recognised by others in its tradition. Michel-Angelo Fardella, a Franciscan monk of Sicily, was persuaded by Malebranche and in one of his works, the *Logic*, asserted much the same doctrine. Berkeley mentions him at C79 as a 'sceptic'. Simon Foucher of Dijon went further, embracing the sceptical consequences of Cartesianism as a means of tempering its votaries' dogmatism; in 1675 he published a *Critique de la Recherche de la Vérité* with this end in view. It is likely that Berkeley knew both of Fardella and Foucher as a result of reading Bayle (Popkin 1 *passim*, cf. Luce 3 p71.) Indeed it is Bayle who provides the most potent characterisation of scepticism in that period, particularly in the articles on Zeno and Pyrrho in his *Dictionaire historique et critique* (1694), which is arguably the prime source for the sceptical problem Berkeley sought to solve (Popkin ibid. *passim*).

In Remark B in the article on Pyrrho, and remarks G and H in the Zeno article, Bayle sets out arguments for scepticism which are echoed, even in phraseology, by Berkeley. The 'new Philosophy' – that is, Cartesianism – had it, as noted above, that material objects possess in themselves such primary or 'original' qualities as extension, figure and motion, but that the secondary qualities of objects exist only in relation to the minds of perceivers. The distinction was held to be important because even if secondary qualities are variable and at least in part subjective, as indeed they appear to be, knowledge of primary qualities, as measurable properties of objects themselves, were thought to provide access to mind-independent reality; and on this the 'new Philosophers' insisted, for it furnished part of the basis of a rising natural philosophy with whose subsequent developments, in the form of physical science, we are now familiar. Bayle marked his contemporaries' acceptance of the mind-dependence of secondary qualities as a recognition that the Sceptics of antiquity were right: 'none among good Philosophers now doubt that the Sceptics are in the right to maintain that the qualities of bodies which strike our senses are only mere appearances'; but he went beyond them in arguing that from this there follows a general scepticism. For, if the secondary qualities are in the mind rather than in objects, he argued, and here he cited Malebranche in support, the same must be held of the primary qualities: '[The new Philosophers agree that] heat, smell, colours etc are not in the objects of our senses; they are only some modifications of my soul; I know that bodies are not such as they appear to me. They were willing to except extension and motion, but they could not do it; for if the objects of our senses appear to us coloured, hot, cold, smelling, though they are not so, why should they not appear extended and figured, at rest, and in

1. Context

motion, though they had no such thing. Nay, the object of my senses cannot be the cause of my sensations: I might therefore feel cold and heat, see colours, figures, extension, and motion, though there was not one body in the world. I have not therefore one good proof of the existence of bodies' (ibid p380).

In Zeno Remark G Bayle again stressed that if secondary qualities are subjective, so are primary qualities; here the argument focusses on the 'overthrow of the reality of extension' which follows from accepting the view that secondary qualities are mind-dependent, for just as secondary qualities are relative to the state or situation of perceivers – the same thing tastes sweet to one person but sour to another – so likewise is extension relative: 'the same body appears to us little or great, round or square, according to the place from whence we view it; and certainly, a body which seems to us very little, appears very great to a fly' (ibid. p381). The conclusion is that if one cannot affirm *which* quality, whether sweetness or bitterness, largeness or smallness, belongs 'absolutely' to an object, one cannot affirm that nevertheless the object *has* 'taste in general' or 'extension in general' at all. And Bayle goes on to argue in Remark H that a belief in there being external bodies is not in any case required to explain the nature either of experience or the world, for 'whether or not [matter] exists, God could equally communicate to us all the thoughts we have' (ibid.). He again cites Malebranche, and with him Fardella, in support.

These arguments seek directly to impugn the view that, however relative or subjective secondary qualities may be, by means at least of empirical access to the primary qualities of things there can be assurance concerning the existence and nature of an independent reality. Their net effect is to say that once a gap is opened between sensory experience on the one hand, and an external material reality on the other, scepticism follows immediately, for the external material reality cannot be known given the inescapable subjectivity of sensory experience in respect not only of the secondary but of the primary qualities of what is sensed. Add Malebranchian doubts on the efficacy of reason, and the scepticism is total. Bayle was by no means alone in seeing these consequences; Arnauld likewise saw them leading directly to 'the establishment of a very dangerous Pyrrhonism' (ibid.).

The sceptical tendencies drawn in these ways from Cartesianism form one part of the background to Berkeley's concerns. The other part arises from developments in natural science, and in particular the expression given to some of its chief philosophical assumptions and implications by Locke. The motive forces in this were the science of mechanics, begun by Galileo and completed, for the time being, by Newton, together with Gassendi's revival of the atomism of classical antiquity. Together these developments constituted the groundwork of the 'corpuscularian theory'. On this view, what there is in the universe, leaving aside questions of mind and God, are atoms and space. Atoms are 'solid, massy, hard, impenetrable, movable particles, of [certain] sizes and figures' (Newton *Optics* Qu. 30), which act upon one another by impact, and whose interactions therefore are to be explained solely in terms of the principles of mechanics. Objects are to be described in terms of their primary properties – that is, their measurable attributes of magnitude, position, motion and so on – which accordingly are to be distinguished from the effects produced in perceivers' minds, namely ideas of colour, odour, and the rest, by the interaction between the primary properties of things and perceivers' organs of sense. The classical atomist, Democritus, had long before separated ideas of secondary qualities from 'reality' as it is in itself (cf. Sextus Empiricus *Adv. Mathem.* VII), but the distinction was now to have major significance, owing to the influence of Galileo, Descartes and Boyle, who were among the first in the modern period to insist upon it.

One of the clearest statements of corpuscularianism is to be found in a short tract by Boyle called *The Origin of Forms and Qualities* (1666; see bibliography). Boyle had a considerable influence on Locke, and also in my view a direct and not always negative influence on Berkeley, although I shall not attempt to make out the case to that effect here (see however pp189, 198 below). In summary form Boyle's corpuscularian views are as follows. There is first the acceptance of the 'Epicurean' view 'that the world is made up of an innumerable multitude of singly insensible corpuscles endowed with their own sizes, shapes and motions'; in the absence of consciousness, that is, of awareness of material things, there would be in the world only 'matter, motion, bulk and shape'; God created the world and imparted motion to its material constituents, as a result of which it runs on mechanical principles, so that 'in explicating particular phenomena' we need only consider 'the size, shape, motion (or want of it), texture and the resulting qualities of the small particles of matter'; and, finally, secondary qualities are dependent upon the 'simpler and more primitive affections of matter', and sensation is the result of corpuscles impinging upon sense organs and exciting motions which are communicated to the brain, where they give rise to perception (ibid. pp18-53). This familiar-sounding view – familiar because it articulates the founding conceptions of modern science – was largely accepted by Locke, who conceived his philosophical task to be the fashioning of a modest propaedeutic to the onward development of science (cf. the 'underlabourer' passage in the *Essay's* 'Epistle to the Reader').

Locke's applications of the corpuscular theory is a product not only of developments in natural philosophy, however, but is in some part informed by Cartesian views, and in part a deliberate reaction against them On many crucial questions arising from the interplay between Cartesian metaphysics and the new natural philosophy Locke was forced to take subtle and often agnostic stances, a fact that explains the considerable difficulty which attaches to giving an accurate interpretation of his views. In outline his position may be characterised as follows (more particular theses will be discussed in the relevant places below).

First, there is Locke's distinctively hesitant conception of substance. In Aristotelian physics each kind or species of thing constituted a substance, but Descartes, as noted above, had reduced their number to three – God, thinking substance and extended substance. The second kind of substance, called *spirit*, has the properties of sensing, thinking and willing. Descartes believed that this member of the set can be known to us in its intrinsic nature, and directly, but Locke disagreed; we might, in his view, be aware of the fact that we sense and think, but the essence of what senses and thinks – thinking substance itself – is unknown to us. Indeed he allowed that the fundamental nature of what thinks might be material, as Hobbes had argued, which demonstrates that the corpuscular view is not *necessarily* dualist. Our ignorance concerning spiritual substance is paralleled, however, by an equal ignorance concerning material substance. The very term 'substance' served for Locke as a reminder of the restrictions to which human epistemic capacities are subject, for the term denotes 'a something we know not what' which underlies and supports the properties of things, and which we must suppose to constitute their inner reality in ways perhaps accessible to beings better equipped than humans for ascertaining what that reality is, but anyway not available to human investigation (cf. *Essay* II.xxiii.2 and *First Letter to Stillingfleet*. This way of putting things accords with Ayers' view that substance and real essence are the same for Locke, cf. Ayers in Tipton 2 pp77ff).

The primary qualities of extension, figure, number, motion or rest, and solidity, which last was Locke's addition to the usual list and is perhaps intended to denote impenetrability or exclusive occupancy of a given space, were regarded by Locke as inseperable attributes of body. The secondary qualities he defined as 'nothing in the objects themselves, but powers to produce various sensations in us by their primary qualities'. Our contact with bodies, and hence our knowledge of both categories of their qualities, is the causally mediated one described by Boyle; corpuscles reflected or emitted from bodies strike our sensory surfaces, imparting motions to the nerves which are thereby transmitted to the brain (II.viii.12). This gives rise in us to 'ideas'. Locke's use of the term 'idea' is notoriously broad; he applied it not only to the results in consciousness of sensory input but to 'whatsoever the mind perceives in itself, or is the immediate object of perception, thought, or understanding' (II.viii.8). As to sensory perception in particular, Locke's view was that the ideas caused in us by external objects in some way *represent* the objects to us. (It is a matter of controversy whether Locke in fact held a representative theory of perception, although on the basis, among other texts, of IV.iv.3 and IV. xi.2 I do not see how it can be denied that he did, although perhaps he subscribed to it reluctantly. This is not the place to enter the controversy, however, and I here adopt the standard line.) Our ideas 'agree' with objects (cf. IV.iv.3); they *resemble* objects in respect of their primary qualities, which cause in us perception of their secondary qualities. In neither case do we have direct access to objects; our ideas are effects, the termini of causal chains, and hence perception is mediate: 'Ideas of primary qualities of bodies are resemblances of them, and their patterns do really exist in the bodies themselves; but ideas produced in us by these secondary qualities have no resemblance to them at all. There is nothing like our ideas existing in the bodies themselves' (II.viii.15).

Locke was untroubled by scepticism concerning the senses. He was aware of but unmoved by arguments of the general character sketched earlier on this head, which is evidenced among other things by the comments in his *Examination of Malebranche* (cf. sect. 20) where he accurately identifies the chief weakness of representative theories, his own not excepted. Nevertheless his representative realism and commitment to the corpuscular theory ran too deep, and his response was to say 'when we have well surveyed the power of our own minds, and made some estimate what we may expect from them, we shall not be inclined to sit still, and not set our thoughts to work at all, in despair of knowing any thing; nor on the other side to question every thing, and disclaim all knowledge, because some things are not to be understood' (I.i.6). He was somewhat more troubled, rather, by what Garber calls 'corpuscular scepticism' (Garber in Turbayne pp174ff), which concerns the question whether we shall ever, given the limitations of our human capacities, be able to succeed in grasping the true inner nature of things; 'There is not so contemptible a plant or animal, that does not confound the most enlarged understanding' (III.vi.9). But he shrugged this aside too, and without too great a show of regret, in the comment that, despite our limitations, 'the candle, that is set up in us, shines bright enough for all our purposes' (I.i.5).

In addition to the representative theory of perception, its attendant primary-secondary quality distinction, and the agnostic acceptance of a doctrine of substance, there is another feature of Locke's thought which is especially relevant to an understanding of Berkeley. This is his view concerning abstract ideas, and it is a product of his theory of meaning. In Locke's view, words 'stand for' ideas. The function of language is to communicate one person's ideas to another; 'the end of speech is, that those sounds, as marks [of the ideas in the mind of him that uses them], may make known his ideas to the hearer' (III.ii.2) At the outset all words are particular in signification, standing for *individual* things (III.iii.7); but it quickly becomes necessary for words to have a general use, that is, to stand for ideas of collections or classes of particulars, because the greater part of our knowledge consists in a conversance with sorts or kinds of things and the properties common to their members. Accordingly many words come to be 'general names' and thus to stand for 'general ideas' (ibid.). Such ideas are formed by 'separating from [particular things] the circumstances of time and place, and many other ideas that may determine them to this or that particular existence' (III.iii.6 and cf. III.iii.12). And so we come to have a general or abstract idea of, say, *man* or *triangle*, which is not an idea of any particular man or triangle, with determinate properties, but of something possessing only those sortal characteristics which make the idea of it the idea of that kind of thing in general. Locke thought that the framing of abstract ideas was a matter not only of importance but of difficulty: 'For, when we nicely reflect upon them, we shall find that *general ideas* are fictions and contrivances of the mind, that carry difficulty with them, and do not so easily offer themselves as we are apt to imagine. For example, does it not require some pains and skill to form the general idea of a triangle (which is yet none of the most abstract, comprehensive and difficult), for it must be neither oblique nor rectangle, neither equilateral, equicrural, nor scalenon, but all and none of these at once. In effect, it is something imperfect, that cannot exist; an idea wherein some parts of several different and inconsistent ideas are put together' (IV.vii.9). To this theory Berkeley had profound objections which are central to his position.

2. Aims

The foregoing is a brief sketch of the philosophical background against which Berkeley developed his views. In the light of it the content of his aims can be identified with accuracy. It was noted at the beginning of this discussion that Berkeley sought to attack scepticism and correlatively to defend 'common sense', and to attack atheism and correlatively to defend religion. In doing so he further aimed to eradicate 'causes of error and difficulty in the sciences'. These aims are summarised in the full titles to both P and D. The former reads: '*A Treatise concerning the Principles of Human Knowledge.* Wherein the chief causes of error and difficulty in the sciences, with the grounds of Scepticism, Atheism, and Irreligion, are inquired into', and the latter reads: '*Three Dialogues Between Hylas and Philonous.* The design of which is plainly to demonstrate the reality and perfection of human knowledge, the incorporeal nature of the soul, and the immediate providence of a Deity: in opposition to Sceptics and Atheists. Also to open a method for rendering the sciences more easy, useful, and compendious'. Both works seek to do what their titles promise, but the opposition to atheists, though present in both, takes second place to the attack upon scepticism. Berkeley treats more fully of atheism and the 'grounds of Irreligion' in other places, most notably in *Alciphron*, which is a set of dialogues specifically written to confute the free-thinkers. In P and D theological considerations proceed rather at the metaphysical than the doctrinal level, although aspects of doctrine make their appearance. When Berkeley is writing as a divine rather than as a philosopher, as he does in the sermons and, for example, his *Guardian* articles, the argument depends barely at all on his metaphysics, but has the character of straightforward Christian apologetic. So far as I can see, however, no inconsistency arises from this for Berkeley's philosophical position; the two respects in which difficulties arise, namely the creation and the problem of evil, he gives special consideration at P151 and 3D256ff. It is suggested by certain comments in the notebooks that Berkeley was careful to avoid committing himself to anything that might appear doctrinally unorthodox (cf. C713, 715, 720), but, again as far as I

2. Aims

can see, this does not force upon him false positions or compromises from the point of view of his overall intentions, although it does make for certain difficulties (see Chapter Three section 4 below).

A probable reason for Berkeley's subordination of the expressed religious to the philosophical aims in these works is that he intended P to be a treatise of two or more parts, only the first of which was published. To this day P continues to be printed as 'Part I'. In a letter to the American Samuel Johnson, Berkeley says that he succeeded in writing much of a Part II, but lost it while travelling in Italy, and could not bring himself to start again (Works II p282). The evidence of C suggests that Part II was intended to deal more fully with God in particular and spiritual substance in general. The absence of a detailed treatment of these issues means that Berkeley's philosophy is present to us in truncated form, as a major fragment of a theory rather than a complete theory. This has significant implications for the business of interpreting Berkeley, which I discuss below.

In one respect Berkeley's central arguments constitute a contribution to natural theology, in that they furnish what could be thought of as a new argument for the existence of God. The argument itself, and attendant considerations about God, have an exceedingly important role in his contentions, and will be discussed at the appropriate places in the body of what follows.

As to atheism itself in P and D, Berkeley's claim is that its rebuttal follows directly from his position. At P92-6 atheism is identified as the impious outcome of the doctrine of 'matter or corporeal substance', which leads its votaries into 'deriding immaterial substance, and supposing the soul to be divisible and subject to corruption as the body; which excludes all freedom, intelligence, and design from the formation of things, and instead thereof make a self-existent, stupid, unthinking substance the root and origin of all beings ... [thus denying] a providence, or inspection of a superior mind over the affairs of the world, attributing the whole series of events either to blind chance or fatal necessity, arising from the impulse of one body on another' (P93). This also gives rise to idolatry (P94) and makes for unnecessary difficulties over the doctrine of the resurrection (P95); but worst of all it makes 'matter to be uncreated and coeternal with' God (P92), which directly controverts not only the first article of Christian faith as expressed in any standard *credo* ('I believe in one God, the father almighty, maker of heaven and earth' etc.) but the doctrine that God keeps the universe in being by a continual act of creation, as its substance in the most literal acceptation of this term. Leaving aside anything else, *this* feature of doctrine is fundamentally important in Berkeley's work; a passage in his second letter to Johnson (*Works* II p280) shows that his way of treating the question in P and D differs only in manner, not in essentials, from the established doctrine of 'divine conservation'. This aspect of his attack on atheism is central, then, for it settles a number of issues in what has come to be called 'the continuity argument', after Bennett's discussion of the matter, and I examine it more fully below.

Important as the attack on atheism was to Berkeley, however, his overriding concern in P and D is scepticism, and this requires more detailed discussion.

Scepticism can take many forms and be addressed to a variety of different subject matters; one can be a sceptic about some things without being a sceptic about others. So, for example, one might be a sceptic concerning whether it is possible to have knowledge or at least justified beliefs about the past, or other minds, independently of as well as in connection with scepticism about the existence of an external world or our capacity for attaining insights to its character. Additionally there is scepticism about the existence or, more weakly, the nature of God, which takes the forms either of atheism or agnosticism of one or another kind. The types of scepticism which concerned Berkeley were religious scepticism, discussed above, and the two matters of, first, whether we can be assured that there is a world, and secondly whether we can know what it is like. These are *different* scepticisms, but they are related in that the same sorts of argument are relevant to the substantiation of both. Thus a sceptic might argue from contingent facts about our perceptual capacities and the nature of the experience to which they give rise, and from the feebleness or inadequacy either in general or in some relevant respect of our powers of reason, to the strong conclusion that we have no grounds for asserting that there is an external world, or failing that to the weaker conclusion that we cannot know the external world in its real and intrinsic nature. Berkeley was aware of these two options for the sceptical attack, and he took it that his response dealt with both at once. It is worth noting this fact, for a reply to the stronger sceptical challenge does not *ipso facto* constitute a reply to the weaker; one might in some way establish that there *is* a world without being able to say what it is like. Nevertheless a refutation of the stronger form of scepticism can, and most proffered refutations do, turn in part on considerations about what the world is or must be like, and Berkeley's arguments take this form.

2. Aims

Berkeley describes the 'root' of scepticism as the opening of a gap between the world on one hand and experience on the other, which results from 'supposing a twofold existence of the objects of sense, the one *intelligible*, or in the mind, the other real and without the mind' (P86), because 'for so long as men thought that *real* things subsisted without the mind, and that their knowledge was only so far forth *real* as it was conformable to *real things*, it follows, they could not be certain that they had any real knowledge at all. For how can it be known, that the things which are perceived, are conformable to those which are not perceived, or exist without the mind ?' (ibid.). One argument showing how scepticism arises is in essentials the one set out by Bayle. If secondary qualities are mind-dependent, that is, are perceptions, so too are primary qualities; and since our perceptions are subjective, and vary, and constitute dreams and hallucinations as well as what we take to be standard veridical experience, it follows that an absolute distinction between what we perceive and what we take our perceptions to be perceptions *of* arises; 'so that, for aught we know, all we see, hear, and feel, may be only phantom and vain chimera, and not at all agree with the real things, existing *in rerum natura*' (P87). But a much more dangerous consideration, which these Baylean arguments help to foster, is the separation or abstraction of the existence of things from their being perceived, for then not only does scepticism concern whether we can know the true nature of things, but amounts to scepticism as to whether there is a world at all: 'So long as we attribute a real existence to unthinking things [viz. matter or corporeal substance] distinct from their being perceived, it is not only impossible for us to know with evidence the nature of any real unthinking thing, but even that it exists. Hence it is, that we see philosophers distrust their senses, and doubt of the existence of heaven and earth, of every thing they see or feel, even of their own bodies' (P88). The same consequence is insisted upon elsewhere. In the Preface to D Berkeley writes 'Upon the common principles of philosophers, we are not assured of the existence of things from their being perceived ... Hence arise scepticism and paradoxes' (D167); and in the second dialogue Philonous says to Hylas 'You indeed said, the reality of sensible things consisted in an absolute existence out of the minds of spirits, or distinct from their being perceived. And pursuant to this notion of reality, you are obliged to deny sensible things any real existence: that is, according to your own definition, you profess yourself a sceptic' (2D211-12. See also pp228-9, 246, 258, and P92, 101).

The source of scepticism, then, is in Berkeley's view the thesis that what there is exists independently of perception, for this permits arguments opening an unbridgeable gap between experience and experience-independent reality. From the fact that we are only ever acquainted with our perceptions, and never with the items which putatively lie inaccessibly beyond our perceptions but which somehow give rise to them – and which they are therefore supposed in some way to represent or even (but how could we know?) resemble – it follows that we have no justification for asserting that there *are* such items, still less that we can know anything of their intrinsic nature. And this scepticism arises directly from the philosophical view that there is matter, that is, corporeal substance, existing independently of our perception of it, having properties which belong to it 'absolutely' – namely, the primary qualities. In sum, 'the supposition that things are distinct from Ideas takes away all real Truth, & consequently brings in a Universal Scepticism, since all our knowledge is confin'd barely to our own Ideas' (C606).

Berkeley's refutation of scepticism, for all its surface simplicity, is a complex matter, for it consists in arguments which move at different levels with subtle relations of dependence on each other. The main body of what follows is devoted to exploring those arguments, but here a sketch is in order. In essentials Berkeley's manoeuvre is to deny the appearance-reality gap by saying that appearance *is* reality; there is no divide between ideas and things because things are ideas, not independently existing items in some way lying inaccessibly behind or beyond experience. At first blush this looks an improbable doctrine, but before the temptation to think so takes hold, two things should be noted. First, as this sketch of Berkeley's position stands, it bears strong similarities to the twentieth century phenomenalist view, subscribed to (with certain important qualifications) by Russell and Ayer among others, to the effect that physical objects are logical constructions out of sense-data, which is to say that statements about physical objects are shorthand for sets of statements, perhaps indefinitely large, about actual and possible perceptions. The central motive for the phenomenalist view is identical with Berkeley's motive, namely to overcome scepticism by laying an axe to its root, which is the perception/perception-independent-object dichotomy. Some commentators, notably Warnock (see bibliography), take it that Berkeley's contentions in this respect are squarely phenomenalist, but I shall argue that the story is more complex than this, not least in ways which suggest that Berkeley was more sophisticated than some of his successors on this point. And secondly, it is just wrong to see Berkeley's denial of the sceptical gap as a reduction of physical objects to ideas in a way

2. Aims

which directly entails subjective idealism with tendencies, if not actual consequences, of a solipsistic kind; for as the detail of Berkeley's arguments shows, there is a serious and interesting point in his saying that he is not so much concerned to show that things are ideas as the other way round, which is illustrated by his making Philonous say to Hylas 'I am not for changing things into ideas, but rather ideas into things; since those immediate objects of perception, which according to you, are only the appearances of things, I take to be the real things themselves' (3D244). A detailed account of this conception appears in its due place below. One among the things it connects with is the correlative of Berkeley's attack on scepticism, namely his claim to be defending 'common sense'.

Entry C606, quoted above, where Berkeley says 'The supposition that things are distinct from Ideas takes away all real Truth' etc., provides an important clue here. His saying in that passage that 'Universal Scepticism' arises from taking it that 'all our knowledge & contemplation is confin'd *barely* to *our own Ideas*' (my emphases) suggests that he construes the sceptical arguments as giving a subjective or even solipsistic result which is utterly opposed to our common sense belief in a public and objective realm transparent to our epistemic capacities. It is this common sense conception he is anxious to defend, at any rate in its essentials. The charge that P offers anything but a defence of common sense moved Berkeley to prove his earnest in this respect when he wrote D, not just by means of repeated avowals and attempted demonstrations, but by opening both the first and second dialogues with speeches by Philonous, who serves as Berkeley's mouthpiece on the whole, on the subject of the beauty, colour, and variety of nature (lD171, 2D210-11). These panegyrics have a serious persuasive intent; they are offered in support of Berkeley's contention that his theory 'leaves things as [it] finds them' (3D229), that is, does not constitute a revisionary metaphysics premissed in part on the thought that common sense views of the world are false. On this he insists to the point of harping. Berkeley's efforts in this direction have, however, been greeted with scepticism by almost all his commentators (see e.g. Pitcher Ch.IX, Tipton 1 pp54-6, 62-7). Against them I shall argue that at least in one crucial respect Berkeley's claims here are not only justified in terms of his own views, but right. Showing how requires the weight of argument to come, but a beginning can be made as follows.

Specifying what the common sense view of the world comes down to is a doubtful enterprise, since it is an armchair activity with all the risks that its being so entails. Nevertheless it is reasonably clear that there is a residuum of conceptions about the world which can safely be described as forming part of a common sense view, once one has allowed for the effect of what happens at any point to be the current theory interpreting those conceptions – something we can exemplify by noting, say, the shift in outlook between our ancestors and ourselves on the question of whether or not the earth is at the centre of the universe, or is round or flat, and so on. At the level only of what we can safely suppose remains invariant in alterations to the theories which putatively explain these facts, then, the common sense view can be described as a commitment to the propositions:

(a) things are just as they are perceived to be, and
(b) things exist independently of particular acts or states of perceptual awareness of them.

Common sense is a species of realism, in virtue of (b); and in virtue of (a) it is what, with some disparagement, philosophers call '*naive* realism', since it has it that our perceptual access to the world is direct, suggesting a model in which the eyes are windows we look through onto a world which in itself has the colours, smells, tastes, textures and sounds just as it appears to have.

The term 'realism' has to be handled with some care, for it has been used to mean a number of things, among which, despite connections, there are important differences. A traditional use applies to the Platonic doctrine of the real existence of universals, to which nominalism is opposed. Thus in addition to there being white houses, white horses, and white shirts there is, on this species of realism, whiteness or perhaps Whiteness; particulars which are white are white because they 'participate' in the universal, or 'instantiate' it. Nominalists, by contrast, do not regard universals as separately existing entities but as concepts attaching to a name. There are, nominalists argue, only particular white things, and realism concerning the property all the white things possess 'in common' is a result of false abstractionism. This opposition applies in other connections; if one thinks there are numbers, one is in this Platonist sense a realist about numbers; and if one thinks there are no numbers, only numerals, or otherwise that numbers are fictions or constructs which do not exist independently of being thought of, manipulated, added together, and so on, then one is rejecting a realist account of numbers. More generally one can label someone who repudiates realism concerning a given class of entities an 'anti-realist' about that class. In contemporary philosophy the labels have come into sharper definition as a result of discussion about what form a theory of meaning for natural language should take. Here a realist is someone who subscribes to the view that a distinctive concept of truth is to be used as the key to explaining meaning, a concept of truth which makes it a property of sentences which those sentences may bear or fail to bear independently of whether or not anyone knows which; and since there is something in virtue of which sentences are true or false – namely, the facts, the way things are in the world – these facts exist and have the character they possess independently of whether or not we have epistemic access to them. The facts in question, in other words, may be and often are verification-transcendent, that is, may and often do lie beyond our capacities to discover what they are. And on the grounds that understanding language consists in grasping the truth-conditions, realistically conceived, of its sentences, a theory can accordingly be stated which yields for each sentence a well-defined pairing between that sentence and a statement of the conditions for its truth. In contrast, an anti-realist in this connection is one who denies that any concept of truth which is to occupy the key position in a theory of meaning can be a verification-transcendent one, that is, can be such that the conditions for the truth of sentences lie in fact or in principle beyond the capacities of speakers to recognise whether or not they obtain. The reason is that if understanding a language consists in grasp of truth-conditions, then these must be available both to the learner and to the user of the language, so that the learner can attain, and the user display, mastery of the language, neither being possible if the truth-conditions of sentences in the language can lie, as on the realist view they do, beyond the learner's and user's capacities to recognize whether or not they are fulfilled. In this arena, accordingly, realism comes down to the view that there are facts of the matter, that is, states of affairs, existing independently of anyone's knowing or even being able to come to know anything about them; in the jargon, it is the view that there exist 'recognition-transcendent states of affairs'. What is central is the thought that the states of affairs in question, or more generally things or situations involving them in the world, exist independently of any knowledge or experience of them.

The independence of items in some class from experience of them can be taken as defining of realism with respect to that class. Given the heterogeneity of the classes of items about which one might be a realist – universals, numbers, other minds, past facts, future facts, God, angels and demons, physical objects – it has to be remembered that different *specific* accounts need to be given in each case of what it is to be a realist concerning that class; but the independence thesis is central to them all, and that is what matters here. Common sense proposition (b), as noted, expresses the independence claim, and does so in the sense described, for it states that things – stones, rainbows, rivers – exist apart from perception or awareness of them. For this reason the common sense view is often labelled 'common sense realism'.

As it stands, the characterisation given here of common sense realism is consistent with Berkeley's position if one significant adjustment is made to (b); but it is not consistent with the representative realism of Locke and the corpuscularians, for representative realism involves a denial of (a). Things are *not* just as they are perceived, on this view, for the reason that the secondary qualities are powers in objects to cause ideas, in the minds of perceivers, of colour, odour, and the rest, which latter, since they are ideas, are subjective and not in the objects themselves. It is because of the subjectivity of colour and the rest that naive realism is so called, since its espousers fail, it is said, to recognize the relevant facts. In Berkeley's view, however, the denial of (a) is one of the chief sources of scepticism, for the reasons given; which is precisely why he resists it.

On the face of it Berkeley and representative realists might appear to disagree only over (a), but in fact they disagree also over (b). This is because (b), in the form in which I have so far stated it, is neutral as between competing accounts of what explains it. The representative realist takes it that things are independent of perceptual awareness of them because they are self-subsistent material particulars, 'determinates' of matter or corporeal substance, which would exist even if there were not or had never been the phenomena of consciousness or experience in the universe; their independence is 'absolute', to use Berkeley's term, in that their existence is in no way contingent upon their being actual or possible objects of experience. Accordingly a form of (b) apt for capturing what I shall from now on call the 'absolute realist' view is:

(b′) things exist independently of any acts or states of perceptual awareness of them.

Berkeley denies (b′); his denial of it is indeed central to his philosophical outlook. To capture the reason for his opposition to (b′) it has to be noted that just as (b) is not explicit enough to convey the absolute realist's view, it is likewise not explicit enough to convey Berkeley's view. The variant of (b) to which Berkeley is committed is:

(b″) things exist independently of any particular finite perceiver's awareness of them.

The intended implications are clear enough; Berkeley's view was of course that (c) all things are perceived at all times by God, and (b″) is a step towards that thesis.

The route from (b″) to (c) is however a complicated one which depends on yet further detailed commitments on Berkeley's part, discussion of which, because they are central, forms a major part of what follows. At this juncture it is enough to note that since what common sense holds, at this level of description, is indifferent to what theory is offered in explanation of (b), Berkeley's position is, so far, in accordance with its basic intuitions. Absolute realism of the materialist variety offers an account of (b), namely (b′), which we must suppose is more immediately plausible from the common sense point of view (because it is the one which has by and large prevailed) than (b″) and its intended implication (c); but it is so, as noted, only at the cost of controverting (a), which Berkeley's position not only does not controvert but deliberately defends. Accordingly, as these contrasts are set out here, they suggest a rethinking of a criticism often levelled at Berkeley, to the effect that his views offend common sense rather than, as he claims, support it; for it is obvious that before we begin to reflect on the nature of the relation between experience and the world we hold both (a) and (b) and have no particular theory which explains (b), and that in learning the rudiments of scientific theory, which in effect alters (b) to (b′), we come by a *special* variant of common sense – a new or 'educated' common sense – in which although we continue to believe (a) for all practical purposes, we acknowledge that in the light of theory (the theory which explains b′) it must strictly speaking be false. Berkeley's view of what explains (b) does not involve a denial of (a) at the level of theory and therefore does not invite us to think one thing for practical purposes and another for theoretical purposes. If a measure of the initial plausibility, at least, of a philosophical theory consists in the distance at which it lies from common sense conceptions, then at the level of basic intuitions, and leaving aside what is invoked to explain them, Berkeley's views are less revisionary than materialist absolute realism or the science with which it is associated. In more religious times than our own it may have seemed just as reasonable, if not indeed more so, to hold (a), (b″) and (c) as to hold (b′) together with the denial of (a) and indifference to the acceptance or rejection of (c). Certainly it seemed so to Berkeley. Given the fact that how we depart from the basic intuitions of common sense depends on theoretical commitments which in part concern how we explain (b) and perhaps in larger part how we construct an interpretation of our experience in general, it is therefore simply wrong – because it assumes that one particular interpretation is *unquestionably* the right one – to see Berkeley as 'the most outrageous affronter' of common sense, as Tipton does (Tipton 1 p56) and as Pitcher in effect does also (cf. Pitcher Ch. IX *passim*). So far as the basic intuitions of common sense go, Berkeley would appear less an affronter of them than his competitors, and this remains true even at the level of theory, where Berkeley's results are no more *strange* than those arrived at by, say, contemporary physics, with its wave-particle duality at the quantum level, and the prospect, held out by recent efforts to formulate a unified field theory, of our having to think in terms of, say, an eleven-dimensional universe.

There are in fact reasons why Pitcher, Tipton and others have gone astray in arriving at their assessment of Berkeley on this score, some of which will become apparent shortly. What makes them apparent is a consideration of Berkeley's method and the questions this raises for an understanding of how he is to be interpreted. To these issues therefore I now turn, reverting to the matter of common sense shortly.

3. Interpretation: method, meaning and empiricism

Berkeley's arguments move at three levels: (1) the strictly empirical or phenomenological level, which has to do with the basic data of sensory experience; (2) the phenomenal level, that is, the level of ordinary thought and talk about everyday experience and its objects; and (3) the metaphysical level, which provides the ultimate framework of explanation for levels 1 and 2. Failure to grasp the threefold nature of Berkeley's approach leads to muddled interpretation of his views (examples of which follow presently); evidence not only that he adopted this approach but did so deliberately is abundant in his texts.

In numerous places Berkeley distinguishes between a 'strict and speculative' approach to matters, on the one hand, and 'received opinions' established by 'use' or 'custom' on the other (eg. P34-40,

3. Interpretation: method, meaning and empiricism

45-8, 51-2, 54-7, 3D234-5, 237-8, 247, VV10, 13); sometimes he puts the contrast in terms of taking matters either in a 'philosophic' sense or a 'vulgar' sense (eg. C724, P34, 37, 3D237). The vulgar or customary understanding of concepts like time, causality, and the perception of objects, constitutes level 2. The strict or philosophical understanding of these same concepts is either level 1 when the subject under consideration is the content of sensory experience as such, that is, what is actually present to awareness in states of awareness, considered independently either of ordinary or of metaphysical accounts of what it portends; or it is level 3 when the subject in hand is the explanation of what is going on at levels 1 and 2. An example will help to clarify this.

Consider Berkeley's account of causality (cf. P25-9, 51-2, 2D216). At level 3 the contents of the world are specified as 'spirits' and their ideas; spirits are active, ideas inert. What at level 2 we take to be natural causes – the fire causes the water in the kettle to boil, etc. -is in fact, Berkeley claims (and compare Hume) a bare succession of strictly unrelated ideas – level 1 – caused in us by God – level 3 – in such a way that the regularity and constancy of those ideas succeeding each other in that way gives rise in us to the custom of thinking that there are natural causes – level 2. Indeed the nomological character of the relations between ideas consequent upon what is explained at level 3 permits us to talk at level 2 of 'Laws of Nature', by thinking, planning and acting in accordance with which we promote our well-being (P30). It is not only, on the whole, unexceptionable to talk in level 2 terms, Berkeley says, but unavoidable; it is unexceptionable because 'In the ordinary affairs of life, any phrases may be retained, so long as they excite in us the proper sentiments, or dispositions to act in such a manner as is necessary for our well-being, how false soever they may be, if taken in a strict and speculative sense' (P52), and it is unavoidable, since 'language is suited to the received opinions' by custom and use (ibid), and does not have the precision required for a correct level 3 account. On these grounds, a term like 'material substance' can be used at level 2 to mean what is ordinarily encountered in experience provided that this is not taken to entail that the correct level 3 account involves reference to it (P37).

Another example – one could cite many – of how the difference between levels operates in Berkeley's thought is afforded by what he says of distance vision (V2-51, 1D201ff, P42-4). At level 2 we take it that the objects of visual perception lie at various distances from us and that this is something we judge on the basis of the visual data we have. Berkeley argues that the visual data, considered as such apart from the interpretations we place upon them – that is, considered at level 1 – themselves provide no grounds for judgements of distance, but rather that it is the correlations between visual ideas and certain others – ideas of touch, sensations of the movements of our eyes – which, in the course of experience, enable us to make those judgements. Accordingly at level 1, where only the content of actual awareness is considered, without any of its customary interpretations or implications, the investigation is purely phenomenological; and it is this which, as I shall shortly show, constitutes Berkeley's empiricism and the austere constraint he places on the conceptions both of meaningfulness and possibility.

The relation between Berkeley's views and common sense is illuminated by these considerations. Propositions (a) and (b) capture the level 2 content of what our ordinary common-sensical views come down to, whereas competing explanations of (b), between which it is neutral, are level 3 accounts. Berkeley's contention is that his level 3 account, arrived at for other and more fundamental reasons, namely those constituted by his central arguments, disturbs level 2 less than materialism does. And in this respect he is right. The failure to note this has led some commentators to make heavy weather of Berkeley's insistence that his views leave everything (at level 2) as it is; which is illustrated by looking, for example, at Pitcher's treatment of the question, as follows (Pitcher pp140-62).

Pitcher begins by distinguishing between conciliatory and non-conciliatory metaphysical systems, the former being those which accord more, the latter those which accord less, with common sense views; and he argues that whereas Berkeley professes to be a conciliator – 'I endeavour to vindicate common sense' (3D244) – he is in fact not one, although he might like to be, for he says things like 'It is indeed an opinion strangely prevailing among men, that houses, mountains, rivers, in a word all sensible objects have an existence natural or real, distinct from their being perceived by the understanding' (P4). In short, Pitcher says, Berkeley is in the 'awkward position' of having to be both a conciliator and a non-conciliator on the basis of his own principles; but as it turns out from an inspection of these principles, he is in fact 'decidedly' a non-conciliator (p143). In substantiation of this Pitcher at one point says: 'In his system, so-called physical objects are not at all what we take them to be. Recall, to begin with, that according to Berkeley we never touch and see the same object [this refers to V49ff where Berkeley argues that the immediate data of sight and touch are

3. Interpretation: method, meaning and empiricism 25

specific to their respective sensory modalities]; this doctrine ... is not abandoned in the later works (cf. 3D245 etc). Our language hides this metaphysical complexity; for example we refer to a fig tree, and not to a visual fig tree, a tangible fig tree – nor to the fig trees that correspond to our other senses. The truth, however, is that what we refer to, and ordinarily think of, as a single object is in reality a complex of several different objects' (ibid.). And this way of looking at things, Pitcher says, is in direct conflict with common sense.

The non-conciliatory character of Pitcher's rendering vanishes, however, when recast in the idiom of levels. For Berkeley is saying that at level 2 we engage in the successful and convenient practice of talking about fig trees, whereas at level 1, paying attention only to the content of states of sensory awareness themselves, we see that the immediate objects of visual, tactual, olfactory, and the rest, experience are unique to their proper sensory modalities – to vision, light and colour; to touch, texture and resistance; to smell, smells; and so on. Thus what at level 2 we think of and refer to as a single object is at level 1 a complex of ideas – and these are caused in us, Berkeley elsewhere argues, by an external source, namely God, which is the level 3 explanation of our taking these level 1 data to constitute the level 2 fig tree, because the ideas we have are independently caused, and hang together in a regular, coherent, and lawlike way. Accordingly when Pitcher says 'In his system so-called physical objects are not at all what we ordinarily take them to be', this is true of Berkeley's views about the matter at levels 1 and 3 – but this is also he case, *nota bene*, in Lockean representative realism and for modern physics and psychology – but false of Berkeley's views about level 2 – although *still* true, *nota bene* again, for Locke's views and for modern physics and psychology. Therefore since the degree to which the appearances are saved, that is, the degree to which common sense is left undisturbed, marks the degree to which a set of views is conciliatory or otherwise, as Pitcher himself has it, it follows that for the foregoing reasons Berkeley's views are *more* conciliatory, when properly understood in the light of his three-level approach, than Locke's views or those of modern physics and psychology, contrary to what Pitcher asserts.

Again, Pitcher thinks that Berkeley's non-conciliatoriness is demonstrated by his handling of identity (p146-7). For, Berkeley is committed to the view that since all we ever perceive are ideas – our *own* ideas – we never perceive numerically the same objects as others perceive. Berkeley has Hylas say 'But the same idea which is in my mind, cannot be in yours, or any other mind. Doth it not therefore follow from your principles, that no two can see the same thing ? And is this not highly absurd ?' (3D247). Philonous replies that indeed 'different people can perceive the same thing. If the term *same* be taken in the vulgar acceptation, it is certain (and not at all repugnant to the principles I maintain) that different persons may perceive the same thing; or the same thing or idea exist in different minds' (ibid.). Here Philonous is saying, Pitcher rightly points out, that the ideas different perceivers have are *qualitatively*, not *numerically*, the same; and therefore Pitcher concludes that since common sense has it that two or more perceivers looking at a fig tree see numerically the same thing, it follows that Berkeley's views are far removed from common sense.

Here too the distinction of levels shows that this is a false result. At level 1 the numerical difference of the ideas in one perceiver's mind as against those in another's is admitted; and it is admitted that at level 2 the perceivers take themselves to be seeing numerically the same thing, an assumption enshrined in the discourse which reports level 2 interpretations of experience. But this is unproblematic, for the fact that this level 2 assumption is justified in practice is accounted for, as one would expect, by a level 3 explanation of it; the source of all the qualitatively similar level 1 ideas which at level 2 perceivers refer to the same object, is indeed single and external to the perceivers, viz. the relevant causal act of God (3D248). This not only explains the practical justification of the level 2 view but the qualitative similarity of the level 1 ideas which give rise to it. Berkeley points out, aptly enough, that on *any* view which has it that the content of a perceiver's experience is private to himself and hence numerically distinct from that of someone else, the same difficulty arises; in the 'philosophic' sense, no two perceivers will perceive numerically the same object, but, in the vulgar sense, will refer their perceptions to numerically the same object, and accordingly an explanation is required. That explanation will be given at level 3; for Berkeley it is God's activity in causing our ideas, for corpuscularians it is streams of corpuscles emanating from *one* object and impinging on the sensory surfaces of *different* perceivers, giving rise to ideas in each perceiver which in some way represent the object to him. For reasons having to do with his denial of matter and allied contentions, Berkeley opts for the former explanation. And a result of his doing so, familiarly by now, is that common sense proposition (a) remains uncontroverted, and hence his views remain closer to common sense than do those of his competitors. Among the charges Berkeley can be seen to be laying at the door of his predecessors is the fact that not

3. Interpretation: method, meaning and empiricism 27

only does their level 3 view (whether corpuscularian or Cartesian) fail to cohere with level 2, but it is unsupported by the level 1 facts. And this charge captures much of what is central to his contentions in all of his first three major works.

What looms large in the immediately foregoing comments is Berkeley's theory of perception, which will be considered more fully in due course. From what has been said it should already be apparent that the 'phenomenalist' aspects of Berkeley's theory have inbuilt advantages over certain alternative varieties of phenomenalism, which can be recognised by noting that, leaving aside the *nature* of the level 3 account, the fact that there is such an account in the offing, as an explanation of the relation between levels 1 and 2 and as a way of filling the gap between those levels, constitutes an advance over any theory which has no level 3 but tries to argue that level 2 can be exhaustively explained in terms of level 1 alone, perhaps, familiarly, by means of a reductive or equivalence thesis of some sort.

The distinction of levels explains a great deal in Berkeley's work, not least concerning his method and his views on sensefulness, from which most of what is crucial in his views follows. Note the choice of 'sensefulness' rather than 'meaning': it is not wholly appropriate in my view to talk of Berkeley or indeed of his near contemporaries as having a '*theory* of meaning' in anything other than a loose sense; to think otherwise is to read too much of contemporary concerns into their work and hence to distort it. Locke, it is true, paid enough attention to questions of meaning to invite the attention, unremittingly critical, of recent commentators (cf. e.g. *Essay* III.ii), and earlier entries in C show that for a time Berkeley accepted Locke's ideational theory. But even in Locke the talk of meaning – of words 'standing for' ideas – is unsystematic and ancillary to his chief purposes, so that what occurs there is a sketch, even if it is enough of one to show that it is on the wrong lines. Where Berkeley talks expressly about meaning, which is chiefly in C and the Introduction to P, it is to point out the sources of the false doctrine of abstract ideas (Intro. P18ff). His noting that many expressions in natural language have *uses* rather than the function simply of standing for ideas (Intro. P19, 20) has been excitedly hailed as an anticipation of Wittgenstein, especially by those who take this to be an ultimate, as opposed to just a good, insight; but nothing like a full-blooded theory of meaning is recoverable from these remarks any more than they are from the somewhat more extensive treatment Locke gives these matters. What Berkeley does, rather, is to place sharp constraints on what makes a concept – for focal examples, those of matter or existence – *senseful*; and this is to give only part, although an important part, of a theory of meaning, with a restricted range of application in Berkeley's concerns. It also provides him with his main type of argument, the 'conceivability' argument, which is employed at almost all crucial stages in the development of his position. Berkeley's theory of sense and conceivability is therefore extremely important. Understanding it first requires that the character of his empiricism be understood, however, so I turn to that now.

The traditional bracketing of Berkeley with Locke and Hume, misleading in some respects, is at least right in having it that they share a commitment to the view that the ultimate source and test of contingent knowledge is sense-experience. But there are differences between them: Hume is the most thoroughgoing empiricist of the three, and Locke's rationalism is apt to be overlooked because of the label. In Berkeley's case, the empiricism to which he is committed is very austere, but it is only part of the story, for it plays no role in the metaphysically more important matter of our knowledge of spirit in general and God in particular. Rather, he is a strict empiricist in that he pays deliberately exclusive attention to the content, and no more than the content, of states of sensory awareness when dealing with the question of what our sensory experience, which they constitute, yields in the way of information about what that experience is of. Only what is 'grounded in experience' is 'certain' (cf. P28); he says, with contingent knowledge in mind, 'I approve of this axiom of the Schoolmen, nihil est in intellectu quod non prius fuit in sensu' (C779 and cf. C539). But it is not so much in avowals about method as in the practice of argument that Berkeley's empiricism is manifested. Consider again, for just one example, his arguments about the visual apprehension of distance. Berkeley enjoins us to note only what is given 'immediately' in visual experience (V2), for doing so shows that estimates of distance are acts of judgement, grounded on the general course of experience, rather than acts of sense as such (V3). The 'appearances', that is, the contents of states of visual awareness, do not 'immediately and of themselves' suggest distance, but do so in connection with certain other ideas, rather as we infer from facial expression to mood (cf. V49). The case of 'one born blind' illustrates this (V41): his visual experience, strictly considered, would be on all fours with his hedonic states or 'the most inward passions of his soul' in being 'in his mind', and until he learned to interpret them, by means of their connections with tactual experience and other signs, they would, far from being attributable to objects at a distance, have

3. Interpretation: method, meaning and empiricism

no external reference at all. At this level, then – level 1 – the focus is strictly on the *phenomenology* of experience. It is for this reason that Hylas, speaking for Berkeley as he occasionally does, says 'in truth the senses perceive nothing which they do not perceive immediately: for they make no inferences. The deducing therefore of causes or occasions from effects and appearances, which are alone perceived by sense, entirely relates to reason' (lD175). But 'the appearances, which are alone perceived by sense' are the source and test of what can legitimately be inferred from them; hence the scrupulous attention Berkeley pays to them. This is what he means by the 'strict enquiry concerning the first principles of human knowledge', and by the 'close and narrow survey' which he promises in the Introduction to P (Intro. P4, 5).

The level 1 restriction to the phenomenology of sense experience gives rise to what I shall call Berkeley's austere empirical constraint on the sensefulness or conceivability of concepts, which is that unless such concepts can be cashed out in terms of the phenomenology of experience, thus strictly understood, they have no content. He applies this test repeatedly, as we shall see, but chiefly in connection with the concepts of existence and corporeal substance. This manoeuvre is indeed what substantiates his 'New Principle', which is fundamental; in the two places where he stakes 'the whole upon this issue' (P22, 1D200) his austere constraint on sensefulness is the key.

The attack on abstract ideas lies at the heart of this issue. Berkeley locates the source of much philosophical error and perplexity in the supposition that we are capable of 'framing' abstract ideas (Intro. P6). He identifies two related sorts of abstraction; abstraction as separation (Intro. P7), and abstraction as universalisation (Intro. P8). The first concerns the supposed ability of the mind to single out and separately consider a property of something despite its being the case that it never in fact exists apart from the other properties of that thing. It is claimed, for example, that from the 'mixed or compound idea' of something coloured, extended, and moved, the mind can pick out just one of these properties and view it by itself, excluding the rest. 'Not that it is possible for colour or motion to exist by itself without extension: but only that the mind can frame to itself by *abstraction* the idea of colour exclusive of extension, and of motion exclusive of both colour and extension' (Intro. P7). The second concerns abstraction to universals. 'The mind having observed that in the particular extensions perceived by sense, there is something common and alike in all, and some things peculiar...which distinguishes them from one another; it considers apart or singles out by itself that which is common, making thereof a most abstract idea of extension' (Intro. P8), that is, an idea of 'extension in general' prescinded from particular extended things. And so with 'colour in general', which is the concept not of some particular colour, red or blue or whatever, but of that property taken in abstract; and 'motion in general', the concept of motion considered apart from particular moving things and from particular directions and speeds. In the same way, again prescinding from particular differences between them, abstract ideas of more complex entities are formed; noting what is common to various human beings, for example, and leaving aside what individuates them, we come by the abstract idea of man or humanity (Intro. P9).

Berkeley chooses Locke as his target in discussing 'what can be alleged in defence of the doctrine of abstraction' (Intro. Pll) and locates the doctrine's source in the idea that words come to have a general signification 'by being made the signs of general ideas' (cf. *Essay* III.iii.6). What Berkeley objects to is not that there are general words and ideas, for there are indeed both, but that there are *abstract* general ideas formed in one of the ways described above, and that general words function by denoting them (Intro. P12). Rather, he argues, an idea becomes general when, while itself remaining particular, it is made 'to represent or stand for all other particular ideas of the same sort' (ibid.); hence the universality of a term consists in the *relations* it bears to particulars signified by it, not in the supposed fact that it names an abstract idea (Intro. P15). To demonstrate the incomprehensibility of the abstractionist doctrine Berkeley cites Locke's example at *Essay* IV.vii.9 of the abstract triangle which is 'neither oblique nor rectangle, neither equilateral, equicrural nor scalenon, but *all and none* of these at once', and fastens on Locke's admission that such a conception is of 'something imperfect that cannot exist, an idea wherein some parts of several different and *inconsistent* ideas are put together' (Locke ibid., Berkeley's emphases Intro. P13). In the same way, Berkeley says, it is incoherent to suppose that one's general idea of *man* is of a being 'neither white, black, nor any particular colour ... (of) neither tall stature nor low stature, nor yet middle stature, but something abstracted from all these' (Intro. P9).

There is one sense of abstraction that Berkeley allows, in which one can consider something apart, like an arm or a leg, say, which although it does not usually exist detached from other things, like torsos, nevertheless possibly could do so, as when for example an arm is severed in an accident. 'But I deny that I can abstract one from

3. Interpretation: method, meaning and empiricism   31

another, or conceive separately, those qualities which it is impossible should exist so separated; or that I can frame a general notion by abstracting from particulars in the manner aforesaid. Which two last are the proper acceptations of *abstraction*' (Intro. P10).

The uses to which Berkeley puts the attack on abstract ideas – an attack which, as almost all commentators agree, is successful – will become manifest in the course of the discussion in the following chapters. It plays such a fundamental role in them that one can only greet with incredulity Bennett's remark that he has 'trouble finding the supposed link between the theory of abstract ideas and materialism' (Bennett p45). One crucial way in which the rejection of abstractionism enters into Berkeley's thought requires comment now, however, for it helps explain the nature of his chief form of argument, namely the 'conceivability' argument.

In rejecting abstract ideas Berkeley argues that one cannot abstract, in the sense of separate, for example colour from extension. The same argument is at work at V130, where he asks whether it is possible for anyone 'to frame in his mind a distinct abstract idea of visible extension or figure exclusive of all colour: and on the other hand, whether he can conceive colour without visible extension?' And he replies, 'For my own part, I must confess I am not able to attain so great a nicety of abstraction: in a strict sense, I see nothing but light and colours, with their several shades and variations' (ibid.). The 'strict sense' is the level 1 or phenomenological sense, and the insistence is, as with the attack on abstraction in the Introduction to P, that ideas of sense are particular and concrete. Now, the claim is, to remain with this example, that colour cannot be conceived of apart from extension nor extension apart from colour; the idea of something coloured is *ipso facto* an idea of something extended, and vice versa. Berkeley uses the expression 'frame an idea' in place of 'conceive' at times (cf. 1D177, 3D194); he also, and I shall return to this point, talks sometimes of conceiving as imagining. And he frequently talks of what is inconceivable as what is 'repugnant', 'contradictory', or 'meaningless' (cf. e.g. P4). He is accordingly talking about *sensefulness*, and correlatively is employing a notion of possibility which, in a very interesting way, is tied to that of sensefulness.

In short order, the idea is that what is conceivable is what makes sense, and what makes sense is what can be cashed in terms of the sensible ideas we can have. 'My conceiving or imagining power does not extend beyond the possibility of real existence or perception. Hence as it is impossible for me to see or feel anything without an actual sensation of that thing, so it is impossible for me to conceive in my thoughts any sensible thing or object distinct from the sensation or perception of it' (P5). By 'distinct from the sensation or perception of it' Berkeley means 'apart from any reference to actual or possible perceptual experience of it in general' (cf. P3; this reading acquires substantiation in the detail to come). Sense therefore is constituted by evidence; to grasp the sense of a term – or in Berkeley's terminology, to make sense of a concept – is to be able to apply it in possible experiential situations, and if nothing counts as experientially-grounded conditions of application for the concept, it is empty. This thesis will have a familiar ring to those persuaded by anti-realist attitudes in the theory of meaning, and it connects directly with the idea, briefly described above in connection with those attitudes, that the conditions for the use of terms in a language cannot transcend speakers' capacities to recognise that the conditions for their use are fulfilled or otherwise, which is to say in jargon precisely what Berkeley is urging here. Accordingly it is senseless, 'repugnant', 'meaningless', to talk of visible extension *as such*, abstracted from coloured surfaces or lines, that is, objects encounterable in experience and having determinate shapes and widths and breadths. What is going on here, then, is that strict attention to the level 1 facts is placing what I earlier called austere constraints on the sensefulness of the concepts deployed in discourse about the experience which those facts constitute; and only if those concepts arise from and can be tested by those facts do they have content. This form of argument, as noted, is fundamental to Berkeley's strategy, and it will be met with again frequently. It ties together questions of Berkeley's empiricism and his method by showing how, in thinking about all matters of sensory experience, any theory constructed to account for it (at level 3) and to explain how it gives rise to our everyday beliefs (level 2) must be licensed by a 'narrow survey' of the level 1 facts in which sensory experience consists (cf. VV18).

That Berkeley sometimes talks of 'imaginability' and 'conceivability' interchangeably (cf. C254, 415, 572) might seem to offer grounds for complaint, on the basis that a theory which conflates the two must have it that conceived ideas are mental pictures; and this, it could be argued, is an inadequate account of conceiving. A complaint to this effect would be justified if imagining were restricted only to *visualising*, to seeing pictures 'in the mind's eye', which is indeed what it is often enough taken to be, to an extent that explains the predominance of the visual model in Berkeley's own writings, as

3. Interpretation: method, meaning and empiricism 33

is also the case with Locke. But neither in fact nor in Berkeley does this restriction apply. Consider the invitation to 'imagine what it would be like to be rich'. Presumably certain pictures will attend doing so – a beach in the Bahamas, a Porsche, diamond pendants, say, if one is prone to think of being rich in hackneyed terms – but that is not the whole story, for what is more significant is the family of conceptualisings which imagining this state of affairs involves, as for example being free from certain constraints and commitments while being bound to certain others, being free to do certain things or to realise certain ambitions while being barred from certain states or satisfactions to which not being rich typically admits one. These aspects of the matter are not pictorial but conceptual. More narrowly, since one can imagine, say, an aria from *Don Giovanni*, or the taste of lemon sorbet, or the irritation of being attacked by mosquitoes in the night – and sounds, tastes, itches cannot be pictorially imagined – it is clear that the tendency to restrict imagining to having mental pictures is simply misleading.

There is a sense of 'imagining' which is in competition with 'conceiving', however, in that one can imagine (one can even write a novel, or make a film, about) some state of affairs which is empirically unrealisable and which depends for any plausibility it has on spurious concepts and jumps of the fancy from what is strictly conceivable to what is strictly meaningless on a narrower scrutiny. Most if not all science fiction trades on the capacity we have to be fanciful. But this is not Berkeley's sense of 'imagine'. In his use of the term imagination as conceiving or 'framing an idea' is restricted to what can be 'copied' from ideas acquired in sense experience (C823, 818); imagined ideas are the 'effect or consequence' of such ideas (C843) and hence presuppose them (C582). Imagining as conceiving is strictly distinguished from 'actually' perceiving by Berkeley (cf. C777), that is, actually having ideas imprinted on the senses on a particular occasion; but a definite relation between them is specified, which is that one cannot conceive or imagine x unless x is something actually perceivable, actually encounterable in experience (cf. C843 and 582 again). And this of course is another way of putting the point about empirical constraints on sensefulness. At C843 a distinction between imagining in Berkeley's sense and fancying is given, and he pointedly contrasts what is 'real', that is, what is senseful, from what is 'chimerical' more than once in the published writings, which is an allied matter (cf. e.g. P39-40, 41, 3D234-5). In short, then, conceiving or imagining, or being able to 'frame an idea' of something, is to form a conception which is secured by or cashable in sense experience at level 1 – and correlatively, a term or expression is senseful just if it is applicable to experience. This – the austere constraint on sensefulness or conceivability in empirical matters – is the key to Berkeley's philosophical position. (What can be encountered in or derived from sensory experience does not exhaust the realm of what can be known; we have knowledge also of spirit and God, but our epistemic access to them takes a different form. See Ch. 3 below.)

The nature of Berkeley's conceivability argument has been widely misunderstood by his commentators, and the importance of the argument itself is accordingly underrated. Pitcher, for example, in remarking Berkeley's 'fondness' for conceivability arguments (which epithet suggests that he does not appreciate their significance) says that Berkeley appears to be committed to the principle 'If property x is inconceivable apart from property y, and vice versa, then x is identical with y' (Pitcher p54.). Pitcher's comment is that this seems plausible in some cases but not in others; for example, 'being a brother' and 'being a male sibling' are identical properties and cannot be conceived apart, whereas 'being triangular', that is, being a plane figure enclosing three angles, and 'being trilateral', that is, being a closed plane figure having three sides, are he says inconceivable apart, but it is not clear whether they are identical (pp54-5). He concludes that we have nothing to go on here but our intuitions, and states that 'Most people's intuitive judgement about the properties of visible extension and colour, I suspect, would surely contradict Berkeley's; it strikes us as highly implausible to hold that visible extension is the very same property as colour' (p55). There are several problems here. To begin with, even if in general we allowed ourselves to think in terms of property identity (which we would express,using predicate variables, as $F=G$), doing so is not to the point here. Berkeley has scant use for a concept of identity, and when he talks of 'identical propositions' he has what contemporary philosophical logicians would recognise as other concerns in mind, for he classes them among Locke's 'trifling propositions' (cf. *Essay* IV.vii. 10) as examples of the way words can be used without ideas: 'A stone is a stone. this a nonsensical Proposition' (C592); 'Homo est Homo etc. comes at last to Petrus est Petrus etc. Now if these identical Propositions are sought after in the Mind they will not be found. there are no identical mental Propositions tis all about sounds and terms' (C728). Berkeley's examples are drawn from that subset of 'identical propositions', namely tautologies, which are most visibly uninformative (although at C592 he cites Locke's example of 'the

3. Interpretation: method, meaning and empiricism   35

whole is equal to the sum of its parts', *Essay* ibid.), and there is nothing at work here to sort the senses in which statements can count as assertions of identity, as being true in virtue of their logical form alone, and as having the semantic property of analyticity. This is hardly surprising, given that the connections and distinctions between these concepts, in the form in which they are now chiefly familiar to us, are of relatively recent articulation. (There is nothing to suggest that Berkeley was aware of Leibniz's contributions in these respects. It was some time indeed before Leibniz's work in philosophical logic came to be appreciated – in fact, by Russell.) Discussions of identity, as we now conduct them, stem largely from Frege, and turn on his distinction between the 'is' of predication and the 'is' of identity, which itself trades upon a distinction between concepts and objects in Frege's technical senses of these notions, in terms of which they are defined as occupying different logical categories. Concepts are introduced by predicate expressions, and objects by proper names; a name can never appear in predicate position, hence a statement of the form 'a is b' – taking, in the standard way, the letters as individual constants – is not a subject-predicate proposition, but a statement in which the copula functions much as does the sign '=' in mathematics (cf. Frege pp43-4). This distinction was not drawn in pre-Fregean term logic, in which names can sometimes function predicatively, and identity was not construed as a special kind of dyadic relation. For these reasons it is at least distorting to read Berkeley as committing himself to a principle of identity by means of his conceivability argument, and this is not just because he did not have the required concept to hand, but, as we shall see, because such a concept is in any case irrelevant to his purposes. Moreover Pitcher's examples introduce further difficulties, in that he appears to ignore the difference between the relation of intensional equivalence, which holds between 'being a brother' and 'being a male sibling', and extensional equivalence, which holds between 'being triangular' (henceforth 'F') and 'being trilateral' (henceforth 'G'). On Frege's terms, again permitting ourselves talk of property-identity, we might say that F and G are coreferential, that is, intersubstitutable for one another in sentential contexts *salva veritate*, but that they differ in sense; since a and b do likewise in the identity statement 'a is b' where, say, 'a' stands for 'Hesperus' and 'b' for Phosphorus', it follows that F=G is clearly enough an identity statement on that theory. If one thought it informative to fit Berkeley's conception of the unabstractability of properties into this mould, it would be tempting to note that, if in addition to talk of property-identity one also allowed talk of necessity as truth in all possible worlds, then $F=G$ entails $\Box(x)(Fx \leftrightarrow Gx)$; and then one might point out that this is of course true consistently with the denial of the intensional equivalence of F and G, so that predicate-expressions like 'being visibly extended' and 'being coloured' do not *mean* the same but apply to all and only the same objects – which thought might clarify the intuitions of which Pitcher speaks.

But to talk in these terms is to lose sight of Berkeley's crucial intention. His intention is to say that what cannot be conceived is what does not make sense, and that what does not make sense is what is not secured by the experiential facts. It is a condition for the legitimate possession and application of a concept that it should have cash-value in experience; what it does not make sense to talk about is what cannot be met with in the world. ('Notions' in Berkeley's technical sense are of course excluded from this account; see below p. 5) The modality is to be taken seriously here; what on these terms in inconceivable, that is, does not make sense, is *impossible*. An illuminating way to explain the equation is as follows.

In setting out ways of importing the modal operator $\Diamond$ into his systems S5 and QS5 Kirwan considers the adverb 'conceivably' to see whether it shares the truth-conditions of $\Diamond$ as previously specified in those systems. He argues that if 'conceivably' were to do the job of acting as the pronunciation of $\Diamond$ then it would have to have the following truth-condition ('T' and 'w' respectively stand for a formally specified truth-predicate and a world): ' "conceivably s" is T in w if and only if s can be used to express a proposition which would be true given some possible facts' (Kirwan p241). But, he argues, this will not do because 'what is possible may be inconceivable ... Some possible worlds may be too strange to conceive', and moreover – and more fundamentally – the 'received axiom' upon which Berkeley relies (cf. the Draft Introduction to P, *Works* II p125), namely that an impossibility cannot be conceived, is false because of 'the really quite obvious fact that impossibilities, e.g. denials of mathematical and logical truths, can even be believed' (Kirwan p242). It is neither here nor there, for present purposes, whether the truth-conditions for 'conceivably' match those for $\Diamond$ in Kirwan's systems; what is interesting is the way Kirwan detaches conceivability and possibility, having it that what is conceivable may not exhaust the domain of the possible, and that at least some of what is impossible is conceivable. This raises a number of questions.

It is implied by the first claim Kirwan makes that the limits of

3. Interpretation: method, meaning and empiricism 37

conceivability are the limits of our power to imagine how things are or could be, which limits are contingent ones lying under constraints imposed by the finitary access we have to experiential and conceptual resources for framing ideas of what is or could be the case beyond our ken. Conceivability and possibility therefore appear to fall apart because the former is an epistemic notion whereas the latter is a metaphysical one. And it is implied by his second claim that conceiving is in effect a propositional attitude, like believing, fearing, hoping, and so on, so that unlike cognitive attitudes it can be true that one conceives x whether or not x is true or even possible. That is, the truth of 'S conceives that ...' is independent of the truth-value and modal status of the embedded proposition, as in 'S believes that ...', which is not the case with 'S knows that ...' for which it is a logically necessary condition that the embedded proposition should be true and hence at least possible. Now, in connection with the first of these thoughts, one can grant that what finite minds can conceive may and almost certainly does fall short of what is or could be the case, as Berkeley himself allows; at 2D211, in talking of the universe, he says 'neither sense nor imagination are big enough to comprehend the boundless extent with all its glittering furniture. Though the labouring mind exert and strain each power to its utmost reach, there still stands out ungrasped a surplusage immeasurable', which recalls his talk at P81 of 'my own few, stinted, narrow inlets of perception'. Berkeley is making just the granted point, namely that what finite minds can grasp is limited in comparison to what there is or could be, and this indeed is a mark of his finitary realism (See Chapter Two Section 6 below where the character of that realism is discussed). But this is neither to say that some of what is possible is *inconceivable*, rather than, contingently, *unconceived* owing to finitary limitations, nor that the bounds of conceivability and imaginability are coextensive, where imaginability is understood in the sense, described above, in which it is opposed to conceivability, and which is not Berkeley's sense (for the present let us call this 'Imaginability'). Rather, and this now brings Kirwan's second claim under consideration, one wants to have a distinction between conceivability and Imaginability in order to bring the notion of conceivability under constraints preserving the thought that the concepts which are formed as a result of experience and which apply to actual or possible experience must, in some way, both reflect their source and function and be governed by them. In line with this one at least requires it to be a condition on what is *conceivable* that it be *consistent*, and that therefore it should in principle be possible to discern connections between how things are known or believed by us to be with how things can be, either in the sense of being consonant with them or in showing, consistently with what else is the case, how we were mistaken, whenever we were so, in what we believed or took ourselves to know. Conceiving is forming concepts; to conceive x is at least to be able to give an account or description of x, to *specify* x, in ways which are consistent with what we have grounds for taking to be possible. By what is possible, in turn, we would therefore mean not just what involves no contradiction, but what does not arbitrarily conflict with our best-attested theories, however defeasible these may be. In sharp contrast, Imaginability is cognate to fancying, to the extravagances of science-fiction and the invention of places and beings like the Land of Oz, Hobbits, Mowgli, and Medusa. It is not *conceivable* that there should be, for example, a Gorgon one glance at whom turns mortals to stone, any more than it is conceivable that there should be a round square. One might fancy or Imagine or even believe such things, but doing any of these is far from having a concept of how it could be true that such things are the case. Berkeley's austere constraint makes the demand that the content of what can sensefully be conceived should be supplied by or consist in, or at very least be consistent with, the evidential basis for our thought and talk of the world; from which it follows that to have and to be able to apply a concept – as *opposed* to Imagining – is something that must be constrained by experience. What is impossible cannot, banally, satisfy that constraint; which is precisely the burden of the axiom upon which Berkeley relies, namely that impossiblities are inconceivable. This shows that Kirwan's rejection of the axiom rests on the too loose employment of 'conceiving' in the sense rather of fancying or Imagining than senseful conceptualising. His counter-example, which is that one might believe a necessary falsehood, can in fact be employed against itself to illustrate the claim Berkeley wishes to urge: one might *believe* that 4 x 5 = 12 (and, with Alice down the rabbit-hole, even be right), but if one is working to the base ten it is, however believable a small schoolboy, say, might find it, quite literally and straightforwardly *inconceivable* that 4 x 5 = 12. The point Berkeley makes in the Introduction to P is well expressed by Tipton's encapsulation, 'Anything can be said but not everything can be thought' (Tipton 1 p131), where what is thinkable or conceivable is, in line with the axiom at issue, specifically being *distinguished* from what can be fancied, thus tying the notions of sense, possibility and conceivability tightly together.

A couple of ancillary remarks are in order here. In Kirwan's view it

3. Interpretation: method, meaning and empiricism   39

is proper to say that the realm of the possible could or does contain things of which we cannot even in principle conceive. But what does this remark *mean*? The notion of a bare possibility, about which nothing whatever can be said other than that it *is* a possibility, is just empty. The remotest possibilities, one supposes, are those so utterly divorced from what our capacities for speculation can yield that they can only be specified negatively – for example, that some remotely possible x is not, say, spatial, is not detectable by anything at all akin to the sensory equipment of any known creature, and so forth. In considering talk of such cases, Berkeley aptly comments 'I do not find that there is any kind of effect or impression made on my mind, different from what is excited by the term *nothing*' (P80). The point is well made. It connects with a further thought, which is that the concept of possibility standardly deployed in philosophical discussion is in any case too loose in virtue of the degree of freedom it enjoys from epistemic and semantic constraints (on certain views, such as Berkeley's, these will be closely allied). Standardly, what is possible is what involves no contradiction. But there is a difference between what one might call *mere* or *bare* possibility and, say, *genuine* possibility, the first being specified only by the absence of contradiction, the second by definable accessibility-relations to the actual. For example: suppose we characterise a possible world as a 'book', that is, a set of propositions. One can say, there is a world-book in which all the propositions are consistent with respect to each other but which are otherwise logically unrelated (except individually to their own negations). Such a world would be 'merely' possible in contrast to a 'genuinely' possible alternative whose structure is not in this way null or, if mere consistency is structure, minimal, but admits of connections being traced, predicted, and explained, and which therefore evinces regularities and patterns – in short, is a world which makes sense in respect of its admitting the application of concepts, among them those of regularity, explicability, and so on, which have their source in the experience we in fact enjoy as a result of the actual world's itself being a 'genuinely' possible one. We say of such worlds, as I have just done, that one can 'make sense' of them, and it is the connection between that thought and the nature of conceivability which informs Berkeley's view. To say that what is possible is what makes sense is to place the notion under tighter controls than to say merely that the possible is what is non-contradictory, and this reflects an implicit tradition of thought about legitimate conception which has surfaced in a number of different guises in the history of modern philosophy. Consider for example what Strawson calls Kant's

'Principle of Significance', which is 'that there can be no legitimate, or even meaningful, employment of ideas or concepts which does not relate them to empirical or experiential conditions of their application'(Strawson 2 p16, cf. Kant e.g. B195, B724). Kant's 'Principle' indeed captures a dominant strand of thought in empiricist attitudes, applied with varying degrees of strength; compare the Positivists' reason for distinguishing between 'the dove is in his cote' and 'God is in his heaven' and Locke's emphatic rejection of innatism. Kant's 'Principle' is a highly apt statement of Berkeley's intentions, for it is just this thought which underlies his major form of argument.

A final point on the issue of conceivability and abstraction is this. In discussing the virtues of traditional formal logic Sommers notes that a distinction between properties and 'features' is employed in that logic which in his view is important, but which has been lost to sight as a result first of empiricism and later of the dominance of modern predicate logic (Sommers pp303-4). The distinction is relevant to Berkeley's reasons for holding that abstractionism is illegitimate. It is this: a property is, familiarly, something like redness or smoothness, whereas a feature is, correlatively, something like Colour or Texture, and is an essential attribute of whatever possesses it. Thus, a thing x may be wet, wetness being a property, and if it is not wet then it is dry; so properties come in pairs. But there is nothing privative to features; a mathematical proposition has no Colour, but neither does it *lack* Colour, for a mathematical proposition is not the kind of thing which is Coloured – it does not fall into the range of things, as Sommers puts it, which can be tested for having that feature. 'The apple I have is red and smooth. It need not have *those* properties. But it must have Colour and Texture' (Sommers p303). The distinction is found in Aristotle's doctrine of substance, features constituting substrata with the potential for taking on determinations; for example, the Colour of an apple is the potential for the apple's being a determinate colour like red or green, and its actually being, say, red is an actualisation of that potential (ibid. p304). In Sommers' view this distinction is ignored by the empiricists to their cost: 'In a classic empiricist argument one is aked to perform the *gedanken* experiment of stripping a thing of its attributes. Having done this the empiricists say we are left with "something I know not what" (Locke) or with nothing at all (Berkeley and Hume). This line of thought ignores the difference between properties like redness and features like Colour. One can imagine the apple without its colour; one cannot imagine it without its Colour. So the empiricists' *gedanken*

3. Interpretation: method, meaning and empiricism 41

experiment cannot be done' (ibid.).

On the most plausible rendering of these remarks they would, contrary to what Sommers implies, be accepted by Berkeley. For on the best rendering of them, Sommers is to be read as saying that one can imagine (or conceive, taking 'imagine' in Berkeley's sense) an apple without its colour in the sense that one can imagine it without *that* colour – say, red – but with some other colour instead – say, green or russet; but one cannot imagine it without *some colour or other*, that is, without Colour. So Colour is not, on this rendering, an abstract idea of an indeterminate colour, neither red nor green, or a universal, but is a *logical* category – it might be treated as a label for a class of predicates one of which an apple must take because it is the kind of thing it is. On this view the Colour of x is x's attribute of 'being coloured', whereas the colour of x is its 'being green' or 'being red'. It is a contingent matter that x is red, say, rather than green, but necessary that it is some colour or other. These thoughts are harmless enough; they do not carry deep commitments to a metaphysics of essence, but simply reflect inescapable facts about the structure of experience. The force of talking about 'categories' is that it shows what predicates something must take in order to fall into that category; the point is the same as the one being made when one says that a teapot is not the kind of thing that can either be or fail to be bankrupt, or that a physical object must always have a spatial location, and so on. A related notion is that thinking of an object is always to think of it *as* an object of a certain kind, that is, as falling under certain descriptions which it must satisfy in order to count as an object of that kind (the point is neutral as between essentialist and conventionalist interpretations of what underwrites it). A gloss on Berkeley's view that one cannot abstract colour from visible extension, say, would in these terms be that to conceive of something visibly extended is in this sense necessarily to conceive of something coloured, since anything which takes the one kind of predicate takes the other in virtue of its falling into the category which takes both if it takes either. And this view might be taken to explain a claim to the effect that 'anything visibly extended is coloured' is, like 'all bodies are extended' and 'all bodes have spatial location', *analytic*, which in Berkeleian terms would be wholly explained by the fact that anything which satisfies 'is visibly extended' satisfies 'is coloured' and *vice versa*.

If, however, by 'feature' Sommers intends an *ontological* category, as unfortunately it seems he does (cf. p303), then Colour *is* an abstract idea – it is not any particular colour, a *determinate* colour, but nevertheless is an attribute of x which can be actualised as such a colour. To this rendering Berkeley would have obvious objections. However the point here is that he would agree with Sommers that the *gedanken* experiment at issue cannot be done, providing the first and more plausible rendering of the property-feature distinction is understood, for what one is per impossibile invited to 'think away' is not *this* particular colour or texture of an apple, but its Colour or Texture. What is shown by the fact that one cannot do so is in Berkeley's view the illegitimacy of abstraction as separation – one cannot conceive an apple without Colour, that is, without some or other particular colour, it does not matter which; or Texture, that is, some or other particular texture, regardless of which. But the fact that the experiment cannot be done does not entail that one can conceive of Colour or Texture *as such*, that is, of an indeterminate abstract idea, which is the second reading of 'feature' and the one Sommers apparently intends.

Interpreting Berkeley correctly, then, involves recognising the fact that he distinguishes between levels 1, 2 and 3; that he applies an austere constraint on sensefulness or conceivability in all matters of empirical discourse, which is that whatever is strictly senseful or conceivable is what is ultimately licensed by reference to the level 1 facts alone; and that, in connection with this, his major form of argument is the conceivability argument, which he applies – often in the form of a denial that certain things can be conceived in abstraction from one another, like visible extension and colour, or existence and perception – to show that certain concepts, for example the concept of matter, are empty and therefore cannot serve in a level 3 account of what explains level 2, that is, the ordinary course of our experience. There are however further and other points touching on the interpretation of Berkeley's arguments which it is valuable to bear in mind, some of which add clarification to the points just made; and to these, in conclusion, I turn.

A theme in Berkeley's attack on abstract ideas is that language can be misleading, for example in making us think that because we have words of general signification we therefore have abstract general ideas. At the end of the Introduction to P (Intro. P21-5) he says that he proposes to take whatever ideas he considers 'bare and naked into my view' (Intro. P21) in order to escape being 'imposed upon by words' (Intro. P24), as far as it is possible for him to do so. In the notebooks he frequently iterates the point that language misleads (C176, 220, 223, 537, 553, 561, 564, 596, 636, 641-2, 693, 702, 719) and in doing so reinforces the considerations about

3. Interpretation: method, meaning and empiricism 43

sensefulness and level 1. He says 'If men would lay aside words in thinking tis impossible they should ever mistake save only in matters of fact ... certainly I cannot err in matters of simple perception' (C693, cf. 731a), and this appears at Intro. P22 as the claim that one cannot be deceived about the actual contents of states of sensory awareness as one has them. Accordingly if we are not to be misled by words we must give them a precise signification which 'never goes beyond our ideas' (C584; cf. 591, 606). In saying this Berkeley is acknowledging, despite the 'bare and naked' remark, that one cannot in practice dispense with words (Intro. P23); his recommendation to himself and others to do so is not, except as an ideal, a recommendation to wordless thought so much as a warning against being misled (Intro. P24). It is indeed very doubtful whether thought above a rudimentary level is possible without language *in principle* (cf. Grayling 2 pp52-3). But this does not affect Berkeley's point, which is in essentials similar to the points made on the same head by Bacon and Locke before him, and Russell and Wittgenstein after him.

There is a rather interesting feature of Berkeley's efforts in this direction, which further illuminates what he has to say about level 1, and this is the conception of the 'solitary man' (cf. C560, 588, 648, 727), a conception sometimes expressed by means of examples about people without language, and children, and sometimes in terms of what 'the vulgar' do and do not say. In the Draft Introduction to P (*Works* II p121f) Berkeley uses the conceit of the solitary man to claim that without the embarassment of words such a man would attend only 'to the constant train of particular ideas passing in his mind', that is, would have a pure level 1 experience unprejudiced by a baggage of language-embodied theory interpreting it for him; and who would consequently, Berkeley says, 'be nearer the discovery of certain great and excellent truths' than any language-using or educated person (ibid. p141). Now, whether or not this conception has much to recommend it – and it strikes me as simply implausible – it nevertheless shows part of what Berkeley has in mind regarding method, in particular concerning the principle that the actual content and character of sensory experience – level 1 – is to govern whatever else we say if we are to say it sensefully. For the thought is that such a man would have 'bare and naked' in his view no more than the intentional content of his states of awareness, making no inferences from them and imposing no theoretical constructions upon them; and so would have a wholly undistorted view of the facts as his awareness reveals them. Among the things such a man would think, presumably, would be that his ideas are inert, with nothing of causal power in them and with no necessary relations obtaining between them; and his only experience of agency would arise from his own felt capacities in that regard, as a being with a will. In particular he would not suppose that behind or beyond his ideas lay an inaccessible realm of material particulars which cause his experiences in him, or at least contribute to their production in virtue of their interactions with his organs of sense; and not only would he not have the concept of matter, he would further not have any of the abstract ideas Berkeley proscribes as illegitimate. Above all he would not have the abstract idea of *existence*, for what is understood by that term would be wholly exhausted by what he perceives. Nor would he be a sceptic, for he would take it that the things he perceives are as he perceives them; there would be no gap between experience and reality for the solitary, since reality *is* his experience, coterminous with and exhausted by it. It is not clear how Berkeley would establish on this basis the final point he would doubtless wish to include, namely that such a man would immediately perceive the handiwork of an infinite spirit in everything about him; but we must suppose that he might be intended by Berkeley to conclude this or something like this from the observation that his ideas are effects and are not caused by him, which are the premises of Berkeley's causal dependence argument for God's existence, as we shall see. If it is true that early humans were animistic, this could be less implausible than it seems. Of course it is entirely a matter for conjecture what a Robinson Crusoe (from birth) might do in the way of producing a conceptual scheme; analytic reconstructions of what would have to be the case in such circumstances have been offered (cf. Ayer 2 pp91-106), but the device is anyway heuristic, and Berkeley did not publish it.

Finally, the matter of the completeness of Berkeley's theory has to be taken into account. We have it, as noted earlier, in truncated form. Only the first part of P was published; V is in a sense an introduction to some of its theses, and D a restatement and amplification of some others of its theses. The theses in question largely consist in the expounding and defence of the 'New Principle', and much that needs to be argued in connection with what the 'New Principle' entails and requires is only sketched, in particular questions about the nature of finite spirit and God, our knowledge of them both, and the precise character of the relationship between them – an account of which would further clarify the nature both of sensible ideas and notions. Moreover, Berkeley has a moral theory in prospect, also promised for Part II of P, and what he says of it in his notebooks shows that Part II would have amplified his theory

3. Interpretation: method, meaning and empiricism

concerning spirit and God: 'The 2 great Principles of morality, the Being of a God & the Freedom of Man: these to be handled in the beginning of the Second Book' (C508). Entries C626-31, 649-52, 736, 792 and 878-9 make clear, in some cases explicit, reference to the 'sequel' or 'the Second Book' (cf. esp. 736, 792, 878), and a consideration of them shows that a considerable number of the entries in Notebook A marked 'S' for 'Spirit', 'Mo' for morals, and 'G' for 'God' are preliminary studies for it, as are some of the 'M' for 'Matter' and 'E' for 'Existence' entries. There is even a reference at C583 to a *third* book; the entry, marked 'M', reads 'That which extremely strengthens us in prejudice is that we think we see an empty space. which I shall demonstrate to be false in the 3rd Book'. This suggests that level 3 issues were to be thoroughly pursued in the sequels to Part I, and it may have been in a third book that Berkeley's speculations about time (with which the notebooks begin) would have received an adequate treatment. Indeed the treatment of time both in the notebooks and the published writings shows just how truncated Berkeley's theory is, for we get an account of time considered for the most part phenomenologically only, that is, at level 1, with barely any hint of how our level 2 employment of the concept works, and even less of a hint as to how it is explained, if indeed it *can* be explained, by an inclusive level 3 account. As they stand, therefore, Berkeley's views on time are drastically incomplete, and have given rise to much puzzlement among the commentators.

Two decades after the publication of P Part I the American Samuel Johnson concluded his first letter to Berkeley with the hope that Part II would soon appear, because in addition to clarifying points of difficulty in Part I and elsewhere – (Johnson in the body of his letter chiefly questions Berkeley about spirits and God and their relations, in particular how God causes ideas in finite spirits) – it will surely, he says, apply the theory of Part I to a further range of issues which, in the light of that theory, require explanation (*Works* II pp271-8). Berkeley replied that he had earlier written a substantial portion of Part II but had lost it while travelling in Italy, 'and I never had leisure since to do so disagreeable a thing as writing twice on the same subject' (ibid. p282). In his second letter Johnson pressed Berkeley again: 'I can't but express myself again very solicitously desirous that the noble design you have begun may be yet further pursued in the second part. And everybody that has seen the first is earnestly with me in this request' (ibid. p290). The plea availed nothing; Berkeley in his first letter had already said that what was published would be enough for a reflective reader to fill in details and supply them further (cf. ibid. p282). Now, this invitation would be well enough if Berkeley had not himself, from the time of his earliest reflections, placed a barrier in the way of accepting it, which is that he sought to introduce his views in a gradual and sometimes veiled manner, with the intention of promoting their acceptability by making them appear less radical or novel than they are. At C163 he ponders a suitable method of presenting his views, for unless done correctly 'a demonstration tho never so exact will not go down with most'; shortly afterwards he notes 'Tis prudent to correct mens mistakes without altering their language. This makes truth glide into their souls insensibly' (C185). Proof that the strategy was in fact adopted is given at P46, where Berkeley remarks that in V he had allowed tangible objects, unlike visible objects, to exist without the mind, whereas in fact his view, argued for in P, is that none of the objects of the senses exist without the mind; but he had not mentioned this in the earlier work because, he says, it was beside his purpose there to do so.

Accordingly a question mark hangs over some of the less fully argued points in the published writings, and were it not for the notebooks the commentators' difficulty in respect of them would be large. Even with the notebooks to hand, a cautious acceptance of Berkeley's invitation to reflect on his 'hints' (*Works* II p282) is necessary. Fortunately for present purposes, however, which are to explore Berkeley's *central* arguments, the sketchier regions of his thought pose somewhat less of a problem than they otherwise would – which is not to say that they pose none.

The writings we have do not contain changes of outlook over time; Berkeley was remarkably consistent in his views, and in *Alciphron* and *Siris* the doctrines of V, P and D are still in all essentials maintained. Rather, there is an unfolding as opposed to a development of views between V and D, and the theory as we have it is extraordinarily tightly-knit and internally coherent. It is also extraordinarily rigorous, a fact which the lucidity and beauty of Berkeley's prose to some extent masks, but which a closer acquaintance with his texts quickly makes evident.

CHAPTER TWO
Esse est Percipi: Against Matter

1. The New Principle

Berkeley's 'New Principle' is central to his philosophical theory. He gives it a condensed statement at P1-7, which runs as follows (and I make liberal use of Berkeley's own words because they will be recalled frequently): The 'objects of human knowledge' are 'either ideas actually imprinted on the senses, or such as are perceived by attending to the passions and operations of the mind, or lastly ideas formed by help of memory and imagination, either compounding, dividing, or barely representing those originally perceived in the aforesaid ways'. Ideas of sense – colours, shapes, and the rest – are 'observed to accompany each other' in certain ways; 'collections' of them 'come to be marked by one name, and so to be reputed one thing', for example an apple, a stone, a tree (P1). Besides this 'endless variety of ideas or objects of knowledge' there is 'something which knows or perceives them'; this 'perceiving, active being is what I call *mind, spirit, soul,* or *my self*', and it is 'entirely distinct' from the ideas it perceives (P2). It is universally allowed that our thoughts, passions, and ideas of imagination do not 'exist without the mind'; likewise it 'seems no less evident that the various sensations or ideas imprinted on the sense, however blended or combined together (that is, whatever objects they compose) cannot exist otherwise than in a mind perceiving them'. Talk of sensible objects is accordingly talk of actual or possible perceptions. 'For as to what is said of the absolute existence of unthinking things without any relation to their being perceived, that seems perfectly unintelligible. Their *esse* is *percipi*, nor is it possible they should have any existence, out of the minds or thinking things which perceive them' (P3). It is a common opinion that sensible objects like houses and mountains have an absolute existence independent of perception, but this is a 'manifest contradiction. For what are the forementioned objects but the things we perceive by sense, and what do we perceive besides our own ideas or sensations; and is it not plainly repugnant that any of these or any combination of them should exist unperceived ?' (P4). The belief that things can exist apart from being perceived depends at bottom on the doctrine of abstract ideas (P5), but it is 'perfectly unintelligible' to abstract the existence of a thing from its being an object 'perceived or known'; 'consequently so long as they are not perceived by me, or do not exist in my mind or that of any other created spirit, they must either have no existence at all, or else subsist in the mind of some eternal spirit' (P6). And from all this the conclusion follows, that 'there is not any other substance than *spirit*, or that which perceives' (P7). The 'New Principle', therefore, is that because the *esse* of sensible things is to be perceived, and because whatever is perceived is an idea, what the universe contains is minds and their ideas; which is to say, the only substance is mind or spirit.

Most commentators, Luce chief among them, take it that the 'New Principle' is *esse est percipi* (or in fuller form 'Existence is percipi or percipere' C429), and therefore concerns 'the nature & meaning & import of Existence' (C491). Ayers has it that the Principle is 'that the mind is the substance that supports sensible qualities, by perceiving them' (Ayers 1 p49), and is therefore the discovery that the only substance is spirit. In fact the New Principle comprises both, for Berkeley's claim is that the thesis about substance is immediately entailed by the thesis about existence, and the argument of P1-6, terminating in the conclusion stated at P7, is intended to show this. In the notebooks Berkeley makes it clear that the New Principle is the insight that once one has grasped the nature of existence it immediately follows that spirit is the only substance: after heralding his discovery of 'the obvious tho amazing truth' (C279) he sets it out in preliminary form; it is that 'Our simple ideas are so many simple thoughts or perceptions, & that a perception cannot exist without a thing to perceive it or any longer than it is perceived, that a thought cannot be in an unthinking thing' (C280). Later, at C379, he gives what is virtually a definition: 'the Principle, i.e. that neither our ideas nor anything like our ideas can possibly be in an unperceiving thing.' These are statements which in effect assert that mind is the only substance because to exist is nothing other than *to perceive*, which is to be a mind, or *to be perceived*, which is to be mind-dependent.

But the key to the New Principle, the claim which makes the conclusion about substance possible, is *esse est percipi aut percipere*: ' 'tis on the Discovery of the nature & meaning & import of Existence that I chiefly insist .... This puts a wide difference betwixt the sceptics and

1. The New Principle

me. This I think wholly new. I am sure 'tis new to me' (C491). At P24 the insistence is repeated: 'It is on this therefore that I insist, to wit, that the absolute existence of unthinking things are words without a meaning, or which include a contradiction. This is what I repeat and inculcate, and earnestly recommend to the attentive thoughts of the reader.' Berkeley indeed rests his case on his claim about the nature of existence and what it entails: at P22 he says 'I am content to put the whole upon this issue; if you can but conceive it possible for one extended movable substance, or in general, for any one idea or anything like an idea, to exist otherwise than in a mind perceiving it, I shall readily give up the cause'; and this offer is repeated at 1D193 where Philonous says to Hylas: 'Now I am content to put our dispute upon this issue. If you can frame in your thoughts a distinct abstract idea of motion or extension, divested of all those sensible modes, as swift and slow, great and small, round and square, and the like, which are acknowledged to exist only in the mind, I will then yield the point you contend for'.

What the New Principle is designed to show is that there is no matter or corporeal substance, because there is only, and can only be, spiritual substance; and the force of showing this is that if there is no matter or corporeal substance, then there is no gap between perception and a supposedly real material world lying beyond it – and hence no occasion for scepticism: 'The reverse of the Principle introduced Scepticism' (C304 and 411). It not only defeats scepticism concerning whether we can know that there is a world, but also scepticism about whether we can know what the world is intrinsically like; for the world is the perception of it, and therefore is as it is perceived. In showing this, Berkeley claims, the New Principle defends common sense proposition (a), provides the materials for showing how common sense proposition (b) is both to be understood (namely as b″) and defended (by his level 3 account), and – since it makes spirit the only substance – defends, or at any rate provides material for defending, religion against atheism, all which are Berkeley's express aims.

The task here is to unpack, explore and assess these claims, for they constitute Berkeley's central arguments. Their expression at P1-7 is, as noted, summary, and the rest of that work and D is devoted to their fuller exposition and defence. The major part of the task in hand is to look at the related concepts of ideas, existence, and substance, which are the lynch-pins in Berkeley's position. I begin with the first of them.

2. Ideas and things

The argument summarised above opens with a Lockean catalogue of the mind's furniture; there are ideas of sense, there are 'such as are perceived by attending to the passions and operations of the mind', and there are ideas of memory and imagination (P1). For Locke, ideas are 'whatsoever the mind perceives in itself, or is the immediate object of perception, thought or understanding' (*Essay* II. viii.8), that is, 'idea' is the generic label for whatever is before the mind in any of its operations whether of sensing, reflecting, remembering, and so forth. Berkeley's decision to employ the term in much the same way is marked by his saying at V45 'I take the word idea for any immediate object of sense or understanding, in which large signification it is commonly used by the moderns'; but although he trades upon its use as a generic label for the mind's contents in the manner of his predecessors and contemporaries, he does so in a deeply qualified way and has his own sorting among them. The opening account of the mind's contents at P1 is carefully phrased, for the second category, 'such as are perceived by attending to the passions and operations of the mind', is not as it turns out a category of *ideas* at all, but of *notions*; the distinction is deliberately suppressed by Berkeley here to maintain, for the time being, the familiar Lockean flavour of the list, and to maintain also the initial expository flow of P1-7, which would be broken by an explanation of the distinction there. It is in any case more easily and pointfully drawn later. The distinction is this: *ideas* are always *sensory* ideas, that is, are either the content of states of sensory awareness, or the copies of these in memory, reflection, and imagination; and *notions* are concepts focally of the self, spirit or mind, and God, none of which have their origins in sense experience and which are therefore not ideas (cf. P42 and especially P142) but which are apprehended either by immediate intuition, in the case of one's own mind, or by 'reflexion and reasoning', as in the case of God (3D232 and cf. P140). Although the *term* 'notion' is introduced for the first time in the 1734 editions of P and D, the *distinction* is present in the first editions, and this marks a departure from what had come to be standard usage in Berkeley's time.

Berkeley calls any act or state of having ideas *perceiving*, hence perceiving x is sensing, conceiving, imagining, remembering, thinking about x. The liberality of this use of 'perceive' threatens mistakes, which commentators have duly fastened upon, although

2. Ideas and things

not everything claimed to be mistaken in Berkeley on this score is actually so, as I shall argue. In fact Berkeley was himself conscious of the possible difficulties, and even, as a result, sceptical about the propriety of using 'ideas' and 'perceiving' in a way generally accordant with their then standard use. He sometimes employs a 'call them what you will' idiom regarding ideas; at P25, for example, he says 'all or ideas, sensations, or the things which we perceive, by whatsoever names they may be distinguished', to show that it is not the question of terminology which matters so much as the fact that whatever is present to awareness, other than notions, either is, or has its origin in, *sensory* awareness. Since this is so he deliberates for a long time in the notebooks over whether he should rather use 'thing' than 'idea' to denote the objects of such awareness (C757, 775, 807-8, 872), concluding at P38-9 that despite the risk of misunderstanding which might arise from saying such things as 'we eat and drink ideas, and are clothed with ideas' (P38), it better captures the philosophical import of his principles to use 'idea' rather than 'thing', 'for two reasons: first, because the term *thing*, in contradistinction to the term *idea*, is generally supposed to denote somewhat existing without the mind; secondly, because *thing* hath a more comprehensive signification than *idea*, including spirits or thinking things as well as ideas. Since therefore the objects of sense exist only in the mind, and are withal thoughtless and inactive, I chose to mark them by the word *idea* which implies these properties' (P39). But the hesitation is significant; *things* like apples, stones and books are *ideas* or clusters of them, and this constitutes a central Berkeleyan tenet, understanding the import of which – and seeing how it can be defended – forms much of the business to come.

The remarks just quoted encapsulate what is chiefly important about ideas for Berkeley, namely their mind-dependence and their inertness. That they are the former follows from their being *ideas*. Their inertness is another matter, with important consequences for Berkeley, and this requires explanation. In a way which markedly foreshadows Hume, Berkeley argues that there is no necessary connection between ideas; they are particular entities with 'nothing of power or agency included in them. So that one idea or object of thought cannot produce, or make an alteration in another' (P25). To test the truth of this we are invited simply to introspect. Since ideas exist in the mind, we know them completely – 'there is nothing in them but what is perceived' – and it is manifest upon inspection that 'power or activity' is not part of what is perceived (ibid.: see Jessop's note 1 *Works* II p51 which shows how this principle is adopted from

Malebranche and Locke). We have a 'continual succession' of ideas, some changing or disappearing and others arising; since they are causally inert, they cannot themselves be responsible for these changes, and therefore there must be some other cause of them (P26). Since ideas *qua* sensible things are causally inactive, and since the only candidate for causal efficacy, or activity in general, is spirit (P27), spirit is therefore what causes both ideas and their succession or change. But not all ideas and their changes are subject to *my* will (P28), hence 'there is some other spirit that produces them' (P29). 'The ideas of sense are more strong, lively, and distinct than those of imagination; they have likewise a steadiness, order, and coherence, and are not excited at random, as those which are the effects of human wills often are, but in a regular train or series' (P30); these 'set rules or established methods' are 'called *Laws of Nature*: and these we learn by experience, which teaches us that such and such ideas are attended with such and such other ideas, in the ordinary course of things' (ibid.). From this Berkeley concludes that God, the 'Author of Nature', is the ultimate source both of ideas and their connections. Accordingly although all that exists is mind-dependent, it is not dependent on particular or finite minds – *my* mind, say – but has an objective source and structure, and this is what defends common sense proposition (b), and constitutes Berkeley's realism (cf. section 6 below).

A central feature of Berkeley's account of ideas and these direct implications of it is the fact that it shows, or is intended to show, that an explanation of the nature of experience requires no invocation of a concept of matter or corporeal substance. This is one of the ways therefore in which Berkeley applies and defends the New Principle; it is effectively an argument from exclusion. Starting from the agreed fact that the immediate contents of sensory awareness are private data – agreed, that is, between Berkeley and his predecessors – a theory is constructed at level 3 (God's causal activity) which explains the levels 1 and 2 facts (the contingent regular associations – level 2 – between particular, causally inert, mind-dependent contents of states of sensory awareness – level 1), and does so, Berkeley claims, in a way which accurately captures the character of, and does not go beyond, the level 1 facts, namely that the only constituents of awareness are inert, particular, mind-dependent ideas. This is only one part of the argument against matter, however, for what is additionally required is that not only must the redundancy of the materialist view be shown, but, more importantly, its incoherence, which is what the argument about existence is designed to show.

2. Ideas and things   53

Much turns on how far Berkeley's conception of ideas is acceptable, and whether he is right about what consequences flow from it. For one thing, there is a need to be quite clear about what is meant by saying that an idea is the immediate object of sensory awareness or what is derived from this in memory and imagination. There are two difficulties here, one concerning '*immediate* object' and the other concerning 'immediate *object*', which latter is in effect the problem of what relationship obtains between minds and their ideas. Other difficulties follow; if all we are ever acquainted with is our ideas, how do we distinguish between those which are to count on the one hand as being independently caused, that is, those which constitute reality, and on the other hand those which are 'chimerical'? And further, what is it to say they are independently caused – and how can we know what causes them?

Discussion of these questions proceeds best in connection with the substantive issues which give rise to them. A start can be made upon them, however, by considering a standard objection to Berkeley which focusses on his identification of sensory ideas with the qualities of objects, a thesis whose truth he takes for granted in the early sections of P but, in response to criticism, devotes the first half of 1D to arguing. An important part of the argument reported above essentially turns on this.

Berkeley's argument is that the sensible qualities of objects – their colours, shapes, odours and the rest – are sensory ideas; objects are collections of such ideas; therefore objects exist 'in the mind'. The objection in question to this is that the identification of sensory ideas with sensible qualities of objects is a straightforward mistake, for there is a large difference between saying 'the table is brown' and 'the table looks brown to me', since the truth-conditions of each statement are independent of the truth-conditions of the other; the table could quite simply be, without appearing to be, brown, and vice versa. Hence, according to the objection, the argument fails (cf. Armstrong pp7-9).

It is however the objection which fails, for it begs the question against Berkeley by resting on the assumption that the content of assertions about what qualities objects possess is independent of questions about how anyone could recognise what qualities they possess – which is exactly what Berkeley is seeking to deny – and therefore rests on the assumption that there are recognition-transcendent facts of the matter about the qualities of objects which can be stated without any reference to experience of them. But this as it stands is so over-strong a claim that it issues in absurdity. If questions about what sensible qualities an object has are completely detachable from questions about how they can be known to have such qualities, then what we are being asked to conceive, on this line of reasoning, is its being possible that something should possess a sensible quality – a colour, say, or an odour – even when it is *in principle* impossible for that colour or odour to be detected by a suitably equipped being; which is to licence saying of some object 'it has sensible quality F even although nothing could count as acquiring by investigation knowledge to that effect'. The incoherence of the view becomes manifest when it is stressed that the qualities in question are *sensible* qualities, that is, able-to-be-sensed-qualities; for what content can be given to the conception of an object's possessing such a quality when the independence from perception of such a quality is to be understood in this absolute way?

This result might prompt one to think that the objection cannot be intended in quite the sense that yields it, but rather that it is based on something like the innocuous fact that, as is often enough the case, objects can on occasions appear to have qualities they do not have, and vice versa. Of this, more in a moment. Some who have urged the objection, however, do so on the grounds that (i) 'x is F' and (ii) 'x looks/appears F' do not 'mean' the same (this is Armstrong's tactic, ibid.), and if this is taken in the minimal sense to mean that the truth-conditions of (i) and (ii) are wholly independent, then the above result follows as demonstrated. Any weaker claim must in some way connect the truth-conditions of (i) and (ii), by having it either that the truth-value of (i) is determined by the truth-value of (ii) because statements of form (i) are reducible to (or perhaps are translations of) statements of form (ii), or at least that the truth-value of (ii) is, together with certain other statements, ineliminably relevant to settling the truth-value of (i). On either of these options the 'meaning' of statements about what qualities an object possesses is, respectively, wholly or partially determined by the sensory evidence which constitutes the grounds for their assertion or denial. Two thoughts are to be borne in mind here. One is that we are dealing with *sensible* qualities, the whole evidence for the existence and character of which originates in sensory awareness. The other is that it is a readily testable fact – and one which will come up for discussion again – that variabilities in the sensible qualities of things are systematically correlated to variations both in the circumstances under which they are perceived and in subjective states of perceivers themselves (so providing us with a conception of 'standard conditions', which enables us to say 'these

2. Ideas and things

conditions are not standard, so the colour the table now appears to have is not the colour we usually ascribe to it'). These thoughts are both true; and their truth makes it impossible to detach our *understanding* of what sensible qualities are from questions about how they are perceived. And this is to say at the very least that something like the weaker of the above claims is irresistible.

It might nevertheless be thought that a case like Armstrong's could be sustained by holding that what it is for an object to be brown or to smell like a rose consists in certain facts about, say, its microscopic stucture, which would still be facts whether or not they were ever discovered or even were discoverable. But this familiar move will not do either, for it is to mistake a model constructed to explain the nature and content of sense experience – one, moreoever, ultimately generalised from sense experience – for an account of what is true independently of that sense experience, as though what the latter demands by way of explanation – 'what explains why the table *looks brown to me*?' – is met by a description of how light-waves, emitted from such and such surfaces, are received by the retina, transmitted along the optic nerves, and so on. But 'browness', familiarly, is not identical with light-waves, retinal stimulation, or neural saltations; and the same facts about light-waves and physiological events, which are now associated with tables looking brown in appropriate circumstances, could remain what they are consistently with the table's looking green to normal perceivers in those circumstances, for the association is contingent. Accordingly an explanation of what it is to predicate browness of the table *essentially* involves taking into account the content of perceivers' experience in the relevant respects, which is in short to say that what sensible qualities something x possesses rests at least in part on how x appears.

But where the objection fails most markedly is in its missing the point by assuming without defence the realist distinction between how things are and seem which Berkeley is precisely concerned to deny, his chief motive being that such a distinction leads straight to scepticism. The motive for the realist distinction is not, because it cannot be, that episodes of sense experience themselves show how objects can at the same time have but fail to appear to have, or vice versa, a given quality, for one cannot detect both the being but not appearing brown of a table at one glance, as it were; hence, on any view, if the table appears brown but is not judged to be brown (which will, note, be the judgement: 'this table does not usually or standardly appear, as it now appears, brown'), it will be a matter of inference from additional facts about the case together with our theory about how things sensibly are and seem, and what the relations between its being and seeming so-and-so are. (Consider the case of someone looking at a white wall through rose-tinted glass; he will judge that the wall is white although it looks, in those circumstances, rosy.) Rather, the realist's motive is the desire to explain the causes of our experience – something which any theory must explain – in terms of objects whose existence is independent of thought or experience in general, so that the objects in question can be describable without reference to the conditions under which they are perceived, thus permitting repeatable, 'objective', description or – in the case particularly of primary qualities – measurement. This indeed is the motivation of the kind of thesis one finds for example in Locke and the corpuscularians, to the effect that the sensible qualities of things are powers in objects to produce in perceivers' minds the sensory ideas of colour and the rest. But to this and its successor conceptions Berkeley has a powerful objection. It is that since all we have available to us are our sensory ideas, which we cannot set aside to inspect what if anything lies 'behind' them as their independent causes or correlates, the assertion that there *is* something lying behind them is unverifiable; and indeed, even if we could set them aside, what we should have is not access to the supposed noumenal reality which gives rise to them, but just more sensible ideas (cf. P8). This poses the central dilemma for any theory, whether realist in Lockean or relatedly more recent forms, which has it that the sources of experience are something other than and independent of experience; for what is being said is that if the sources of sensory experience lie inaccessibly beyond experience, we have no grounds for asserting that they exist; and if they are accessible to experience, then they are, tautologously, not experience-independent. That the force of this is at least tacitly acknowledged by *some* espousers of more recent forms of materialist realism is marked by a shift in views about the status of the motive for adopting it. This is that even although facts about the content of states of sensory awareness do not themselves necessitate commitment to there being a realm of items describable without essential reference to the conditions under which their existence and character can be known, nevertheless such a commitment constitutes the 'best hypothesis' available to us, as Mackie puts it, for explaining the course of our experience (cf. Mackie pp62-7). Putting matters this way intentionally **dodges** questions about whether the hypothesis is *true* – unless perhaps it is intended to invite **a Pragmatist**

2. Ideas and things

reading of truth; but either way it remains open to questions about its intelligibility – and Berkeley's challenge to materialist realism proceeds not only on the grounds that experience itself does not license it, but that it is intrinsically incoherent, as we shall see.

Questions about the relation between how things are and seem have been intensively debated in recent philosophy, with the result that the dependence of how things are on how they seem, at least with respect to secondary qualities, and a resulting commitment to the ineliminability of subjective aspects in thought about the world – both Berkeleyan points – have been accepted even by those whose resistance to other Berkeleyan claims is strong. Peacocke and McGinn come to mind in this connection (cf. Peacocke pp31-44, McGinn pp6-11). In Peacocke's view the concept of something's having a certain secondary quality, for example its being red, has to be explained in terms of definitionally prior experiential concepts, which explanation can in his view be given without either circularity or prejudice to the semantic complexity of 'looks red' (Peacocke pp31, 37-40). Similarly McGinn holds that 'the ultimate criterion for whether an object has a certain colour or taste (etc.) is how it looks and tastes to perceivers', and an immediate consequence of this 'is that secondary qualities are subjective in the sense that experience enters into their analysis: to grasp the concept of red it is necessary to know what it is for something to look red, since the latter constitutes the satisfaction condition for an object's being red' (McGinn p8). There are (on the whole very minor) differences between the reasons each gives for arriving at this view, but their taking it has the same outcome in one crucial respect, which is that they both agree with Berkeley, and therefore with the tradition on which Berkeley himself relies, that any account of *secondary* qualities, at least, must proceed in terms which essentially involve reference to perceptual experience. They both further agree with Berkeley that primary and secondary qualities always come together, and cannot be abstracted from each other, which is directly relevant to issues shortly to be discussed (Peacocke p45, McGinn pp80ff). Neither of them agree with Berkeley's more substantial claim, however, that sensible objects just *are* collections of ideas, for both hold that primary qualities are specifiable without reference to experience of them (which Berkeley denies) and correlatively defend absolute realism. Their views are of special interest in these respects, and I shall have occasion to revert to them – most particularly, and with more general concerns in mind, to McGinn's views in Chapter Four below.

Some of the argument Berkeley gives in 1D in support of the thesis that sensible qualities are sensory ideas has invited criticism on the grounds that it identifies the qualities of temperature, taste and smell with acknowledgedly subjective states like pleasure and pain (1D175-80), and so turns on a conflation of these qualities with the hedonic states we sometimes but not always associate with them. It is notable that when Berkeley comes to consider the case of sounds and colours he argues, instead, in terms of familiar considerations about perceptual relativities rather than hedonic states; and this argument turns out to be more important for Berkeley's case in 1D, since not only are the supposed hedonic qualities of temperature, sound and smell relative in the same way, but so too are the primary qualities, which is the reason given by Berkeley for holding that they are mind-dependent in the same way as secondary qualities (1D187-94). It has been pointed out by commentators that the weight Berkeley places on relativity arguments in 1D accords ill with his comment at P15, where he says that such arguments do not show that the qualities of objects are not in the objects, but give only the weaker result that we cannot know which, among the variable qualities objects seem to have, are their true qualities. He asserts at P15 that it is the 'foregoing' arguments, that is, certainly those in P1-8, and probably also those in P9-10, none of which turn on considerations about perceptual relativities, which show that all sensible objects are in the mind, and therefore that there is no matter but only spiritual substance. This shows that the *esse est percipi* component of the New Principle is the key to making out the claim that sensible objects are sensory ideas, and that the reason why Berkeley gives the argument of 1D (and P11-15) at all is simply to show how that thesis applies in a case-by-case analysis of the objects of the sensory modalities, with these analyses not constituting the chief argument for the thesis, but, rather, having adminicular status, that is, being intended to support the *esse est percipi* claim by showing that the attribution of sensible qualities to things does not turn on a supposed capacity of perceivers to recognise that some of those qualities are possessed by objects independently of their being perceived, but in every case on the fact that perception of such qualities turns out, on analysis, to consist wholly in perceivers' being in certain sensory states. At 1D175 the *esse est percipi* thesis is stated – in a denial of it by Hylas: 'to *exist* is one thing, to be *perceived* is another' – and Philonous responds by going through each of the senses in turn to show that their objects do not exist 'exterior to and distinct from their being perceived' (ibid.) and hence that Hylas' separation of existence from perception is mistaken.

Because in P1-7 and elsewhere the *esse est percipi* thesis is justified by a briefly stated but powerful and complex conceptual argument, it

2. Ideas and things

might seem unecessary to consider the 1D discussion, which, even if it had all the appearance of being conclusive, is after all merely another and longer way of establishing the same result; and that therefore it would be as well to proceed directly to consideration of the *esse est percipi* thesis itself. But although this is so there are two reasons for not neglecting 1D. One of them is that its arguments are so far from appearing conclusive that it has attracted considerable critical attention, most of it aimed at showing that its implausibilities weaken if not wreck the *esse est percipi* thesis itself. The second is that it shapes the content of much discussion about perception in more recent philosophy, in the light of which fact alone it deserves reconsideration. I shall accordingly look at each of the three forms of argument Berkeley uses there.

Berkeley's aim in 1D is to substantiate the claim that 'by *sensible things* [is meant] those only which are perceived by sense' (1D174), and this is to be shown to hold good in discussion of each of the sensory modalities and their objects. Its intended force lies *not* in its detachment of what is *immediately* present to awareness – colours, odours, and the rest (1D175) – from what we typically attribute these qualities to, namely sensible objects, for the claim is that sensible objects are collections of sensible qualities; but rather in its detachment of these from *external* objects, that is, the supposed (material) *causes or occasions* of sensory ideas, somehow lying behind sensible objects. So Berkeley takes the problematic distinction – the one he wishes to resist – to be one between (a) sensible objects, which as collections of sensible qualities are what is immediately perceived, and (b) independently existing objects which are the causes of them; and not one between (a') something like sense-data in the contemporary sense, that is, uninterpreted contents of sensory states, and (a) sensible objects. It is important to note this because it matters to Berkeley that what is *immediately* present in awareness are sensible objects; we do not infer from red patches in our visual field, and so forth, to *books* and *roses*, but see (and feel etc.) books and roses. But what this means, he claims, is that books and roses are composed of 'sensations' – that is, contents of sensory states – of colour, smell, and the rest, which 'being observed to accompany each other ... come to be marked by one name, and so to be reputed one thing' (P1) Now this on the face of it appears to involve a difficulty, for it seems illegitimately to be having things both ways; the familiar objects of sense-experience, books and the rest, are immediately perceived, while at the same time what is immediately perceived are colours and smells; and one temptation is to say, as some in the more recent debate have argued, that if it is to be claimed that the former are constituted by the latter, then they are so as an interpretation of, or an inference from, the former – and indeed what we are committed to in talking of the former 'goes beyond' what the latter strictly permits (cf. Ayer 1 *passim*.) for the familiar reasons that among the things we think about objects, for example books, is that they exist when they are not perceived by me, are public to more than one perceiver, and so on, none of which is true of the sensory ideas I have when looking at and handling a book.

This objection can however be met by unpacking Berkeley's intentions in terms of the interpretative idiom of levels. In this idiom, a book is a level 2 object, and our capacity to detect its presence involves no inference – we are *immediately* aware of it when we are aware of it. (There are certain complications here which can be deferred for a moment; one concerns the classificatory conventions which lead to our discriminating objects as objects of certain kinds; another, much more important, is Berkeley's 'suggestion'-'inference' distinction and the celebrated coach case. I deal with these matters shortly.) But when asked to explain what it is to be aware of an object, perhaps by being asked 'how do you know there is an object there?' the answer will be 'I see it', 'I see and feel it' (cf. P3, 3D234) – and such innocuous, even banal, replies contain what is for Berkeley philosophically crucial: for they show in his view that there is no more to being aware of a book than that certain level 1 facts hold true, that is, that one has certain sense experiences. In particular, states of awareness as such do not of themselves settle which of different level 3 options is to be chosen as explaining them in some more inclusive way – but it *begins* to do so, by excluding *one* such option, and does this by showing that what is perceived, namely the sensible qualities of things, cannot be independent of their being perceived. Thus, as the argument so far has it, there are not colour patches *and* felt textures and resistance or weight *and*, in addition to these, a book, considered as something *in itself* undetectable by any means, in which the perceived qualities or powers to produce them inhere. This is the interpretation we are invited to give by the materialist hypothesis. Nor however are there colours *and* textures etc. *and* a book, in the sense that there are sensible qualities – the colours and textures – and over and above them something else sensible, namely the book *qua* sensible object, at which we arrive, logically speaking, later. This is an interpretation suggested by some forms of phenomenalism, which have it that we 'advance' from sense-experience to claims about objects, if not as a matter of

2. Ideas and things

psychological fact then at any rate as a logically reconstructable move from evidence to judgement. Although therefore what is immediate present to awareness is the book, *ipso facto* what is immediately present to awareness is the book's colour, its shape, its feel – and since colours and feels are sensory ideas, that is, the contents of sensory states, the book of which we are directly aware – the sensible or perceived object – is as such a congeries of those sensed qualities. At levels 1 and 2 we have, then, a part of each of two theses about sensible objects, one of them ontological and the other epistemological. The ontological thesis is that level 1 items taken together – the contents of sensory states taken as such – and level 2 items, that is, sensible objects like books, awareness of which is awareness of a determinate collection of level 1 items, stand in a relation of what might be called 'constitutive identity' in the sense intended by Berkeley's talk of 'collections' at P1 and immediate perception at P3 and 1D174ff; and the epistemological thesis is that there are not *two* acts of perceiving going on, namely one of perceiving the level 1 items and one of perceiving the level 2 items, with inferential or cognate relations between them, but a single act of perception. But note that these are only *parts* of the correlative theses at issue; for what remains to be explained is the theory – at level 3 – which accounts for the origin of the experience in which such awareness consists and the further, non-perceptual, character of its objects, for example those non-sensible properties we attribute to them of being public, persisting, and so on, possession of which fits them into a world view and provides among other things criteria for distinguishing between what is 'real' and what 'chimerical'. It is essential for an understanding of Berkeley's claims in the relevant parts of 1D that the argument there concerns levels 1 and 2 only: 'Our discourse proceed(s) altogether concerning sensible things, which you defined to be the things *we immediately perceive by our senses*' (1D180, Berkeley's emphasis); this excludes level 3 considerations, which 'entirely relate to reason' not sense-experience (1D175), except in the one matter of whether the sensed qualities of objects have 'an absolute existence without the mind'. The move from levels 1 and 2 to 3 is forced on Philonous in the celebrated gardener discussion in 3D when it becomes pressing to take into consideration the wider theory by which what we perceive is to be explained; but at this point what is alone relevant is the groundwork for showing which of competing level 3 interpretations is open and which is closed.

The interpretation so far given of Berkeley will doubtless invite the protest that it ignores Berkeley's talk of mediate perception,

II. *Esse est Percipi: Against Matter*

'suggestion', and inference, and the complications which arise as a result of the relations between these concepts. There is in particular Berkeley's much discussed example of the coach heard rumbling down the street outside, which some commentators have claimed shows that there is a muddle in his views about perception (1D2040 cf. e.g. Dicker in Turbayne pp48ff, Tipton pp190ff). These claims, as I shall now show, rest on a misunderstanding of Berkeley's position, resulting in part from the fact that Berkeley's treatment of the issue is not systematically presented, but appears in fragments, as demand for the relevant fragment arises, in all of V, P and D. Nevertheless his view is consistent and its central thesis is as just presented.

By 'immediate' perception Berkeley means exactly what the phrase says, namely that it is perception without intermediary or inference (compare Pitcher pp9ff). Ideas are fully present to awareness, are no more than as they appear, and do not stand for, represent, or transmit information about something other than themselves in the sense intended by representative theories of perception in general. Since objects – tables, trees – are collections of sensible qualities, and sensible qualities are ideas, it follows that objects are immediately perceived; and the sense in which objects and the ideas which constitute them are thus immediately perceived is to be understood in the way just described. Moreover the fact that what is perceived is perceived *as* something – a table or tree – is not an *additional* fact about the content of the perceptual experience itself, but is a fact about our thought and talk of the level 2 world based on that experience (cf. what Berkeley says about seeing a picture of a man *as* a picture of Julius Caesar, 1D203). This is a matter of our classificatory conventions. Nor is it an *additional* fact about the contents of sensory states themselves that objects *qua* collections of ideas are individuated as they are – that is, that the ideas constituting a given object are collected in just this or that way, for it is, as the foregoing shows, not the case that collections are constructed by a process of synthesis out of perceptual atoms, but are themselves the objects of immediate perception, with its *ipso facto* being the case that what is perceived are collections of *ideas*. At P1, it will be recalled, Berkeley says that ideas which go together 'are accounted one distinct thing'. Their being so is not in some way a conceptual result of their *first* being noted to hang together and *then* individuated as a collection, despite the rather misleading phraseology there which might give a hasty reader the impression, most certainly unintended by Berkeley, that some sort of temporal sequence is involved, in which for example naming a given collection

2. Ideas and things

of ideas is *followed* by its being 'reputed one thing' (ibid.). At 1D203 Berkeley cites the example of someone looking at a picture and seeing 'colours and figures with a certain symmetry and composition of the whole', which fills out the implication of P1 to the effect that objects are of course *structured* collections of ideas and are immediately perceived as such; the implication is carried by the talk at P1 of apples and stones, which are definite collections of definite ideas, thus sustaining the classificatory conventions (involving the naming of things) by means of which we pick them out or identify them, tell them apart, and so on.

That, then, is the main substance of Berkeley's account of sense perception. The basic principle is summarised for Berkeley by Hylas at 1D174: 'in truth, the senses perceive nothing which they do not perceive immediately: for they make no inferences.' But in addition to immediate sense perception there are, in Berkeley's view, two *mediate* routes to knowledge; one is inference, the other is sense perception involving what Berkeley calls 'suggestion'. It is this second category which has given rise to misunderstanding among the commentators.

Inference is the familiar matter of 'deducing ... causes or occasions from effects and appearances', and it is a process which 'entirely relates to reason' (1D175) Thus one infers from the presence of fresh fox spoor in the soil that a fox has recently been this way, or from a politician's veiled remarks that a change of policy is likely soon. *Suggestion* is another matter. It is a category of mediate *sense* perception which is by no means to be confused with inference: 'To perceive is one thing; to judge is another. So likewise, to be suggested is one thing, and to be inferred another. Things are suggested and perceived by sense. We make judgements and inferences by the understanding' (VV42). An illustrative case is afforded by visual perception of distance. In V Berkeley claims that distance is not immediately perceived by sight – is not something present to awareness in states of visual awareness as such – but is suggested by those states as a result of our having learned, from their association with other cues such as straining of the eyes, touch, and so forth, that the objects of such awareness lie at a distance from us (cf. V16ff, 45). The claim is that the general course of experience teaches us that certain visual ideas are connected with certain other – say, tangible – ideas, which leads us to expect or even, indeed, simply to interpret the ideas of one modality in terms of the ideas of the other. The main statement of the conception occurs at 1D204, that is, near the end of the first dialogue, throughout the body of which Philonous has been arguing the case in hand, namely that anything perceived by sense is immediately perceived. He here adds: 'Though I grant we may in one acceptation be said to perceive sensible things mediately by sense: that is, when from a frequently perceived connexion, the immediate perception of ideas by one sense suggests to the mind others perhaps belonging to another sense, which are wont to be connected with them'. His illustration is the coach heard in the street outside: 'For instance, when we hear a coach drive along the streets, immediately I perceive only the sound; but from the experience I have had that such a sound is connected with a coach, I am said to hear the coach. It is nevertheless evident, that in truth and strictness, nothing can be *heard* but sound: and the coach is not then properly perceived by sense, but suggested from experience' (ibid.). As with visual distance, the typical case is that in which ideas of one sense suggest ideas of another by experienced association; he gives the yet better example directly afterwards of our 'seeing' a 'red-hot bar of iron; the *solidity* and *heat* of the iron are not the objects of *sight*, but (are) suggested to the imagination by the colour and figure, which are properly perceived by that sense' (ibid., my emphases). Therefore, in the typical case, the ideas which in our level 2 way of talking we say we perceive are in fact ideas suggested, as a result of experience-based association, by that of another sense, and so that ideas we *say* we perceive are strictly speaking those we *would* perceive if we *were* to walk or reach out (in the case of distance) or see (if we look out of the window into the street where the coach is passing) – that is, our level 2 talk in this respect is elliptical for, or is sustained by, subjunctive conditionals. This connects directly with the topic discussed in section 4 below and I defer analysis of it until then.

Berkeley here and elsewhere allows, quite properly, that ideas of one sense can in certain circumstances suggest others of the same sense, as when we see a stick in water which appears bent but which, correcting for the distorting medium, we recognise as straight (3D238), which case falls into that class of cases so often invoked by sense-datum theorists and including white walls seen through rose-tinted spectacles and so forth. Thus the notion of suggestion is adequate to the fact, reported from empirical psychology by Peacocke, that perceptual judgements of, say, the surface colour of objects, when seen through tinted transparencies, are based on the interpretational content of the states of awareness which give rise to them and not, or not only, on the sensational content, whose character is determined by the intervening medium (Peacocke

2. Ideas and things 65

pp38-9 and cf. n.1 p39).

A quotation from Dicker's discussion will serve to illustrate the kind of misunderstanding which has surrounded Berkeley's views on this score (Dicker ibid.). After quoting the coach passage – but leaving out and for some reason neglecting what is stated in the opening sentence, namely 'Although I grant we may in one acceptation be said to perceive things mediately by sense' – Dicker says '[Berkeley's] reasoning, presumably, is that (i) whatever is perceived by sense is immediately perceived, but (ii) the coach is not immediately perceived; therefore (iii) the coach is not perceived by sense ... by (ii) Berkeley must mean to assert that the coach has to be (very rapidly but consciously) inferred from the sound; much as rain may be inferred from thunderclouds, or fire from smoke. But (ii), taken in this sense, is simply *false*; it is just false that the coach has to be ... inferred, however rapidly, from the sound' (Dicker p51). This, as the foregoing shows, is a misapprehension of Berkeley's position. Berkeley does not conclude (iii), but the converse, allowing mediate sense perception by suggestion. Nor does he at all mean to assert that the coach is *inferred* from the sound; Dicker does not appear to be aware of the suggestion-inference distinction. And he would therefore be the first to agree with Dicker that it is false to hold that the coach is inferred from the sound it makes. The remainder of Dicker's discussion is based on this misreading and suffers accordingly.

In Tipton's view, Berkeley is in the right to say that it is strictly speaking the *sound* we hear and not the *coach* (Tipton p193). Nevertheless he does not think that the coach example helps Berkeley's case because, he says, sounds are *made by* things and so are not *qualities* of things; and therefore what Berkeley needs to rely upon instead are examples which turn on visual and tactual qualities if his view is to be made out. (Tipton suggests that tastes and smells are in this respect like sounds, pp193-4.) The comment is interesting because it serves, at least, as a reminder that one cannot simply assume that what applies to one of the sensory modalities automatically applies to the other four. But there is no difficulty for Berkeley's position here. For one thing, whether the sound in question is to be thought of as made by the coach or as a quality belonging to it, it still serves to *suggest* the coach, and therefore the coach case remains a case of mediate sense perception. For another, Berkeley does indeed give visual and tactual examples: distance and the red-hot iron bar are one of each. And thirdly, it is difficult to think of sounds, tastes and smells as non-qualities in the way Tipton suggests, two opposite reasons for which might be mentioned. A rose's scent, for example, is made by, or given off by, the rose, analogously to sounds being made or given off by the coach; but we nevertheless account the rose's scent a quality of the rose, and prize the rose therefore. Our everyday theory which ascribes 'possession' of scent to the rose and noise to Concorde is at least non-arbitrary. The opposite reason is that the model we employ to talk about the structure and properties of objects – the model materialists take to be *true* – has it that colour, for example, is the effect in perceivers' consciousness of their visual equipment's being stimulated by physical impingements on it of photons emitted from surfaces (we loosely say light is 'reflected' from surfaces, but strictly speaking, on the standard theory, it is to be thought of first as *absorbed* by surfaces and then *re-emitted* at a frequency determined by the surface's properties) – so in a sense (it merely involves an awkward locution to put it like this) colour is made by, or given off by, things too, in a way which it is hard to construe as wholly disanalogous to the sound case; and yet colour is the paradigm of a sensible quality. But for Berkeley it is anyway the case that the objects of the five senses are *ideas*, so that the question whether one or more of the five standardly-designated types of sensible qualities should properly be thought of as products rather than properties of things does not arise – it is a problem (another one) for those who hold that sensible qualities have the 'twofold existence' Berkeley attacks, namely as perceived and as dispositions (or powers), or the grounds of these, in things existing independently of perception.

We may now return to the main theme of the present discussion. The parts of the correlative ontological and epistemological theses argued for in the stretch of 1D under consideration (1D175-88) jointly constitutes the claim that sensible qualities – and therefore sensible objects, since these are collections of sensible qualities – are sensory ideas; this follows for Berkeley from seeing that level 1 items, sensed ideas of colour and the rest, stand in the relation of constitutive identity to level 2 items, books and the rest, and that perceiving a level 2 item consists, in all cases other than suggested perception, in a single immediate awareness of that item. What requires explanation is why perceivings of level 2 items are normally reported or thought of in terms of a recognition that a certain quality – say, the colour red – belongs to or is predicable of the object in question. The key lies in Berkeley's remarks at C115 'of & thing causes of mistake' and C660 'The referring Ideas to things which are not Ideas, the using the Term, Idea of, is one great cause of mistake'.

2. Ideas and things

The point is that our manner of talking about things and properties, as when we say 'the book is red', consists in assigning properties *to* things or saying that they are properties *of* things, and accordingly manufactures a conception of sensible qualities belonging to or inhering in things independently of their being perceived. There is no harm, Berkeley remarks, in employing these idioms, which are 'proper or conformable to custom' (P38), provided that we are not misled by them into giving the wrong level 3 account; the corrective resides in the dictum, quoted by Berkeley at P51, that we should 'think with the learned, and speak with the vulgar'. In 'speaking with the vulgar' we talk about the qualities *of things*, and so hypostasize them or detach them from the states of awareness they constitute, in this way leading us to think of them apart from their being what constitutes our awareness of those things. In 'thinking with the learned' we recognise what implicit selection of level 3 theory is being made by so speaking, and resist it on the grounds that the qualities we attribute to things are not perception-independent items but, again, just the exhaustive contents of our states of sensory awareness.

The heat-pain argument of 1D175-8 is often selected by commentators for discussion because it is intended by Berkeley to be one way of showing how the points just made work out in a concrete case. (The other two ways – arguments from perceptual relativity and causation – will be discussed shortly). With few exceptions the view is that the heat-pain argument fails. Pitcher's discussion provides a good example of this majority reaction, and is worth discussing for that reason (Pitcher pp100-4).

Pitcher gives Berkeley's argument as follows: (a) an intense degree of heat is a very great pain; (b) any pain is a sensation, that is, an idea of sense, therefore (c) an intense degree of heat is an idea of sense. Pitcher focusses on (a) as the crucial premiss, treating it as an identity statement, that is, as asserting that 'what we are (directly) aware of when we feel an intense heat is nothing other than a great pain' (ibid. pp100-1). He then goes on to argue that (a) is false, on the following grounds.

It is surely wrong, Pitcher says, to hold that 'feeling the heat of the fire' just is 'nothing other than a great pain' because 'there are two objects whose heat I feel: the heat of the fire and the heat of that part of my hand that is nearest the fire' (ibid. p101). Moreover 'the former heat causes the latter' (ibid.). If the former heat is to be identified with the pain, then 'the pain, like the heat, is in the fire!' – the exclamation mark showing that this is an absurd result (ibid.).

II. Esse est Percipi: Against Matter

What gives (a) a chance of being true, Pitcher says, is that the pain felt could perhaps be identified with the heat in the hand, on the ground, offered by Berkeley, that what one feels is 'simple and uncompounded' (1D176); but Pitcher finds talk of the distinction between 'simple' and 'compound' questionable on Wittgensteinian grounds, namely that what is to be counted as either depends on our interests or purposes, and may therefore be one from one point of view and the other from another point of view (Pitcher pp102-3). He therefore concludes that since Berkeley needs a clear and acceptable demonstration that the sensation in question is simple, but cannot give such a demonstration, the whole heat-pain argument fails (ibid. pp103-4).

This discussion is unsatisfactory. At the outset it begs the question against Berkeley by asserting what Berkeley's argument is aimed at denying, which is that there is an external object, 'the heat of the fire', that is, a sensible quality belonging to the fire independently of its being perceived, and quite apart from this 'the heat of that part of the hand nearest the fire', which Pitcher says caused by the former heat. The latter heat's status *vis a vis* the perceiver is treated rather ambivalently by Pitcher, for it is not clear whether it is a sensation and hence dependent upon being perceived, as his ensuing discussion of the simple-complex distinction appears to presuppose (pp102-3), or whether, since it is the *hand* which is hot, and may therefore be hot without being sensed to be so (for example when its possessor is anaesthetised), it too is a perception-independent heat. If however the hand's heat is the former, that is, a sensation, then Pitcher begs the question more deeply still by commiting himself to a causal theory of perception of the Lockean variety. Yet it is precisely Berkeley's claim that the fire's heat is *not* something independent of its being perceived, and *a fortiori* that it is not the independent cause of the sensation of heat. Pitcher's discussion accordingly comes down to a counter-assertion of the point Berkeley seeks to attack, and that cannot do. What has to be *shown*, not *premissed*, is that there is an intelligible account of how what is *felt* is also an *unfelt* property of something external to the perceiver; such an argument would be interesting indeed, provided it did not beg allied questions by reducing heat *felt* as such to, say, the vibrations of molecules and the release of quanta of energy.

Pitcher's argument turns on the claim that there are in fact *three* felt objects: the heat of the fire, the heat of the hand, and in addition the private sensation of heat; he says 'You feel the heat of the fire, you feel the resulting heat of that part of your hand that is nearest the

2. Ideas and things 69

fire, and you feel a pain' (p102). This is impossible to accept. One might refer the felt heat to the fire as its cause, and that is just what one pretheoretically does; but that is far from a claim to the effect that the cause and its effects – the fire's heat and the hand's heat and the sensation of heat or pain – are together but discriminably present to one in the act of holding one's hand to the fire, as though one could say '*this* component of what I feel is the fire's heat, and *this* the heat of my hand, and *this* is the sensation of pain private to my consciousness'. In claiming that three objects are felt, Pitcher is claiming that they are distinguishable in experience in just this way, which involves the further difficulty that at the outset we are invited to think of feeling a fire's heat as a *compound* matter, decomposable into feelings of different objects; but we are shortly afterwards told that Wittgenstein has shown that the simple-compound distinction is, because it is relative, of no use in this discussion, and hence the basis of discussion is impugned by its own later content. These are not merely *ad hominem* considerations, for the chief point here, and it is a substantive one, concerns how many things we feel in the case in point. There is a simple resource for settling the dispute over whether, when one's hand is in or very near a fire, one can feel *more than one* hot thing *and also* pain, and that is to conduct the relevant experiment. Indeed one need not go to Scaevola's lengths; applying one's finger to a candle flame is sufficient to demonstrate not only that the result is simple or uncompounded in character, but – more importantly – single in its object; in short, that Berkeley is right about (a) If in this case the perception of great heat is indistinguishable from pain, that is, if in this case perception of the sensible quality consists in having a sensation, the same must hold generally true of sensible qualities, for it cannot intelligibly be argued that the less intense the degree of some sensible quality, the more objective it is; on a sliding scale of this sort, the fully real and objective qualities would be all and only the sensorily undetectable ones, which is absurd. This indeed is the point of Philonous' comments about warmth (1D178). Berkeley's claim on this score is rhetorically summarised at C136: 'Qu: what can we see beside colours, what.can we feel beside hard, soft cold warm pleasure pain' (and cf. P3). In line with the account given above in terms of levels – and it is levels 1 and 2 which are at issue – the point is that explanations of what it is to attribute sensible qualities 'to things' are exhausted by specification of the sensory ideas in which they consist. Nothing otherwise particular turns on the fact that certain sensible qualities – temperature, for example – are identified with hedonic states by Berkeley; his point in emphasising this is to show that what, 'speaking with the vulgar', is thought to be a quality 'of' a 'thing' is nothing beyond the reason for its customary attribution to the thing, namely its being an effect in consciousness – that is, its being perceived. Further, the fact that sensory ideas are individuated by reference to what, 'speaking with the vulgar', they are taken to be 'ideas *of*', does not affect the claim that they are sensory ideas; for it is consistent even with subjective idealism that there should be applicable criteria in the subjective idealist's scheme for distinguishing burning pains from stabbing pains, toothaches from tickles, and the rest.

A point which is raised by the foregoing and requires clarification is the use sometimes made by Berkeley of the phrase 'idea or sensation'. Warnock argues that this equating disjunction at least threatens to mislead, for, he says, although it is true that if ideas are sensations then Berkeley's case is immediately made, there is every reason to think that they are not identical, at least not in every case (Warnock p143). Warnock's argument is based on what we say when we talk of sensations and ideas. 'We say that we have or that we feel, that we get or are given, sensations'; but we cannot say these things about ideas – for example, the 'ideas of sight' are light and colours, but 'we do not *have*, or *feel* or *get*, light and colours; on the contrary, as Berkeley frequently says, we *see* them. Furthermore, when we see light and colours, or for that matter anything else, we usually have no sensations at all' (ibid.). It is only with the sense of touch that ideas 'would be naturally called "sensations" ... But here the sensations are not of course *what* we touch; they are what we *have*, *when* we touch things' (p144). These considerations do not refute Berkeley, Warnock says; they simply show that his terminology 'is unfortunate' (p145).

What Warnock says about ordinary usage is of course right, but it makes of 'sensation' something narrower in application than 'content of a sensory state' which is the meaning Berkeley, quite legitimately, attaches to it (cf. 1D181 and P87). For ordinary usage a sensation is an itch, or an ache, or that lurch of the stomach which some fairground rides are designed to provoke, and so may well be something that attends but does not constitute particular sensory ideas, or might even be felt in connection with no *particular* sensory idea. But this is not at all what Berkeley intends. As the content or object of a state of sensing, a sensation *is* in his usage a colour or sound. On this view we can *have* or *get* certain sensory ideas, but we do not *feel* sensations; which simply marks the fact that 'sensation' is not being used by Berkeley in Warnock's 'ordinary' sense, from

2. Ideas and things

merely observing which we would not in any case expect philosophical solutions to follow. The legitimacy of Berkeley's usage is demonstrated by the accepted philosophical employment of 'sensing' to mean the process of acquiring sensory ideas; 'ordinary usage' has 'sensing' not as what we do when we have sensations, standardly construed, but something else again – it is what we do when, say, we become aware, perhaps vaguely, of someone creeping up on us, or when we detect an undercurrent of one or another emotion in someone's tone of voice. But so much by way of aside.

The second form of argument Berkeley uses in 1D is the appeal to perceptual relativities. It is this argument of which he says, in P15, that it shows comparatively little; it does not prove that sensible qualities are not in objects, only that we cannot say *which* of incompatible qualities an object has. Pitcher, taking this cue, pays only brief attention to it (Pitcher p104-6). In 1D however Berkeley gives the argument considerable weight, and various reasons have been offered in explanation of why he came to revalue it and to make use of it again (cf. e.g. Tipton pp236-40). What is suggested to me by Berkeley's employment of the argument in 1D is that, in his view, it establishes two things: first, and very importantly, that the Lockean primary qualities – extension, figure, solidity, number, motion or rest – are on a par with the secondary qualities in being sensible ideas, because they are as relative as these latter to the situation and state of the perceiver and the conditions under which the objects possessing them are perceived (cf. P11ff), and secondly that if one cannot tell *which* of incompatible qualities belongs to an object, one has no grounds for saying that it has *any* of them. At P87 Berkeley says: 'Things remaining the same, our ideas vary, and which of them, *or even whether any of them at all* represent the true quality existing in the thing, it is out of our reach to determine' (my emphasis). This is exactly the conclusion Russell draws from the relativities argument (Russell pp2-3). Tipton approvingly quotes Cummins' remark that even if in water an oar appears bent while in one's hand it appears straight, nevertheless the fact that at least one of these qualities cannot be an actual property of the oar does not entail that neither is (Tipton p241), and this appears to be just Berkeley's P15 view too; but the P87 remark and the Russell conclusion go well beyond this observation in what they claim. On the Cummins version, the perceptual evidence does not exclude the *possibility* that one or other of competing qualities in fact belongs to the object, and that is taken to be enough to show that the fact of perceptual relativities is not a worrying one; but on the Russell version, since it is ruled out that one could ever know which quality belongs to the object, talk of its nevertheless being possible that one of them *does* belong to the object is empty. What is possible is what makes sense for Berkeley; because 'it is out of our reach to determine' which or whether any of the qualities belongs to the object, and because what is possible must fall within the range of what it is within our reach to determine (cf. P5 and the remarks on this head in Chapter One above), the Cummins version fails to persuade. What it requires to be persuasive is a substantiation of the claim – for which Tipton argues at length (Tipton pp241-55) – that we can by some means give content to the idea that something can have a certain quality even although it only sometimes, or even never, appears to have it. But this would either involve begging the question at issue by premissing realism with respect to qualities or their grounds, or it would involve having to specify a means of telling which quality it is that the object in fact possesses, thus having *per impossibile* a non-arbitrary point of vantage from which a judgement to that effect can be made. It is of course the case that we have a conception of 'standard conditions' which enables us to *legislate* that a thing has a certain quality, namely the one it has under those conditions, so that when it fails to have it we can continue to think and speak of it as having the selected quality 'despite appearances'. Nor indeed are our legislations in this respect merely whimsical, for they have cash-value in pragmatic terms. But our conventional practices are not to the philosophical point, which is that since apparent qualities vary, and since there is no independent way of establishing *which* among them is possessed by the object, we have no grounds for asserting that it has *any* of them.

Tipton remarks that Berkeley cannot get an argument from perceptual relativities off the ground unless he assumes what he is in fact concerned to deny, namely that *there is* an external object the appearances of which can vary (Tipton p243). This is a failure to see the relativities argument as a species of *reductio*. Berkeley points out that if qualities are supposed to inhere in material objects, then variations in the qualities might be taken to bespeak a variation in the objects; but it is argued by materialists that the object remains invariant while appearing differently, and so they make of the object a *quid* wholly inaccessible to awareness. One again it is the sensefulness considerations which are being brought into play, for the question this conception immediately prompts for Berkeley is: what sense attaches to the idea of something hidden and unknowable? (1D206).

2. Ideas and things

The point of main interest here, however, is Berkeley's claim that primary qualities do not have a 'real' existence without the mind but, rather, are mind-dependent in just the same way as secondary qualities. At 1D187-8 Hylas capitulates over these latter – 'all those termed *secondary qualities*, have certainly no existence without the mind' – but insists that Philonous' case applies only to them, and that primary qualities 'exist really in bodies'. Philonous says 'what if the same arguments which are brought against secondary qualities, will hold good against these also?' (1D188), and proceeds to argue, by an appeal to relativities, that the same result does indeed follow (1D188-91). The argument here is not much less briefly stated here than at P11-15, although, as noted, it comes without the qualification that attends it at P15.

A question this last point immediately raises is why Berkeley deals with the alleged difference between primary and secondary qualities – in respect, that is, of their relation to mind – so briefly, for his treatment of the issue occupies less than a dozen pages in the whole corpus of P and D. The thrust of his overall argument about qualities is to show that sensible (that is, *both* primary and secondary) qualities are in the mind, and his discussions of the view that primary differ from secondary qualities in being mind-dependent are almost perfunctory. The supposed difference in this respect plays, after all, a crucial role in the materialist conception of the world, because the thought that we have access to the properties of things which things possess in themselves, which in no way depend upon being perceived for their existence, and which therefore are describable – and measurable – without reference to facts about the conditions under which they are perceived, is surely intended to provide a powerful reason for taking it that materialism is true (cf. McGinn ch. 7). One might therefore expect Berkeley to deal with the matter in detail. The reason why he did not do so, I think, is that Berkeley just took it to be *manifestly* unsustainable on his principles to hold that primary qualities exist independently of perception, and that therefore the view is not worth dilating upon. The arguments employed by Berkeley here come directly from Bayle (see pp 00 above). It is very likely that what Bayle had to say on the issue was justifiably assumed by Berkeley to be familiar to his readers, and accordingly it was a simple matter for him to annex the considerations of the Zeno and Pyrrho articles to his New Principle because, unquestionably, if it is true that one cannot distinguish between primary and secondary qualities in respect of their relation to mind, then the New Principle is much reinforced by that fact.

II. Esse est Percipi: Against Matter

(The assumption is widely made that Berkeley had Locke's arguments in mind at P9-15 and 1D188ff. This has given rise to lengthy discussions showing how Berkeley misunderstood and distorted Locke – cf. Bennett pp112ff – or did not misunderstand him – cf. Wilson in Turbayne, Stroud, *passim* – all which, although it constitutes an interesting and valuable debate which clarifies the historical issues and helps to put the argument of P9-15 and 1D188ff in its proper light, I shall not go into here.)

What it is exceedingly important to note is that Berkeley *nowhere denies or sets out to deny* that there is a *distinction* between primary and secondary qualities. Rather, his sole aim is to show that primary qualities are not mind-independent but, like secondary qualities, that their *esse* is *percipi*. *This* is the crucial issue for Berkeley. At P9, where the question of primary qualities is first raised, at P73, and again at 1D187-8, Berkeley both allows that there is a distinction and in the consequent discussions employs the labels 'primary' and 'secondary' without demur. But in both P9ff and 1D188ff where his main discussions occur, his argument is that in the crucially relevant respects affecting the question of mind-dependence or independence – and affecting this alone – both kinds of quality are on a par: they are *ideas*, they are *relative*, and they *always go together* – that is, are unabstractable – and so subsist in the same ground, namely mind.

These arguments are allied to others directed against what materialists claim is the explanatory power of the material hypothesis (cf. P19ff, 25, 50, 104ff, 2D208-9, 3D241-3), since the explanations which that hypothesis afford proceed in terms of the primary qualities which in the materialists' view constitute or inhere in corporeal substance, independently of their being perceived. This aspect of the question I discuss in section 7 below where Berkeley's case against the concept of matter as such is more directly examined. The denial of the explanatory utility of the concept of *matter*, however, does not, any more than does the denial of a difference in respect of relatedness to mind, amount to a claim that there is no distinction between primary and secondary qualities. Berkeley indeed allows that science proceeds in terms of talk about primary qualities, which in his view is wholly unexceptionable provided that it is not taken to involve level 3 commitments to 'natural' – that is, non-spiritual – causes and therefore to non-spiritual substance. This is made clear by what he says at P50 in answer to the objection that his principles conflict with the fact that the material hypothesis has powerful explanatory uses, and in all his talk elsewhere of 'Laws of Nature' and of natural

2. Ideas and things

causes being 'signs' rather than true causes (cf. P30, 60-6).

What therefore has to be asked about these of Berkeley's arguments is not whether they succeed in collapsing the primary-secondary quality distinction, but whether they succeed in showing that primary qualities are mind-dependent. The way he does this is by insisting on the fact that primary qualities are *sensible* qualities; from which it immediately follows, in the light of the general argument for identifying sensible qualities and ideas, that primary qualities are mind-dependent.

His arguments are these. At P9 he asserts the basic case, namely that the primary qualities are sensible, and because P1-8 has established that all sensible qualities are in the mind, it follows that primary qualities are in the mind too. He then briefly gives an assortment of further reasons for putting matters this way, which touch upon, without specifying their sources, related but different theses about primary qualities to which various of his predecessors had subscribed. Secondary qualities are agreed on all hands to be in the mind; primary qualities are 'inseparably united' with them and cannot be abstracted from them; 'where therefore the other sensible qualities are, there must these be also, to wit, in the mind and nowhere else' (P10). All relative ideas, such as '*great* and *small*, *swift* and *slow*', are agreed to be in the mind; what is said to be in things themselves is 'extension in general' and 'motion in general', but these are products of the 'strange doctrine of *abstract ideas*' and have no meaning (P11). Primary qualities are relative in just the way secondary qualtiies are, therefore if the relativity of these latter show them to be mind-dependent, the relativity of the former show them to be so likewise (P14). The relativity argument is employed again at 1D188ff for extension, motion, and solidity, this time clearly echoing Bayle, but Philonous cuts the debate short by saying 'if extension be once acknowledged to have no existence without the mind, the same must necessarily be granted of [the rest] since they all evidently suppose extension' (1D191). And the source of the supposed difference between primary and secondary qualities in respect of their relation to mind is once again attributed to false abstraction (91D192-4). The bottom line of these considerations is that *all* sensible qualities, whether primary or secondary, are on a par in being *sensible*, that is, in being ideas, and therefore in subsisting nowhere but in mind; which is in effect to say that whatever distinction might otherwise be drawn between primary and secondary qualities, it does not turn on the fact that the former are mind-independent.

From the outset Berkeley in any case takes this thesis as read. At P7 he says 'the sensible qualities are colour, figure, motion, smell, taste, and such like, that is, the ideas perceived by sense'. This list comprises both kinds of qualities. These arguments, then, are reminders of, or insistences upon, the fact that primary, just like secondary, qualities are objects of awareness, with all that follows from their being so. Interpretations of these arguments which have it that they are aimed at obliterating the primary-secondary quality distinction draw attention away from this point, and so detach the argument from its setting, which is the general argument Berkeley has for saying that sensible qualities are ideas, together with the consequences of that thesis. The thought that Berkeley was seeking to dispense with the distinction itself is correlative to the exploded view that in *Essay* II.viii. Locke was trying to *establish* the distinction, rather than treating it as an hypothesis whose consequences he was interested to explore. Once one sees this as a 'fictional chapter in the history of philosophy', as Stroud puts it (Stroud p150), the *point* of Berkeley's arguments becomes clear.

It might be thought that what would have to be shown against Berkeley's contentions here is that among the reasons for drawing the primary-secondary quality distinction are some which *show* that the ground or at least part of the ground for the distinction itself is that primary qualities are located in perception-independent objects and so likewise exist whether or not they are perceived. But such a manoeuvre, although it appears natural because it well accords with the content of unreflective realist beliefs about how the world is, would be wholly misconceived. There is no question of showing that such a result is obtainable on the basis of facts about perceptual experience – that is, of showing that the distinction is an *a posteriori* one – for precisely the reason upon which Berkeley insists, namely that all qualities are sensible and in *that* respect indistinguishable. Ideas of certain qualities do not come phenomenologically tagged as secondary or primary, still less either as resemblances or, more generally, representations of perception-independent originals. Rather, the tags are affixed by us as a result of theory, something amply shown, for example, by the corpuscularian view of the issue, which is that it is an hypothesis, open to test, that both kinds of quality exist in objects independently of perception, and give rise to experience by causal interaction with organs of sense. Accordingly the fact is that one distinguishes qualities into the two classes on *a priori* grounds – on the basis perhaps of a (non-arbitrary) stipulative definition – governed by theoretical requirements of explanatory

2. Ideas and things

utility and the availability of criteria for establishing reference to the qualities based upon what, in terms of the theory in which the distinction has the explanatory role assigned to it, we regard as grounds for saying that a given quality is instantiated 'in' an object. For secondary qualities these will make ineliminable use of facts about how things appear; for primary qualities they will consist, typically, in measurement. What helps to *sustain* the distinction are certain facts about experience chosen for their relevance – for one example among many, it seems that on the whole, although not invariably, primary qualities can be thought of as 'common sensibles' in Aristotle's sense, that is, as available to more than one sensory modality, whereas secondary qualities are 'special sensibles', available to one modality only. Again, primary qualities are much more elaborately related to each other and to our apprehension of them than is the case with secondary qualities. But to point to these facts is not to assert what was a moment ago denied, namely that the distinction itself is grounded *a posteriori*. Accordingly the thrust of *these* of Berkeley's arguments about primary qualities is not weakened, but is, rather, strengthened, by noting the extent to which it fits the empirical facts: since there is no question but that all qualities are sensible, the central considerations about sensible qualities apply, and the fact that there is a distinction to be drawn does not make a difference in that respect. The question whether the explanatory power of the material hypothesis shows or gives reason for making it intelligible to hold that bodies, and hence primary qualities, exist 'without the mind' is a further although related question, and Berkeley considers it as such. This more general and more important matter, as noted, is discussed in section 7 below.

The third and final argument deployed by Berkeley in the stretch of 1D under consideration is addressed to causal accounts of perceiving. Berkeley himself subscribes to a causal theory, but not one at all like the theory at issue here, which has it that the contents of states of awareness are termini of causal chains initiated by, or at an early stage involving, properties of external objects (1D179ff). Vision affords a standard example (1D186ff). On the causal theory – and we can give it as contemporary a flavour as we wish – light is absorbed and then re-emitted by the surfaces of objects, whose constitution determines the wavelength of the re-emitted light; the light traverses the intervening medium to the eye's surface, which it penetrates, passing thence through the lens which focusses it on the retina, whose assorted receptors are stimulated by it in patterns which are encoded and transmitted along the optic pathway to the visual centres of the cortex, located at the back of the brain; and the firing of the cortical cells thus prompted finally gives rise, in some yet unknown way, to the sensory idea of a coloured shape. Berkeley's argument is that what we are alone aware of is the sensory idea which figures *last* in this account; we have no access to the intermediate links in the causal chain or its origin, and no way of somehow stepping aside to detect, beyond or apart from our sensory ideas, the various events putatively involved in giving rise to them. At best this view constitutes a model designed to explain perception *on realist premisses*. But since all we have, and all we can have, are sensory ideas, and since we could have these – as in dreams, for example, we do – without their being the termini of causal chains, we have no justification for employing the realist premiss, which the causal theory demands, in order to set up that theory – unless the premiss can be independently established; and nor of course can the theory itself be used as a justification for believing that by means of the processes it describes we gain access to external objects. This case against the causal theory stands, despite the revived interest in causal accounts of perceiving following Grice (Grice in Warnock 2 pp85ff). The fact that it persuades less than it once did is not the result of its having been shown to be false, but because post-phenomenalist treatments of perception have been influenced by the two related thoughts that first-person accounts of what can justifiably be believed on the basis of empirical evidence yields very much less than our realist perconceptions lead us to wish to have, and that, secondly, it is simply implausible or unreasonable to believe that those preconceptions are false. Neither thought is however anything like as philosophically persuasive as it has been allowed to be, which a little reflection will show.

Pitcher's discussion of Berkeley on this point is instructive (Pitcher pp107-8). He begins with the attribution to Berkeley of the thesis 'that if one event immediately causes another, the latter must occur at a place contiguous to the former' (p107). It should immediately be remarked that Berkeley comes nowhere near asserting such a thesis; since, for Berkeley, all causal activity is reserved to spirits, chief among them God, and since he does not ascribe spatial location to spirits, this claim about Berkeley's view of causation is simply mistaken. On this basis, however, Pitcher argues that Berkeley 'must reason along something like the following lines': there is an event y which is the emitting of light-waves from an object, an event x which is the resulting brain stimulation, and there is 0, which is the further resulting object of awareness, namely the

2. Ideas and things

sensory idea. Berkeley, Pitcher says, 'imagines that since x immediately causes the occurrence of some object of awareness 0, 0 must occupy a spatial position contiguous to x. But only an idea of sense is close enough to x to be able to fulfil the requirement placed on 0; the object that figures in event y. [The emitting or reflecting of light-waves towards the observer] is too far away' (ibid.). I do not know whether anyone has ever held such an extraordinary theory, but it is at least clear that Berkeley does not, since items 'without the mind' like events y and x are no part of his ontology, and since sensory ideas are not in Berkeley's view caused by brain states, but by God.

The mistake which leads Pitcher to this view is his thinking that Berkeley accepts what in fact he denies, namely that there is a distinction between 'direct' and 'indirect' perception in the sense of one's perceiving something by means of a *re*-presenting intermediary or surrogate (like 'seeing' someone by seeing him on a television screen) – which is *not*, note, the immediate-mediate distinction discussed earlier. Causal theorists appear to be obliged to utilise such a distinction since what is directly present to awareness is the sensory idea *qua* terminus of the perceptual causal chain, and therefore the external object at the start of the chain must by contrast be, in this sense of 'indirectly', indirectly perceived (cf. Locke II. viii. 12). One way of putting Berkeley's point in response is to say that this conception is plausible only if it is already granted that there is an external object and a causal chain at the other end of which it is located (cf. Mackie on this p.64ff); but since what the causal theory purports to tell us is how we get access to such objects, the argument, in premissing what it seeks to prove, is circular. Because, therefore, no grounds have been provided for asserting that there are external objects, nor still less that there is a chain of intermediate events linking them to us, there are no grounds for asserting that something is in this sense 'indirectly' perceived by means of such a chain.

This claim goes beyond the more modest worry Locke felt: 'It is evident the mind knows not things immediately, but only by the intervention of the ideas it has of them. Our knowledge, therefore, is real only so far as there is a *conformity* between our ideas and the reality of things. But what should here be the criterion? How shall the mind, when it perceives nothing but its own ideas, know that they agree with things themselves?' (IV. iv. 3) Putting the question in this form would from Berkeley's point of view beg the question twice over, because it is no longer just a question about whether ideas are caused by 'things themselves', but whether there is a 'conformity' between them and ideas, upon which depends the 'reality' of knowledge. The question is only askable if it is assumed that there *are* 'things themselves', and this has merely been assumed, not shown. Since the causal theory cannot therefore be offered as a reason for taking it that there are external objects, it cannot further be asked whether the causal process gives us ideas 'conformable' to what causes them. Berkeley in fact has a strong additional argument concerning this point, which has been called the 'Likeness Principle' after Cummins' discussion of it (Cummins in Martin and Armstrong pp353ff). It states that 'nothing but an idea can be like an idea' (P8). Any theory which holds that a relation of conformity or resemblance obtains between ideas and something other than ideas falls foul of it, for, as Berkeley puts it, 'I appeal to anyone whether it be sense, to assert a colour is like something which is invisible; hard or soft, like something which in intangible; and so of the rest' (ibid. and cf. lD190, C47, 51, 484). This thought is primarily intended to expose a problem fundamental to representational theories as such, and so goes in scope well beyond causal theories, which constitute just one class of representational views.

It was noted earlier that these arguments are adminicles to Berkeley's central thesis concerning existence, the main account of which does not depend upon a theory of perception but on a conceptual argument whose chief statement occurs at Pl-7. The stretch of lD considered here is chiefly concerned to substantiate and capitalise on what in any case Berkeley's predecessors were largely agreed about, which is that secondary qualities *as perceived* are sensory ideas – even if, notably for the corpuscularians and Locke, they are more strictly to be thought of as powers, or the grounds of them, in material objects, which the sensory ideas they produce in us represent. It is when Hylas, after conceding his ground to Philonous on the secondary qualities, shifts his attention to the primary-secondary quality distinction that lD catches up with where P effectively begins, so far as arguments about perception go. That is significant; it shows that when Berkeley was writing P he took it that it was unnecessary to go into detail on *those* points. But Berkeley's task in lD is much simplified by his preparing the ground from scratch in this way, for the argument thereafter has only to be that primary qualities are on a par with secondary qualities, in the relevant respects, for the first stage of the *esse est percipi* thesis to be established, as shown above. Having demonstrated this, he is able to devote his energies to urging that the concept of an inaccessible and unknowable something supposed to underly what we experience –

3. Existence

namely, matter or corporeal substance – is unintelligible, and this completes the setting out of his grounds for holding that *esse est percipi*. This I discuss in section 7 below. First, however, I turn to that thesis itself and certain considerations immediately allied to it.

3. Existence

It will be remembered that the *esse est percipi* thesis applies only to sensible objects; the *esse* of spirit is *percipere* (plus, as it turns out, a little besides; I discuss spirit in the next chapter). For convenience 'the *esse est percipi* thesis' will hereafter be abbreviated 'EP'.

An initial difficulty in discussing EP concerns whether Berkeley intended it to be understood as stating that to exist is to be an *actual or possible* object of perception, or more austerely – and, some would say, less plausibly – an *actual* object of perception. It is however clear, and in what follows I shall furnish reason for so saying, that the thesis is intended to be that to exist is *actually* to be perceived, but that from the point of view of *finite* perceivers the existence of things consists in their being either an actual or a possible object of perception, the possibility *vis à vis* finite perceivers being cashed out in terms of actuality *vis à vis* God. Indeed Berkeley is committed to, and gives, an interesting and defensible analysis of counterfactuals of the relevant sort; see the discussion of perceivability in the next section. Accordingly from the outset I shall take it that for Berkeley *esse* is properly *percipi* and no more than percipi, but from the finitary viewpoint it is also ' ... *aut posse percipi*' as Luce puts it (Luce 2 p61), and that this expansion is to be understood in terms of the way the level 3 account, in which *esse* is strictly no more than *percipi*, explains what is the case at level 2 where and only where the expansion applies.

Berkeley's thesis about existence can informatively be compared to more recent discussions of the matter, with which it has a great deal in common. It differs from recent discussions more largely in form than in content, and its difference of content on the whole resides in the fact that it goes, if anything, *further* than its successor conceptions, by offering to identify the source of the propensity to think that existence is conceivable apart from what can be met with, in one or another way, in the domains over which experience ranges. A useful way to bring out the comparisons is to work backwards from more recent discussions to Berkeley's view, and this I do shortly. First, however, it is helpful to locate the issue in a general way by noting its chief source. (I traverse some familiar ground, to begin with; the point of doing so emerges shortly.)

A fruitful way of specifying what is at issue is to ask whether existence is a *property* of things, that is, whether among the properties attributable to, say, a tiger, such as being striped, growling, being fierce or tame, and so on, it is in addition pointful or even admissable to count existence as a property of the tiger likewise. There have been objections to treating existence as a property almost from the outset; Aristotle took the view that 'existing' or 'being' is not predicable of things: 'that there is such a thing is not what anything is ... being is not a genus' (*Analytica Posteriora* II. 7. 92b13). Others, among them Augustine and Anselm, treated existence as a property in formulating versions of the ontological argument for God's existence. Critical responses to the ontological argument, indeed, traditionally gave the debate on this topic much of its impetus, for it is an immediate result of denying that existence is a property that the argument fails (although this is not the only reason it does so).

Recent discussions of the question characteristically take an oblique approach; to unearth the reasons why existence does not at least straightforwardly seem to be a property attributable to things on a par with properties like being striped or red, the question 'is "exists" a *predicate*?' has been selected as the right one to answer first. It is a familiar point in current philosophical logic that in providing regimented paraphrases of ascriptions of existence to things in ordinary discourse, 'exists' as a property-introducing term vanishes, and the existential quantifier, objectually understood, assimilates its function. Definite advantages accrue from this in at least certain respects. It is sometimes pointed out that the 'surface grammar' of natural language can mislead – a point Berkeley would find congenial – and because 'exists' is a grammatical predicate – 'this book is red' and 'this book exists' are parsed in the same way – the necessity arises for an analysis which will show that 'exists' is, although grammatically a predicate, nevertheless not a proper (or a logical) predicate. The point is a Russellian one. And the reasons for this, in turn, include the fact that surface grammar might seduce us into mistaken ontologies, as arguably happened with Meinong – and they also include the one already met with, namely that there is something obviously *odd* about thinking of existence as a property of things on a par with others.

One way of spelling out this last point in more detail is to note that saying 'tigers are striped' and 'tigers growl' conveys information about tigers, but to say 'tigers exist' is not to convey information about tigers, at least in the same way; what information saying this

3. Existence

conveys, if information it is, is of a quite different kind. Moreover this quite different kind of information, if that is what it is, is expressly catered for by the apparatus of existential quantification for sentences conveying the ordinary kind of information. This shows what is intended by denying that 'exists' is a 'logical predicate'. A predicate is a logical predicate, on the standard view, if it counts as such in an interpretation of first-order quantified logic. Whenever there is a definite commitment to something's having a certain property in a given domain of discourse, the existential quantifier is employed to 'bind' the variable occuring in sentential functions of the familiar sorts, in which the variable serves as the referential device. This is to say, in effect, that quantifying over something states that it falls within the given domain, or places it there; a quantified function says this and *further* – and *differently* – that it has a certain property or properties, namely the arguments of the predicate variables. To deny that 'exists' is a logical predicate is therefore to deny that there is a place for it in the regimented paraphrases of the sentences of ordinary discourse, on the grounds that anything one might wish to say containing 'exists' has a paraphrase into regimented form which serves the same purpose but does not contain 'exists' among the legitimate predicates. This way of putting the matter originates with Frege, who held that quantification captures the fact that assertions of existence are not ascriptions of a property to something, but a way of saying how many things have this or that property or of showing that something answers to a certain description.

The oddity of treating 'exists' as a predicate does not however turn on one or another particular choice of regimentation as the *right* way to express logical form. The point can be put more generally. Moore, for example, suggests that whereas one is *expressing a proposition* when one points at a tiger and says 'this tiger is tame', one is not doing so when one points and says 'this tiger exists' (Moore p185). Although one can say with propriety 'this tiger might not have existed', which seems to suggest that 'this tiger exists' can be said with equal propriety, nevertheless the fact that in some sense *nothing is being said* when one says this suggests that an alternative analysis is required. Perhaps, Moore says, 'this exists' is part of what is asserted when one says 'this is a tiger' or 'this is striped'; and perhaps, further, what is involved in taking it that predicates like these stand for properties 'is that *part but not the whole* of what is asserted by any value of "x is a tiger", "x is striped" etc., is "this exists"' in which case 'exists' does not stand for a property 'because the whole of what it asserts, and not merely a part, is "this exists" ' (ibid. p187, Moore's emphasis). These ideas are adopted and developed by Pears, who fashions the notions of 'referential tautology' and 'referential contradiction' to display what the oddity of straightforwardly predicative uses of 'exists' involves (Pears pp79-102). Take for example someone's saying 'this room exists'. The expression 'this room' implies that there is a room, namely this one, and does so in virtue of having been used to refer to it. To add 'exists' is to assert the room's existence all over again, as if one were saying 'this room (which exists) exists'. This Pears calls 'referential tautology'. If one says 'this room does not exist' then the room's existence is implied by the reference to it, and therefore one implicity contradicts oneself by denying what is thus implied, as if one were saying 'this room (which exists) does not exist'. This Pears calls 'referential contradiction'. (There are qualifications for times, realms – like the fictional – and contexts, which introduce no special difficulty). What these considerations appear to show, in line with Moore's thoughts, is that 'exists' does not function as a true predicate, that is, as a property-introducing term genuinely capable of filling the gap in 'x (is) __', because what is expressed by its use seems already to have been implied or presupposed by the use made of the subject in the propositions at issue. A similar view is at work in Strawson's earlier treatment of the question (Strawson 1 p191). A proposition like 'the book on the table is red' is capable of truth-value, Strawson there argues, only if the presupposed statement 'there is a book on the table' is true. If the latter is false, the former cannot be said to be *either* true or false. If this is right, then 'x exists' cannot be subject-predicate in form, for to say that the subject expression 'x' in 'x exists' presupposes that x exists is absurd, since it carries as a presupposition what the proposition, of which it is a part, as a whole asserts. Hence in 'x exists' the expression 'x' cannot have a particular-referring role, and so the whole is not a subject-predicate proposition. If we treated 'x exists' propositions as having subject-predicate form, Strawson says, 'we should be faced with the absurd result that the question of whether they were true or false could only arise if they were true; or that, if they were false, the question of whether they were true or false could not arise' (ibid.).

These thoughts show why the formal paraphrase considerations are so attractive, for if in some sense the existence of what one is talking about is implied or presupposed by one's referring to it or saying of it that it has this or these properties, then the equipment of quantification aptly represents a way of showing how 'exists' disappears when what we say is unambiguously and cleanly set out.

3. Existence

It may therefore serve to provide what Quine thinks of as a criterion for testing our ontological commitments, in the sense that we reveal whether we are committed to counting some x into a given domain of discourse just in virtue of our preparedness to quantify over x (Quine 2 p242). There are, nevertheless, numerous difficulties invited by a treatment of the matter in this way, involving among other things the problem of reference, the nature of the relation of 'presupposition' which Strawson and Pears rely upon and the truth-value gaps its employment introduces, and the question whether the quantifiers should be read objectually rather than substitutionally, or more generally whether formal systems should not be altogether free of existential assumptions – and so forth. But even if this is only one approach to showing how we can eliminate talk of existence in ways which make it an attribute, and even if it invites explanations of these problematic issues, it is nevertheless useful because it goes some way to clarifying our intuitions.

It might however be argued that there is something in danger of being lost to sight here, which is that there *are* cases – rather special ones, it is true -where predicating existence of things is informative, namely where there is doubt or question as to whether, say, King Arthur is to be counted a real or legendary figure, or whether Loch Ness has a monster in it. Questions of this sort can of course be asked with 'exists' occurring in their formulation, as has just indeed been demonstrated, but that fact does not, so it might be argued, show that there is logical or any other impropriety in formulating them with 'exists' For when one says 'x exists' in such cases one is saying that x is to be met with, is to be counted among the things which, given the appropriate circumstances, it falls within our competence to encounter. Much this point is in effect argued by Strawson in a later paper (Strawson 4 pp193ff), in which the view is that assertions of existence function as assignments to subclasses of the members of a presupposed class of entities, where the class in question is something like, for example, the class of kingly characters, and the subclasses those of real (like King Alfred) and legendary (like King Arthur) kingly characters, and where what presupposes the class is a discourse. The class is the topic of the discourse; it is what is being talked about. It could be replied that it is open to one to regard questions about the status of these disputed items as settled by what Quine calls the 'systematic considerations' which determine whether or not one is prepared to go from 'Arthur was King at Camelot' to $(\exists x)(Ax \& Kx)$, where 'A' is 'has the property of being Arthur' and 'K' is 'has the property of being King at Camelot', which considerations are a matter of epistemology, not logic; but that, so the argument might go, is simply to say in one way what has already been said, without commitment to there being a preferred canonical representation of its form.

This manouevre does not however succeed in reserving to 'exists' an irreducibly predicative or property-ascribing role, but rather hints at a way of marking its character independently of whatever analysis one might give of sentences containing it. This is to note that 'x exists' statements are, as this approach to them itself suggests, merely shorthand for statements about *what can be encountered or met with*, or in respect of which there are grounds for holding that they count among the classes of items having this character. This is by no means as vague as it seems. It is true that what it is to encounter trees or Myrmidons is radically different from what it would be to encounter, say, numbers if Platonism about them were correct; but at least in the case of the former, namely sensible objects, it is unequivocally clear what encounterability involves. Among other things it involves the items' having spatial and temporal properties, and with them therefore a familiar range of sensible properties such as colours, textures, and the like. We standardly take it that it is the possession by objects of such attributes which provides the grounds of our capacity not just to individuate or identify them, but to recognise their presence in the first place. The point is clearer when put negatively: one good way of explaining what is meant by denying existence of something is to say that it fails of encounterability – that is, that nothing counts as an operable procedure for detecting its presence in the world. The point is not that something x is nonexistent if nothing *in fact* serves as such a procedure, for contingent limitations on our capacities to get in touch with things cannot be the arbiters of what is countable into our ontology. Rather it is that such a procedure must be available at least in principle if sense is to attach to claims that this or that item is to be met with. The point need not be restricted to sensible objects; for any item in any domain we must suppose a means of arriving at it or picking it out – 'no entity without identity', as Quine's slogan has it – for what it would be for something to be an item in a given domain when nothing serves as a means of recognising its presence in that domain is wholly opaque – indeed it is without content.

This way with the matter is promising, for it gives a wholly intuitive insight into what is intended by denying that existence is a property which things have in addition to being red, say, or heavy, and it does so without relying on one's having a preferred theory of

3. Existence

logical form, paraphrases into which reveal the sense in which talk of existence is reducible. Moreover, this comes close to the conception Berkeley articulates. His manner of doing so is more readily assimilable if one looks at arguments to the same effect which are very close both in content and form of expression, because closer in time, to his; for example those of Kant and in particular Hume.

In some versions of the ontological argument for God's existence, it is taken to be a contradiction to assert nonexistence of God because existence is a perfection and God is perfect. Descartes in the fifth *Meditation* argues this, commenting 'I clearly see that existence can no more be separated from the essence of God than can its having three angles equal to two right angles be separated from the essence of a triangle'. Among the reasons for Kant's objections to the ontological argument, which proceeds with this formulation of it in mind, is that existence or 'being' 'is obviously not a real predicate; that is, is not a concept of something which could be added to the concept of a thing', for a real predicate is a 'determining' predicate, that is, one which 'is added to the concept of the subject and enlarges it' (A598/B626). 'By whatever and however many predicates we may think a thing – even if we completely determine it – we do not make the least addition to the thing when we further add that this thing is' (A600/B628). The point of saying that nothing is *added* to the concept of a thing by saying it exists is that, as the metaphor of 'enlargement' is designed to illustrate, true predications convey information about the subject of the sort that might constitute answers to questions like 'what kind of thing is it?', 'what colour?', and so on. That there *is* a thing about which such information might be sought and given is no part of such information, and what is intended by bare assertions of existence is a matter 'external' to this, namely whether the subject of real predications is connected with 'perceptions, in accordance with empirical laws' (A601/B629). There can indeed be no knowledge *a priori* of existence, and hence all questions about what exists are on Kant's view empirical, that is, relate exclusively to sensible objects (ibid). Accordingly to say 'x exists' is not to predicate anything of x but to say that x is an actual or possible object of experience – that is, can be perceived. (Kant is not entirely clear when it comes to the implications of this for the objects of pure thought; by reserving existence to phenomena and excluding *a priori* knowledge of it, the status of the transcendental ego and the 'Ideal of Pure Reason' becomes problematic, for they seem to require a category of being whose nature it is difficult to conceive, even if we know formally that it has, in at least the case of God, to be necessary. But this puzzle does not affect the point in hand.)

There is disagreement concerning the extent to which Hume was influenced by Berkeley, but whatever one might think of the degree of that influence it is difficult to read *Treatise* I.II.VI. without finding something very like Berkeley's thesis expressed there. Hume, familiarly, classifies the mind's contents into simple and complex impressions and ideas, with every idea arising from a similar impression precedent to it. His argument about existence turns on this classification and its implications. 'There is' he says 'no impression nor idea of any kind, of which we have any consciousness or memory, that is not conceived as existent; and 'tis evident, that from this consciousness the most perfect idea and assurance of *being* is derived.' But this occasions a 'dilemma', which is that since no impression or idea is perceived other than as existent, 'the idea of existence must either be derived from a distinct impression, conjoined with every perception or object of our thought, or must be the very same with the idea of the perception or object'. Resolution of the dilemma is not however far to seek, for just as it results from the principle that every idea arises from a similar impression, so that same principle affords a solution. 'So far from there being any distinct impression, attending every impression and every idea, that I do not think there are any two distinct impressions, which are inseparably conjoined'; which is to say that each item of awareness is discrete and particular, with no necessary connexions obtaining between them, so that although 'certain sensations may at one time be united, we quickly find that they admit of separation, and may be presented apart'. And this settles the matter: 'And thus, tho' every impression and idea we remember be considered as existent, the idea of existence is not derived from any particular impression'; there is no impression of existence inseparably accompanying every other impression and idea yet distinct from them. 'The idea of existence, then, is the very same with the idea of what we conceive to be existent. To reflect on anything simply, and to reflect on it as existent, are nothing different from each other. That idea, when conjoined with the idea of any object, makes no addition to it. Whatever we conceive, we conceive to be existent.'

The conception which is being expressed in this and all the foregoing ways is that there is no more content to the idea of existence than that what exists is what is or can be met with; that existence is not a separate attribute of what is or can be encountered in experience of the relevant kind, but just is that encounter or encounterability. Berkeley not only argues for this view but offers an

3. Existence

explanation of why existence should ever have been thought a property – and one, moreover, detachable from others, even if only in thought; thinking which misleadingly suggests that until possession of that property is asserted of something, the concept of it is somehow incomplete or provisional. He also furnishes a means of controlling the Meinongian consequences which on the face of it Kant's account and Hume's do not immediately exclude.

The fullest specification of what Berkeley meant by EP is furnished by C; the relevant entries show why he took himself to be justified in giving such terse expression to the thesis at P3, for they provide the substantiation of the claim at P5 that the argument for it turns in considerable part on the rejection of abstraction set out in the Introduction to P. It turns also on the related identification of sensible qualities with ideas.

The argument itself is as follows. At P4 Berkeley notes that the received view is that sensible objects 'have an existence natural or real, distinct from their being perceived by the understanding', but claims that this view involves a 'manifest contradiction. For what are the forementioned objects but the things we perceive by sense, and what do we perceive besides our own ideas or sensations; and is it not plainly repugnant that any one of them should exist unperceived?' The key element in this thought is of course that 'An idea cannot exist unperceived' (C377); this, together with the equation of sensible qualities ahd ideas, directly yields EP. More fully, since sensible objects are collections of qualities, and since qualities are ideas, and since ideas must be perceived to exist, it follows that the *esse* of objects is *percipi*. The 'prevailing opinion' reported at P4, which is a level 3 view constituting part of the absolute realist theory standardly taken to explain level 2 phenomena, depends, in Berkeley's view, 'at bottom' on the 'doctrine of abstract ideas. For can there be a nicer strain of abstraction than to distinguish the existence of sensible objects from their being perceived, so as to conceive them existing unperceived?' (P5). The objects of sense (at level 1) are 'light and colour, heat and cold, extension and figures ...' in short 'so many sensations, notions, ideas, or impressions on the sense; and is it possible to separate, even in thought, any of these from perception?' (ibid.). Since it is not, it is 'impossible for me to conceive in my thoughts any sensible thing or object distinct from the sensation or perception of it' (ibid.).

The grounds of this claim emerge from Berkeley's reflections, in his note-books, on what levels 1 and 2 license apart from level 3 explanations of them. It is instructive to take a brief survey of the relevant entries, as follows. 'The abstract idea of Being or Existence is never thought of by the Vulgar. They never use those words standing for abstract ideas' (C552). 'NB that not common usage but the Schools coined the word Existence supposed to stand for an abstract general idea' (C752). 'Existence, Extension, etc. are abstract i.e. no idea. They are words unknown and useless to the vulgar' (C772). 'Strange it is that men should be at a loss to find their Idea of Existence since that (if such there be distinct from Perception) is brought into the mind by all the ways of Sensation and Reflection; methinks it should be most familiar to us & we best Acquainted with it' (C670. This irony is directed at Locke's view, II.vii.7, that 'all the ways of sensation and reflection' introduce the idea of existence). 'Will any man say that Brutes have the ideas, unity and Existence? I believe not. Yet if they are suggested by all the ways of sensation, tis strange they should want them' (C746). The conclusion is that 'Existence ... is no simple idea distinct from perceiving and being perceived' (C408). In these last few comments the identity of Hume's view with Berkeley's becomes apparent. The claim is that existence is not an idea that accompanies other ideas; it is not an *extra* idea attendant on them. This conception is given content for Berkeley by reflecting on what the 'vulgar' mean when they talk or think of existence; in full C408 runs 'The Vulgar notion agrees with mine when we narrowly inspect into the meaning and definition of the word Existence which is no simple idea distinct from perceiving and being perceived.' Likewise at C589 Berkeley says 'There was a smell i.e. there was a smell perceived. Thus we see that common speech confirms my doctrine.' In the published works this consideration is given in the form of the celebrated gardener example at 3D234-5: 'Ask the gardener, why he thinks yonder cherry-tree exists in the garden, and he shall tell you, because he sees it and feels it; in a word, because he perceives it by his senses. Ask him, why he thinks an orange-tree not to be there, and he shall tell you, because he does not perceive it. What he perceives by sense, that he terms a real being, and saith, it *is*, or *exists*; but that which is not perceivable, the same, he saith, hath no being.' This passage introduces an important debate about perceivability, considered below; its usefulness for present purposes is that it illustrates Berkeley's contention that the abstract concept of existence is a purely philosophical fiction which has no place in ordinary thought and talk, in which to say that something exists is no more than to say it can be met with, that is, that it can be perceived; it is not something additional to or besides perceivability, and could only ever have

3. Existence

come to be thought so as a result of illegitimate abstraction. Berkeley again uses the idea of the solitary man to reinforce the point: 'A good Proof that Existence is nothing without or distinct from Perception may be Drawn from Considering a Man put into the world without Company' (C88); unprejudiced by abstractionist tenets, so this thought suggests, no one would think that something which could in no circumstances or by any means be perceived or encountered in experience nevertheless exists. The 'something' in question is of course a sensible object, for EP relates only to sensible objects and not to spirits or notions. The 'repugnancy' or 'contradiction' for Berkeley is that there should be 'insensible objects of sense', which is *per impossibile* possible only if abstraction is legitimate.

In Berkeley's view the illegitimacy of abstraction consists, it will be remembered, in the fact that no *sense* attaches to talk of, for example, motion apart from particular things moving, or colour apart from extended surfaces (Intro. P7-8, cf. 1D193). Unperceived existence is 'the most abstract and general notion of all', and accordingly Berkeley describes it as 'the most incomprehensible of all' (P81). In a number of places, for example P24, 3D233 and 244, Berkeley talks of the 'meaninglessness', 'manifest repugnancy' and 'inconsistency' of the thought that existing is something different from being perceived; and again that it is 'a plain contradiction' to suppose this. That it is meaningless or contradictory to abstract the concept of existence from the concept of what can be perceived results from the fact that what is perceivable is what is extended, coloured, textured, and so on – that is, something propertied, indeed which is the sum of its properties, and hence encounterable in perception, whereas a thing which is without properties is nothing, a 'non-entity' (P68). This is the respect in which EP is the obverse of the coin whose reverse is the denial of matter.

We can now note how Berkeley's thesis fits with the other accounts of existence mentioned. In recent discussions, for example those of Moore, Pears and the others mentioned above, the idea that emerges is that the existence of things talked about or referred to – except in those cases where the existence of something is explicitly denied and which therefore count as assertions to the effect that the thing in question is not encounterable in whatever way is relevant to encountering things of that kind – is in a sense 'contained' in talk about or reference to those things *already*, which is what gives rise to the appearance of something like referential tautology or, more generally, redundancy, in 'x exists' locutions. An essential ingredient of this thought is that the fact that talk of x (in all cases other than express denials of there being x) carries this contained commitment to x's existence shows that there are not two conceptions in hand, namely the conception of x and, separately or additionally, the conception of x's existence; and one way of putting this is to say that one cannot separate or *abstract* the conception of x's existence from the conception of x. In Berkeley's terminology, one would say: one cannot conceive x without conceiving of it *as existing*, any more than one can conceive of an existence which is not the existence of something. The case is similar, in Berkeley's view, when we say something extended is coloured, or that something moving has a direction, where what would be genuinely informative (assertions about *particular* colours or directions) is not at issue. One mark of the unabstractability of extension and colour, or motion and direction, is the special kind of *pointlessness* in saying that extensions are coloured or that movements are directional; the same applies to perceivability and existence.

The same basic insight connects Berkeley's claim with the claims of Kant and Hume on this head. At C408 ('Existence ... is no simple idea distinct from perceiving and being perceived') and in those assertions, similar in content, which deny that a recognition of something's existence accompanies, as something extra, recognition of that thing's presence to awareness, the idea is in essentials that existence is not one among the properties a thing has, but is nothing apart from its being a propertied thing and *ipso facto* available to perception. The formulations ' "exists" is not a predicate' and 'existence is not a property' are not of course employed by Berkeley and Hume, but the assertion that what exists is neither more nor less than what is encounterable in experience – that is, is nothing detachable from or additional to what makes an object encounterable in experience – amounts precisely to that. In two respects, however, Berkeley's views go beyond those of Kant and Hume. The first has already been mentioned: it is the explanation of why existence should ever have come to be thought separable from the properties in which a thing consists, the explanation being the 'nice strain' of abstraction which infects philosophical thought. And secondly it takes seriously the consequences of thinking in terms of substance, and does so in rather an unusual way. Ideas are *dependent* items, and as such require a 'substance or *substratum*' (cf. P2, 7). The terminus of the argument summarised at Pl-7 is that there is only one substance, namely mind; ideas and mind are distinct (P2, 142), but they are intimately related – the relation being that ideas 'exist' in the mind, or, 'which is the same thing', are perceived by it (P2).

3. Existence

Since the existence of ideas consists in being perceived, and since sensible qualities are ideas, it follows that sensible qualities can only exist in mind, and not in anything else, a point Berkeley puts by saying 'Now for an idea to exist in an unperceiving thing, is a manifest contradiction; for to have an idea is all one as to perceive: that therefore wherein colour, figure, and the like qualities exist, must perceive them; hence it is clear there can be no unthinking substance or *substratum* of those ideas' (cf. 3D233). This explains Ayers' characterisation of the New Principle as the claim that there is only mental substance, which supports sensible qualities by perceiving them. Ayers points out the Berkeley accepts a conception of substance very like Spinoza's, which is 'that the conception of which does not need the conception of another thing' (Ayers 1 p49). Substance is what is ontologically *basic* in the sense of being self-sufficient, requiring no ground. If one were to grant both that sensible objects are no more than the sum of their properties, and that these are ideas, it follows that the only substance by which they can be supported is mind – which 'supports' them *by perceiving them*. Elsewhere Berkeley attacks the notion of 'support', as applied to the relation between *material* substance and its accidents, as merely metaphorical (P16). By contrast, the mind-idea relation is taken by Berkeley to be perspicuous, on the ground that it is immediately present to awareness whenever it obtains. As we shall see, there are in fact a number of difficulties in Berkeley's account of the relation between minds and ideas, but the difficulties do not affect the main point here, which is that it is a dimension of Berkeley's views, going further than the other accounts of existence mentioned, that they involve a distinctive thesis about substance. Whether or not this is a strength of his account depends on whether the thesis about substance is independently sustainable. Nevertheless although his analysis of existence centrally involves it in its positive aspect, his criticism of the abstract notion of existence does not; and *that* aspect of it is very close to the discussions elsewhere and at other times given of the concept.

A consequence of these two features of Berkeley's account is that EP states not just that anything which exists is perceivable, but that anything which is perceived exists. 'That a thing should be really perceived by my senses, and at the same time not really exist, is to me a plain contradiction' (3D230 and cf. P40, 88). Such a view threatens Meinongian consequences, and accordingly requires that a criterion be furnished for distinguishing between the 'real' and the 'chimerical', which Hylas demands at 3D235 and Philonous, summarising the numerous discussions of this in P (e.g. P29, 30, 33, 36 etc.) gives. Any idea, whether 'real' or 'chimerical', exists in virtue of being perceived; that is what Berkeley means by saying at C473 'But say you then a Chimaera does exist. I answer it doth in one sense i.e. it is imagined. but it must be well noted that existence is vulgarly restrained to actual perception. & that I use the word Existence in a larger sense than ordinary.' For a moment Berkeley was tempted to assert therefore that 'NB according to my Doctrine all things are entia rationis i.e. solum habent esse in Intellectu' (C474); but the entry is marked with the obelus, which means in this case that it is rejected, and there appears *verso* the emendation 'according to my Doctrine all are not entia rationis the distinction between ens rationis & ens reale is kept up by it as well as any other Doctrine' (C474a). The reason is as Philonous gives it at 3D235; ideas of imagination or 'chimerical' ideas are 'faint and indistinct' and have an 'entire dependence on the will' (ibid. cf. P33). Ideas of sense, 'that is, real things', are 'more vivid and clear', and have an independent source; they are coherent and orderly, and their connections lawlike, so that they can be represented in those statements of their regularities we call 'Laws of Nature' (ibid. and P30-1). This criterion, although what Berkeley says about 'chimerical' ideas is in part just false, is sufficient, for whatever level 3 theory is invoked to account for the difference between what is bracketed as real and what chimerical, these empirical characteristics will be the appearances saved by that theory. What is false in Berkeley's characterisation of ideas and imagination concerns their relation to will; not all subjective ideas are 'entirely dependent' on one's will, a fact psychiatrists would confirm on the basis of their dealings with phobic or paranoid patients. Nevertheless it is true that subjective ideas are, among other differentiating respects, less independent of the will on the whole than are 'ideas of sense', one of whose characteristic marks is their haecceity or 'givenness'; echoing Locke, Berkeley says 'When in broad daylight I open my eyes, it is not in my power to choose whether I shall see or not, or to determine what particular objects shall present themselves to my view; and so likewise as to the hearing and other senses, the ideas imprinted on them are not creatures of my will' (P29). This passage gives the misleading impression that Berkeley takes it to follow immediately from their independence of will that these ideas have external sources or at least an external source, but his argument to that effect turns not just on this but on his account of causality also. That account is investigated later.

The convertability of EP has given rise to some interesting discussion on the status of the thesis, not least by Marc-Wogau (Marc-Wogau in Martin and Armstrong pp314ff), who devotes part of his investigation to the question whether Berkeley intends to be committed to holding, in effect, (x) (x exists ↔ x is perceived) or just (x) (x exists → x is perceived). (This way of putting things, in which 'exists' serves as a predicate, and moreover one within the scope of a quantifier – bearing in mind the equivalence of (x) Fx and – (Ex)-Fx – is simply odd, but provided it is not taken to be a question-begging way of representing what is at stake, it will serve). Much of what Berkeley says suggests the former, but Marc-Wogau claims that at most what Berkeley's arguments could establish, if they work, is the latter. (He concludes, on the basis of an investigation into the perceivability issue, that Berkeley's argument fails.) In setting up the contrast Marc-Wogau chooses the formulation (x) (x exists ↔ x is perceived) as interpretatively a better formulation – because weaker – than 'esse = percipi' (p327), but it is interesting that *identity* should be mentioned at all, even in this rather hybrid way. For if – as in Chapter One, section 3 above – we permit ourselves two idioms, that of property identity and that of necessity as truth in all possible worlds, then, as noted before, when it is true of the properties F and G that F = G, it is entailed that necessarily anything is one if and only if it is the other. For Berkeley the commitment is that 'existing' *just is* 'being perceived', which is to say in this idiom that he is committed to the necessary equivalence of *esse* and *percipi*. The arguments he gives can be expressed in this idiom as having *that* conclusion as their aim; they might as they stand bear more on showing that nothing more or less could be *meant* by 'existing' than 'being perceived', but that does not alter the fact that it is a mistake to think therefore that his intended terminus was the weaker matter of proving (x) (x exists → x is perceived) alone.

The discussion here has gone part of the way to showing how EP is to be understood. An immediately connected question is the one raised at the beginning of this section, whether EP is to be taken in the strict sense of *esse est percipi* or in the more liberal sense of that and *aut posse percipi* as well. To this I now turn.

4. Perceivability

That Berkeley's views about perceivability are full of difficulty is amply illustrated by the stark contrasts to be found among his commentators' treatments of them. Luce and Bennett afford examples. Luce claims that 'In point of fact the *esse est percipi* is an elastic principle, meant to stretch ... his formula thus expands naturally into *esse est percipi aut posse percipi*' (Luce 2 p61). One ground for Luce's claim is that at P3, 'on the first occurence of the problem' (ibid. p63), Berkeley characterises existence as actual or possible perception: 'The table I write on, I say, exists, i.e. I see and feel it, and if I were out of my study I should say it existed, meaning thereby that if I was in my study I might perceive it, or that some other spirit actually does perceive it'. Bennett's view stands at the opposite extreme. He distinguishes Berkeley's idealism from phenomenalist views by reference to the former's commitment to the thesis 'that *no object can exist unless it is perceived by someone*', citing P4 as illustrative (Bennett p138), whereas phenomenalism is the claim that '*objects are logical constructions out of sense-data*' (ibid. p137) in the sense that statements about objects are expressible as sets of statements about actual and possible sense-data, therefore including among them counterfactual conditionals (ibid. p136); and with 'logical construction' also, therefore, meaning something quite different from Berkeley's 'collection' (ibid. p137). And he then says, 'Apart from his covertly phenomenalistic theory about (Berkeleyan) "real things" ... there are two isolated phenomenalistic passages' (ibid. p145), namely P3 and P58; but anything which might be inferred from their occurence is negated, says Bennett, by Berkeley's explicit disavowal of phenomenalism at 3D234 where occurs the following exchange: '*Hylas*: Yes, Philonous, I grant the existence of a sensible thing consists in being perceivable, but not in actually being perceived. *Philonous*: And what is perceivable but an idea ? And can an idea exist without being actually perceived?' Interestingly, Bennett takes the notebook discussion of the question of perceivability to show that Berkeley began as a phenomenalist and ended as an idealist.

There is something both right and wrong in each of these attitudes, despite their wide divergence. One way to recover Berkeley's intentions here, and therefore his commitments, is to begin by considering the development of his views on perceivability in C. Luce, in his note to C52, points out that it is one of the more extensively discussed issues in the notebooks; he lists no fewer than thirty-eight entries relating to it, although some of those he cites are, in fact, marginally relevant only. Nevertheless a substantial proportion of the focally relevant entries are revised and annotated, indicating dissatisfaction at least with the *formulation* of the theory adopted early on, which is the 'powers' theory – and which has, as

4. Perceivability

will be seen, nothing to do with phenomenalism despite Bennett's view.

At the outset Berkeley was attracted by the thought that to say an object *could* be perceived is to say that it is a power in God to produce ideas in us: '+Bodies etc do exist even when not perceived they being powers in the active Being' (C52). This accords with two of the theses Berkeley had under consideration at this early stage, one of which was to retain a fundamental importance throughout the notebooks and published writings. This is the familiar thesis that qualities do not exist without the mind: 'Extension a sensation, therefore not without the mind' (C18); 'World without thought is nec quid nec quantum nec quale etc' (C22); 'Extension to exist in a thoughtless thing is a contradiction' (C37). The other thesis, allied to this, is that because qualities exist as powers in God's mind to cause them in us under appropriate circumstances, there is therefore a means of thinking about primary qualities which is somewhat analogous to the corpuscularian view, but which is consistent with the mind-dependence principle: '+Nothing corresponds to our primary ideas without but powers, hence a direct & brief demonstration of an active powerful being distinct from us on whom we depend. etc' (C41). But the seeds of difficulty for this view are already present, for at C50 Berkeley comments 'Nothing but ideas perceivable', which – unless it were intended to apply only to finite perceivers and not to God, who would not on the powers theory *perceive* but merely *intend to produce* all those ideas not currently perceived by finite beings – undermines the powers theory. And ultimately, as the notebooks show, it does so. But the basic idea of the powers theory retained its attraction for Berkeley until C802, only a few pages from the end of the notebooks, despite his having to attempt alternative formulations of it. So, for example, before he drew what is in effect, but not yet in terminology, the idea-notion distinction, Berkeley was prepared to regard God as an *unknown* substance in which it could be 'demonstrated' that bodies unperceived by finite minds exist as 'combinations of powers' (C80), although since these exist as something like *intentions* in the mind of God it seemed proper to Berkeley to ask 'Powers quaere whether more or one merely?' (C84). As powers, things unperceived by finite minds must be 'allowed' existence 'but not an absolute actual existence' (C185); this conception, together with the query at C84, leads Berkeley to say at C282 '+Bodies etc do exist whether we think of 'em or no, they being taken in a twofold sense. Collections of thoughts & collections of powers to cause those thoughts. These latter exist, tho' perhaps a parte dei it may be one simple perfect power'. This view is repeated at C293, and in the annotation to it Berkeley reasserts the existence-actuality distinction of C185: '+Bodies taken for Powers do exist when not perceived but this existence is not actual. when I say a power exists no more is meant than if in the light I open my eyes & look that way I shall see it i.e. the body &c' (C293a). By C461 the doubts which ultimately issued in the rash of obeluses attached to the foregoing entries had begun to set in: '+The simple idea called Power seems obscure or rather none at all, but only the relation 'twixt cause and effect.' This seemed adequate for a short while; at C493 Berkeley says '+Power no simple idea. it means nothing but the Relation between cause and effect.' The option implied by these remarks is that since God, the external source of the ideas we cannot choose but have present to sensory awareness, is the cause of these ideas, perceivability consists in the ubiquitous and unfailing causal efficacy of God (cf. C831, 838, P29-33, 2D213-15). This is the official doctrine; but there is no further development of the idea that *powers* can be reductively explained in terms of the causal relation, despite indications that what Berkeley was thinking in connection with the relation between power and *volition* (cf. C699) might have had a role to play in this.

Concurrently with these entries there appear an increasing number which speak of the existence of bodies independently of 'our Mind' (finite minds) without reference to the powers theory; and after EP is announced in C279 and 280 the 'powers' entries dwindle sharply in number, and the thesis of C50, 'Nothing but ideas perceivable', gains rapidly in importance and number of entries – it is expressed in C301, 347, 377, 408, 427a, 429, 437, 472-4, 477a, 517-8, 550, 606, 609, 646, 692, 775, 792, 801, 802, and 823, and is directly implied by a number more. In view of the central role the contention plays in the official doctrine, this is as one would expect.

At C802 Berkeley drops reference to the powers theory altogether with the remark 'Not to mention the Combinations of Powers but to say the things the effects themselves to really exist even when not actually perceived but still with relation to perception.' This entry is intriguing for a number of reasons. First, Berkeley advises himself not to mention the powers theory, which on the face of it is a matter quite different from rejecting it; moreover 'the things the effects themselves' of these powers are to be accorded the status of really existing as opposed to being existent but not actual; and finally they are to be accorded this status on the grounds of having a 'relation to perception', which two last features constitute part of the official

4. Perceivability

doctrine of P and D. All this requires comment.

One of the least clear aspects of Berkeley's overall theory concerns the form taken by ideas in the mind of God, and in what relation, other than being caused by God, our ideas are supposed to stand to them. That the ideas we have – and therefore nature itself, since it is the overall collection of ideas – are caused by God is clear (P29-33, 150-1, 2D210, 213-15, 3D230-1, 236, 253-4); Berkeley talks of God 'producing' ideas in us (P29, 49, 2D215), 'exciting' them in us (P30, 70), 'imprinting' them on our senses (P33, 150), 'exhibiting' them to us (2D215, 3D231), 'affecting' us with them (2D215), 'actuating' the universe (2D210). But these locutions leave unexplained how God himself perceives ideas, since they are not for him as they are for finite minds, namely the *effects* of his causal activity. He *perceives* them, as these same sources amply testify, but perception is a wide concept for Berkeley, embracing all the ways of having ideas before the mind whether in sensing, imagining, conceiving, remembering and the rest. In resisting a Malebranchian interpretation of his views Berkeley denies that ideas inhere in God (2D213-14); they are, rather, distinct from him just as they are distinct from finite minds (P2, 142); but 'His ideas are not conveyed to Him by sense, as ours are', which is a 'manifest difference' as between God's perceiving and ours (3D241). Accordingly the sense in which ideas are in the mind of God or are perceived by God is not wholly clear. There are at least two possibilities suggested by what Berkeley says. One is that the ideas perceived by God are the archetypes of which our ideas are ectypes (cf. 3D248 and Johnson to Berkeley *Works* II pp285-7 and Berkeley's reply p292). On this view what God perceives and what we perceive are qualitatively identical, in the sense that he perceives this ashtray on my desk just as I do – more completely, perhaps, in that he may have all its qualities in all their aspects immediately and simultaneously present to him – and that he causes in me the idea of at least part of the ashtray whenever my other ideas are such that I am sitting here striking matches and so on. However, God's having qualitatively the same ideas I have, in fuller form perhaps, is logically independent of his causing them in me, since he could cause those ideas in me without himself having them in just *that* form; for quite obviously he could bring it about that I see an ashtray without himself doing whatever is the divine analogue of seeing. This suggests the second possibility, which is that God's willing that finite minds perceive certain ideas is, in God, an intention or volition the content of which is purely formal or propositional rather than one or more of visual, olfactory, auditory or whatever – that is, that since

God's knowledge of things is not sensorily conditioned it does not take or at least have to take a specifically sensory character. This second possibility is one which naturally accords with the powers theory, for if items currently unperceived by finite minds are powers in the mind of God to produce ideas in us under appropriate conditions, then they exist there as *potential causes* but not as *actual effects*, which effects are the ideas themselves. And this would in turn explain the existence-actuality distinction employed by Berkeley in several early notebook entries, as we saw, for on this view the items would exist in potentiality and not as actual ideas, that is, ideas currently perceived by any finite mind. The suggestion that what has a sensory character for finite perceivers has as it were a propositional character for God seems to be allowed at 3D240-1, where Hylas says that it is a derogation from the perfection of God that he should feel 'pain and uneasiness', which is entailed by the principle Philonous holds, namely 'that whatever ideas we perceive from without, are in the mind which affects us' (3D240). Philonous' reply is that God knows what pain is and what it is for his creatures to suffer, that he even indeed causes pain; but the supposition that he suffers from pain himself 'I positively deny' (ibid.). Finite beings are embodied and constrained by what is external to them, Philonous says, and these facts, together with all their implications, are what give rise to pain and uneasiness; but God is affected by nothing whatever, perceives nothing by sense, and is 'absolute and independent' in his activity (3D241), and hence is not subject to the imperfections in which 'to endure, or suffer, or feel anything by sense' consist (ibid.).

Nevertheless it is the first of these two possibilities which turns out to be the official doctrine for Berkeley – that is, the doctrine of the published writings – which doctrine is encapsulated in Hylas' characterisation of the view, just quoted, 'that whatever ideas we perceive from without, are in the mind which affects us', where 'in the mind' is at least to be understood in the non-Malebranchian sense of being distinct from but perceived by that mind. With a certain latitude what Berkeley says in the quoted exchange can be allowed, as it is intended, to be consistent with this doctrine; and everything else said in the published writings accords with it as with the increasingly dominant entries embodying it in the notebooks. But more to the point, it *has* to be this doctrine, as it is clear Berkeley recognised, for the other view is inconsistent with the rest of his theory. That theory assembles, familiarly, the related views that bodies are collections of ideas; all ideas are sensory ideas or copies of these; only ideas are perceivable; bodies really exist when

4. Perceivability

unperceived; to be is to be perceived; nothing exists without the mind, that is, without reference to perception; God causes ideas in regular and coherent trains representable as laws of nature; and so on. All these and allied themes demand the first interpretation and cannot comfortably be squared with the thought that it is not ideas but powers to cause them in which for most of the time the greater part of the universe consists. Moreover a powers theory would conflict with the Likeness Principle – 'nothing can be like an idea but an idea' – one of whose purposes is to demonstrate that whatever we perceive we know in its intrinsic character, so that what exists is not something concealed behind ideas, either in the form of an empirically inaccessible corporeal substance or in the form of powers which are not ideas and hence which are different from their effects, and which therefore also constitute an empirically inaccessible noumenon beyond the phenomena. Accordingly Berkeley makes it plain in P and D that God perceives those ideas his creatures perceive, and that their existence is assured in virtue of that fact. What clinches this reading is the doctrine espoused, as I show in a moment, in the published writings; but it is significant to note that shortly after C802 Berkeley comments 'The propertys of all things are in God i.e. there is in the Deity Understanding as well as Will. He is no blind agent & in truth a blind Agent is a Contradiction' (C812). This suggests that *mere* power or volition to cause ideas – 'blind agency' – is not enough; God perceives them in their manifest character too. This does not settle the vexed issue, noted above, of quite how God's perceiving is to be understood, but it might be supposed that the projected Part II of P would have suggested answers. (I return to this matter below.)

'Not to mention powers', then, suggests that Berkeley saw, by the time he arrived at C802, that the powers theory, at least as it stood, conflicted too deeply with the focal commitments of his other views, and that although he wished to be able to employ the concept of God's volitonal and hence causal activity as his level 3 theory – the metaphysics explanatorily underlying the levels 1 and 2 facts – he did not before C802 have a settled account of how that was to be made out uniformly with the view that the sensible world consists in ideas whose *esse* is *percipi* and which therefore must always be perceived by God, not *just* willed by him. Some commentators, Bennett among them, take it that the relative paucity of discussion in P and D concerning God and his role as conservor of the universe – in particular the very few, and then mostly oblique, references to God in the first eighty-odd sections of P – suggest that Berkeley was simply unaware of how to manage this complex issue. This, as I shall now show, is not plausible.

The key to Berkeley's view of perceivability is to be found in two passages in D. One is the exchange, already quoted at 3D234: '*Hylas*: Yes, Philonous, I grant the existence of a sensible thing consists in being perceivable, but not in actually being perceived. *Philonous*: And what is perceivable but an idea? And can an idea exist without being actually perceived ?' The other is Philonous' remark at 3D235: 'The question between the materialist and me is not, whether things have a real existence out of the mind of this or that person, but whether they have an absolute existence, distinct from being perceived by God, and exterior to all minds.' The passages in P which some commentators take to express a different doctrine, but which I shall show do not, are these: 'The table I write on, I say, exists, that is, I see and feel it; and if I were out of my study I should say it existed, meaning thereby that if I was in my study I might perceive it, or that some other spirit actually does perceive it ... For as to what is said of the absolute existence of unthinking things without any relation to their being perceived, that seems perfectly unintelligible' (P3); 'we may not conclude [that bodies] have no existence except only while they are perceived by us, since there may be some other spirit that perceives them, though we do not. Wherever bodies are said to have no existence without the mind I would not be understood to mean this or that particular mind, but all minds whatsoever' (P48); 'Thus when I shut my eyes, the things I saw may still exist; but it must be in another mind' (P90). In none of these remarks does Berkeley mention God's perceiving, although God is immediately in the offing in each case. It is in 2D212 that the thesis first takes explicit form in the published writings; Philonous says 'To me it is evident, for the reasons you allow of, that sensible things cannot exist otherwise than in a mind or spirit. Whence I conclude, not that they have no real existence, but that seeing they depend not on my thought, and have an existence distinct from being perceived by me, *there must be some other mind wherein they exist*. As sure therefore as the sensible world really exists, so sure is there an infinite omnipresent spirit who contains and supports it.' It is to be noted that this passage brings together three Berkeleyan themes often treated apart by commentators – those of *reality, perceivability* and *continuity*. The themes are closely intertwined, a fact which will become apparent here and again below where the questions of continuity and reality recur.

Some commentators, notably Pitcher, take the fact that the three comments in P make no mention of God to be evidence, as noted, for

4. Perceivability

Berkeley's being 'between theories' when he wrote P (Pitcher p173), or at any rate unclear about how to handle the problem of unperceived objects; and that it was only when he came to write D that a solution offered itself. In the light of the notebook entries alone this is an implausible view, and its usual competitor, namely that Berkeley intended to cash the P remarks in a Part II where God was to have been the chief topic of discussion, that is, where the level 3 account was to be given in fuller form, is greatly more credible. In just the spirit of P44 where Berkeley says 'it was beside my purpose to examine' in V the supposition that tangible objects exist without the mind, so he might justifiably claim that a fully spelled out theory of the nature of God and his activity is beside the purpose in Part I, however anxiously – like Johnson – we might wish to see Part II as a result of what Part I leaves open. But even this defence is not required, although I think it plausible, for what Berkeley says in P both directly implies and exactly fits what is said in D. It is made abundantly clear in P that the *reality* of things consists in their being ideas caused in us by God (P29-33, 34, 35-6 etc), the constancy and regularity of which ideas and their connections permits representation of them as laws of nature, which in turn bespeaks not just the independence of nature from finite perceivers but its continuity (P48). From these theses, EP itself, and P3, 45 and 90, the explicit doctrine of D directly follows. The brevity of Berkeley's treatment of perceivability in P would seem, therefore, to have much more to do with his desiring that the conception should 'glide insensibly' into his readers' understandings, than any confusion or uncertainty on his part as to what that conception should be.

Taking all the relevant passages together, then, the perceivability thesis which results is this: to say that something is perceiv*able* is to say that it is perceived by God (3D234). No idea is ever merely perceivable relative to God, for every idea is in fact perceived by him (cf. 2D212) – the 'merely' is there because of course what is perceived is *ipso facto* perceivable, an instance of the truth *ab esse ad posse* – hence perceivability is strictly speaking relative only to finite perceivers. The possibility that a finite being might perceive x therefore turns on the fact – the actuality – that God perceives it. There are various ways of displaying the content of this thought. One is to compare it with the result of thinking in terms of the subjunctive conditional 'S would perceive x if ___' where the antecedent (following 'if') states a condition the fulfilment of which makes 'S perceives x' true, for example 'if S were in his study'. On one kind of analysis offered for such conditionals, their truth-conditions are to be stated in terms of a possible world minimally variant with respect to the actual world, in which the condition for the truth of the indicative form of the consequent is realised. So for 'S would perceive x if S were in his study' there is a world, differing minimally from the actual world, in which S is in his study and S perceives x. The requirement that the world in which it is the case that S perceives x should be as little different from the actual world as it can be, consistently with its not being the actual world, and where the differences are specific to the state of affairs in which S's perceiving x consists, issues from the fact that understanding the modality contained in the counterfactual turns on the need for something like a sharply constrained relation of 'accessibility', or a cognate of this, between the worlds in question. Explicitly modal propositions involve quantification over all and any possible worlds, and in some or at least one of these 'S is in his study and S does not perceive x' is true. The world reference to which is relevant for making sense of holding a *particular* counterfactual true of the actual world must accordingly have a strict characterisation in terms of the realisation of the state of affairs described in the antecedent of that conditional, together with the consequences of its realisation, and for this the relevant constraints are intended to provide. Therefore the world which makes 'if S were in his study he would perceive x' true is that world in which S is in his study and perceives x, all else being, as far as it can be, the same. A treatment of counterfactuals along these lines might be given more detail by working it out in accordance with one or other of the theories in the current literature which have this character – the proposals collected under the label 'actualism' come to mind; what would have to be excluded are theories involving realism about possible worlds, since in order to give content to talk about how things might be, have been or would be in this world, one requires to stay as 'close' to *this* world as one can. Something like this view would be required to spell out the content of conditional statements which form an irreducible part of phenomenalist conceptions of objects, in which the set of experiential data logically constituting an object include an indefinitely *larger* collection of sensibilia than sensa, the facts about the former being expressible in counterfactual terms, that is, in terms of what would be the case if certain currently unfulfilled conditions were fulfilled.

For various reasons which cannot be gone into here, theories of conditionals of the sort at issue invite difficulties, discussion of which has prompted a variety of alternative formulations, trading on commitments in closely related problem areas (cf. Grayling 1 pp70ff).

4. Perceivability

Fortunately for present purposes, that wider debate is not at issue. Berkeley's view of perceivability requires a single and specific understanding of the implicit modality and how it is to be understood, and this his theory readily provides.

The question for Berkeley is what makes it possible that if S were in his study he would perceive x. What is *not* at stake here are questions about 'possible studies', 'possible desks' and 'possible perceivers'; the issue is not one that requires a metaphysics of possibilia, but, far from it, is one that turns solely on explaining how things have to be for actual perceivers, studies and desks to be so placed that if S were in a given study he would perceive a given desk. This makes the question one about what conditions require fulfilment for it to be true that S stands in the relevant epistemic relation to x, a specification of which sustains the associated counterfactual. And this specification is to be given in terms of the *actual* world, for the possibility that S perceives x in the study entails the actualities of S, the study, and x; if it is possible that S perceives x then trivially it is not possible that there is no S to perceive and no x to be perceived – in this as in other cases of statements of logically necessary conditions the relevant *de dicto* modality is familiar and unproblematic. The key condition for present purposes is that if x is perceivable *it is there to be perceived*. One might put the point in either of two related ways, one starting from consideration of the logic of 'can' and the other from what is in relevant part required for ascriptions to Ss of their being able to have cognitive attitudes to xs. To say that *S could perceive x* is in part to say that there is x; if there were no x to be perceived then S cannot perceive it. This is quite different from the matter of understanding what it is to say that if there were x then S, because he is suitably equipped, say, would be able to perceive it, for in this case the possibility to be explained is that there is x, not the possibility that S perceives x. It is not, in other words, a possible x but a possible perceiving of x which is at stake. Because it is the latter alone which is at stake, it is part of the condition for S's being able to perceive x that there be x. Alternatively, to say that S in the right circumstances is able to take a certain cognitive attitude to x is again in part to say that there is x, for in every *true* statement either of the form 'S knows that p' or 'S sees x', 'S hears x', and so on, it is a logically necessary condition that there be x (or in the 'knows' case that 'p' be true); hence if it is possible for it to be true of S that 'S perceives x' there must be x. Again, the point does not concern what is involved in S's having or coming to have a cognitive attitude to possible xs; it is not possible xs which are at issue, but possible perceivings.

The point is intuitive. If it is possible for S to see a desk, say, then S must be sighted, there must be a desk available, and things must be such that S has the means to position himself relative to the desk so that, for example, no opaque structures block his line of vision ... and so on. (The 'and so on' will include considerations such as its being the case that it is in S's power to open and focus his eyes, that there is enough light ... and so on again.) One cannot say that it is possible for S to see a desk if S is blind, or has no means of getting at a desk, or if there are no desks. Accordingly what makes it *possible* for S to see a desk is the fact that the required conditions are fulfilled, that is, are *actual*: he actually has sight, actually has the means to position himself appropriately relative to the desk, and there actually is a desk. Everything that is here actually the case is contingently so, of course, but it stands to the possibility for S of S's perceiving the desk as a logically necessary condition – of the *possibility*, for S, of perceiving the desk, note; not of S's perceiving the desk. The explanation of what makes it possible for S to perceive the desk is therefore a set of actually fulfilled conditions, one of which is there being a desk.

Now, on Berkeley's view, sensible objects are ideas and the existence of an idea consists in its being perceived. Therefore because to say the desk in the study is perceivable is to say I might perceive it if I were there, then because I can perceive it only if it exists, it exists; and since this by EP is to say that it is perceived, then it is perceived; therefore whether or not it is being perceived by any finite mind, if it is *true* that it is possible for some finite mind (mine, say) to perceive it, it is perceived by God. Accordingly the perceivability of the desk relative to me – that is, its being possible for me to perceive the desk – ultimately rests on the actuality of God's perceiving the desk. This is what Berkeley means by 'And what is perceivable but an idea? And can an idea exist without actually being perceived?' (3D234).

One of the standard criticisms levelled against Berkeley in this connection arises from a mistaken reading of this commitment. As these two interrogatives at 3D234 stand, they appear to commit the kind of fallacy sometimes found, for example, in talk of something's 'being φiable', that is, 'can be φied, implying 'is φied', as in the case of Mill's arguing that the evidence for taking it that x is visible, that is, can be seen, is that x *is* seen (cf. White p21). But Berkeley's view is not at all this; the perceivability and the actual perception are relative to two *different* perceivers, the former to a finite, the latter to an infinite perceiver. In an allied connection Berkeley makes it clear that what is 'relative' or 'hypothetical' from the finitary viewpoint is what *is* from the divine viewpoint. This he does in Philonous' reply to Hylas' question, 'What then shall we make of the Creation?'

4. Perceivability

Philonous says, 'May we not understand it to have been entirely in respect of finite spirits; so that things, with regard to us, may properly be said to begin their existence, or be created, when God decreed they should become perceptible to intelligent creatures, in that order and manner which he then established, and we now call the Laws of Nature? You may call this a *relative*, or *hypothetical* existence if you please' (3D253). This follows immediately upon an agreement between Hylas and Philonous that everything 'always had a being in the Divine Intellect' (ibid.). In direct accordance with this view, perceivability is naturally to be understood 'entirely in respect of finite spirits'. And this makes clear what it is that finally legitimises this conception; it is the fact that what is perceivable for Berkeley is an *idea*, just as what is perceived is an idea – and an idea can exist only if it is perceived. Hence an idea perceivable with respect to finite minds must be perceived, whether or not by other finite minds then anyway, and always, by God; which is precisely the case with the world antecedent to there being finite spirits to perceive it.

The result is that EP, in strict form, states that *esse* is *percipi* and no more. It is only with respect to the finitary viewpoint that '*aut posse percipi* is legitimately added, but its addition, far from affecting the fundamental thesis, is only intelligible on the basis of it. For this reason Berkeley's official thesis cannot be interpreted as in any point having a phenomenalist character, for it rules out the existence of 'possible ideas' and hence the option of describing sensible objects partially in terms of nonactual qualities, qualities whose status is determined by subjunctive conditionals for an understanding of which the notion of possibility remains irreducible.

This way with the matter of perceivability removes a difficulty Foster locates in Berkeley's views (Foster pp22ff). Like others Foster finds what he calls a 'hard-line' thesis and a 'softer' thesis in Berkeley, the former consisting in EP, for which what exists is what is perceived, and the latter in the apparently phenomenalist passages at P3 and P58-9, for which what there is includes possibilities of perception where these are understood conditionally. The soft thesis appears to be required, at least in P, to explain 'the publicity and externality, relative to us, which our concept of the physical requires' (ibid. p30) However, as Foster correctly observes, it turns out that the 'hard-line' thesis is the official doctrine, for, as D unequivocally shows, Berkeley's view is that everything is in the mind of God and hence everything is perceived, and that everything's being in God's mind provides for the publicity and permanence of the world which would be inexplicable on the hard-line thesis alone, that is, without either God or the soft thesis. But this creates a problem for Berkeley, Foster argues, for in taking this view 'he is implicitly rejecting that element in the opinion of the vulgar which he is claiming to vindicate, namely that "those things they immediately perceive are the real things" ' (ibid. p31) This is because if the world is in God's mind, then it lies 'beyond the scope of our immediate perception', and our perceiving is therefore mediate and representative, not, as Berkeley wishes to have it, immediate and presentative (ibid.). And Foster holds that a problem of this sort is inevitable for Berkeley, who cannot have all he wants 'within the confines of the hard-line doctrine', for there is a tension between having it both that perception is immediate and, at the same time, that the world is an objective reality 'public and external in relation to us'; 'there is no way of reconciling ... the immanence required for immediate perceptibility with the transcendence required for objective reality' (ibid.).

These are well-made points. Nevertheless a reply to them is implicit in the foregoing perceivability considerations, which the interpretative idiom of levels will help to bring out. The thesis about God's activity is a level 3 thesis explaining the ultimate character of the world as existing and as having the character it has in virtue of being perceived by God. The finitary viewpoint is the level 2 viewpoint, that is, the level of experience enjoyed by finite minds, having for each individual a highly local and discontinuous character, to which, nevertheless, coherence accrues in the overall course of experience because of the fact that that finite experience is of an independent and orderly realm – describable at level 3 in terms of what Foster calls God's 'volitional policies' (Foster in this respect makes the same mistake as Pitcher, see below). But the levels 2 and 3 descriptions are not descriptions of *different sets of facts*, at level 2 concerning the objects of finite perceptions and at level 3 the causes of these represented as something different – God's fulfilled intentions, perhaps. Rather they are different descriptions of the *same* facts, differing in respect of viewpoint and scope but not, where the scope is the same, in content. This has to be so, for what God causally perceives and finite minds passively perceive are *ideas*, and any idea is known in its completeness, with no hidden content or noumenal aspect, whenever it is present to awareness, its existence depending wholly on the fact that it is thus perceived (cf. P87 etc.). What God's causal activity therefore issues in is, in short, the having of *his* ideas by finite minds. Accordingly the immanent-transcendent distinction does not apply, for in so far as a finite mind perceives an idea or ideas,

4. Perceivability

it has before consciousness a part (a minute fraction, P81) of what is before the divine consciousness. The sense in which objective reality transcends the finitary viewpoint is therefore a matter of scope, not kind; no dualism is implied – indeed such a dualism is often and explicitly rejected by Berkeley (cf. P86-7) – by the fact that the world to which finite minds have partial access is not dependent on those same finite minds for its existence. The perceivability considerations indeed trade on the view that the ideas which a finite perceiver could perceive are as they could be perceived by him, which entails that everything is as it is perceived – just the common-sense view Berkeley is concerned to defend.

Pitcher argues that Berkeley *ought* to account for the existence of unperceived objects on phenomenalist lines (Pitcher pp164). He takes this to follow from the fact that, for Berkeley, objects are collections of ideas only some of which are present to awareness on any occasion, so that a given object consists of certain actual ideas together with 'indefinitely many, non-actual, possible ideas of sense that give an extra degree of reality to any object' (ibid.). To say that there are possible ideas is 'to say that God stands ready to cause those ideas of sense – to make them actual – in case any finite mind should be in a position to perceive (have) them' (pp164-5). Certainly, as the foregoing shows, Berkeley is committed to there being indefinitely many possibilities for *finite* perceivers to perceive further ideas belonging to the collection which is a given object; but Pitcher is mistaken about what this means. The mistake lies in taking it that what it is possible to perceive is itself therefore possible, and this is what leads to Pitcher's saying that Berkeley is or ought to be committed to there being 'non-actual, possible ideas of sense', to be fleshed out by invoking the conception of God's 'standing ready to cause' them. As just shown, however, there are no 'possible ideas' in Berkeley's scheme – 'can an idea exist without being actually perceived ?' (3D234) – for they are all perceived by God and are therefore actual. Moreover Berkeley considered and abandoned the thought that God 'stands ready to cause' ideas – that is, intends rather than perceives them – in the notebooks, and in the published writings consistently has it that God ubiquitously and omnitemporally perceives them. It is a virtue of Berkeley's account that possibility is fully accounted for in terms of actuality, as described, and that consequently the garbled and unintelligible notion of 'existing but nonactual' items vanishes (cf. Grayling 1 pp77-9). On what Pitcher thinks Berkeley ought to think, irreducible possiblities are restored and existing but nonactual items with them. (How their presence might be supposed to give 'an extra degree of reality to any object' is puzzling; but since the – otherwise bizarre – notion of 'degrees of reality' is anyway implicit in that of nonactual existing things, it might be allowed, if one is going to talk in these terms, that the more there are of the latter, the more there are of the former.)

Further, having said what Berkeley ought on his own principles to have held, Pitcher comments that the view thus arrived at 'can easily strike one as inadequate', for 'One wants the object itself to be totally actual at all times and this would mean, for Berkeley, that there must at all times be actual ideas of sense belonging to the object'; but this is 'unjustifiable ... on Berkeley's conception of an object' (ibid. p166). What would satisfy this realist requirement would be 'to say that God perceives all objects, and indeed all parts of objects (even their insides), all the time ... God would be the perpetual observer of all parts of things, thus maintaining them continuously in being' (ibid.). Now, on the foregoing account of Berkeley's theory of perceivability, just this realist requirement is satisfied in just this way; but Pitcher argues that although 'Many readers of Berkeley think that he takes this step' it is his 'opinion (that) it would be both pointless and impossible for Berkeley to try to make God into a kind of cosmic observer' (ibid. pp166-7). His reasons are that 'It would be pointless, because what can ideas in God's mind do for the reality of unobserved objects that cannot be done by an intention on His part to cause suitable ideas of sense in the minds of finite observers, should the need have arisen?' (p167). And it is impossible because 'whatever kind of act or process *perception* may be, it must at the very least be caused in part by something other than the perceiver'; in the absence of this feature it will not be perception but hallucination, or dreaming, or something like. But nothing can affect God (3D241), for he is purely active and being affected by something external is being passive, hence God does not perceive, and *a fortiori* 'cannot be a cosmic perceiver of anything' (ibid.).

These two points are readily answerable. I take them in reverse order. Pitcher is restricting 'perception' here to *sense perception*, that is, the having of sensory ideas or sensory input; and it is clear enough that Berkeley says God does not perceive by means of sense (3D240-1). But it does not follow that God does not *perceive*; for in Berkeley's view, as has often been pointed out, perceiving just is having ideas, whether in sensing, conceiving, remembering, and the rest. Whatever form God's perceiving (other than sensory perceiving) takes, the following heuristic consideration will show that he is not bound merely to be hallucinating or dreaming because his perceiving is not as perceiving is for finite minds, that is, is not a relation between his mind and states of affairs independent of but affecting it. The heuristic consideration is this: It is open to a finite perceiver to imagine, vividly and coherently, some complex train of ideas, which he might, perhaps, write down and publish, and hence communicate to others – novelists do just this; and if he is a Tolkein, say, he might create a world, and people it, and do it so vividly that readers will enter into quite a rich and familiar acquaintance with that world. It is of course facile to say that if there were a God like Berkeley's then this is roughly how he might do things, but it at least shows that the Berkeleyan conception is by no means incoherent. Moreover it is plausible, on this conception, to take it that God would represent to himself how things are for finite perceivers (with Berkeley we make the assumption that he is crucially *interested* in how things are for finite perceivers) and that this is what Berkeley means by saying at 3D241 that God *knows* how things are. This answers Pitcher's question 'What conceivable motive could He have for wanting to cause perceptual [Pitcher means sensory] ideas of actual things in his own mind ?' (ibid.). Pitcher anyway suggests that if God causes ideas in his own mind then he must be partially passive (ibid); but that is a *non sequitur*.

The pointlessness charge is answered by EP and Berkeley's theory of perceivability. An idea exists if it is perceived; only an existing, that is perceived, idea is perceivable; therefore it is not enough that God *intend* that an idea should come to be perceived in suitable circumstances, for the idea in question, since it exists only if perceived, does not exist if it is not (yet) perceived but merely intended, and therefore in Berkeley's theory is not perceivable. So, what 'ideas in God's mind do for the reality of unobserved-by-finite perceivers objects' is that their being there constitutes *reality*. Only the unintelligible doctrine that x can be real but not exist, to which Pitcher (together with Meinong and some possible worlds theorists, among others) is committed, makes any apparent sense of the thought that God's *intentions* can do all that is necessary for the reality of unobserved objects. That Berkeley dropped this theory in the notebooks and opted for realism marks one sense at least in which Berkeley follows his own advice to 'be eternally banishing Metaphysics and recalling men to common sense'.

In line with his belief that Berkeley should have opted for phenomenalism Pitcher approvingly quotes C293a: 'Bodies taken for Powers do exist when not perceived but this existence is not actual.

when I say a power exists no more is meant than that if in the light I open my eyes and look that way I shall see it i.e. the body &c', and says that this comes close to the view Berkeley ought to take (ibid. p169). It will be remembered that C293a results from Berkeley's dissatisfaction with making powers in God a noumenon to which our ideas of things stand as the phenomena, thus reintroducing a Lockean dualism he is elsewhere eager to combat. But C293a is in turn rejected, for the admirable reason that it simply does not *explain* the existence of objects unperceived by finite minds. The doctrine he eventually settles upon is the one described above. That this is so is agreed by Pitcher (p171), although he thinks the earlier, phenomenalist, doctrine partially survives in P and is only finally replaced in D. For the reasons given earlier this view of the matter is to be regarded as incorrect. But Pitcher's main point is that the official doctrine 'is by no means an attractive one' (ibid.). This is because it has to take, in Pitcher's view, either of two forms; it has to be a Perception Theory, that is, that God perceives everything always, or a Conception Theory, that is, that God thinks of everything always. The Perception Theory has been ruled out, says Pitcher, by the above reported considerations; hence Berkeley is committed to the Conception Theory. And Pitcher contests this by saying it is 'little more than a bad joke to claim that a thing exists simply in virtue of the fact that someone has an idea of it in his understanding' (ibid.). What motivates this remark is Berkeley's notorious argument concerning the tree which Hylas imagines existing unperceived (1D200) and which Philonous says, in reply, exists in virtue of the fact that Hylas is thinking about it. As to this argument, more shortly; for present purposes it is enough to note again that Pitcher is restricting 'perception' to 'sense perception', which enables him to draw a distinction not drawn by Berkeley, that is, between perception and conception, for in Berkeley's view conceiving is one way of perceiving; and then to argue that merely conceiving of something does not make it exist. He gives the following example: 'Imagine ... what your response might be to someone who asserted that there is a purple man with three heads, and who explained his remark by saying, "Yes, he exists in my daughter's mind, since she is thinking about such a man"' (ibid.). One might first note that Pitcher allows reality, though not existence, to what God *intends*, as noted earlier, but now apparently does not allow the same of what God *conceives*. This surely requires some explanation on his part. If Pitcher were to agree that my intending to build a bookcase does not make the bookcase real, he

4. Perceivability 113

might nevertheless claim that *God's* intentions are very different from my finite intentions, and that God's intentions are, in virtue of being divine and omnipotent, quite capable of doing the trick. But then by parity of reasoning God's *conceptions* are very different from those of finite minds thinking about purple three-headed men, and therefore equally capable of doing the trick. Hence even if one allows the unBerkeleyan separation of perception from conception, on Pitcher's own arguments it is legitimate to take it that God's conceiving the world is enough to make it real. This is an *argumentum ad hominem* and not a defence of Berkeley, it is true; but it shows that Pitcher's objections fail, and that, at any rate so far, the theory of perceivability Berkeley holds has not been shown either to be inconsistent with his principles nor, yet, incoherent itself.

What, then, of the notorious tree argument? It occurs in three places: C472, P23, and lD200. It is on the face of it a bad argument; Tipton prefaces his discussion of it be referring to the commentators in whose view it is, variously, 'contemptible', 'entirely specious', and so forth (Tipton p160). If it is indeed an irremediably bad argument then it infects the theory of perceivability and therefore EP itself, for it is allied to both in that it concerns the existence of objects unperceived by finite minds. In none of the three formulations of the argument is God's perceiving invoked, and this requires particular explanation. I shall try, against the odds, to show that although the argument is *badly put*, it is not *bad*, for from it can be recovered a train of thought, actually present in the formulations of the argument (especially at P23), which is consistent with what Berkeley elsewhere argues and which is defensible on his principles.

I shall quote only one of the three statements of the argument, the one occurring at P23: 'But say you, surely there is nothing easier than to imagine trees, for instance, in a park, or books existing in a closet, and no body by to perceive them. I answer, you may so, there is no difficulty in it: but what is all this, I beseech you, more than forming in your mind certain ideas which you call *books* and *trees*, and at the same time omitting to frame the idea of any one that may perceive them? But do not you perceive them or think of them all while? This therefore is nothing to the purpose: it only shows you have the power of imagining or forming ideas in your mind; but it doth not shew that you can conceive it possible, the objects of your thought may exist without the mind: to make out this, it is necessary that you conceive them existing unconceived or thought of, which is a manifest repugnancy. When we do our utmost to conceive the existence of external bodies, we are all the while only contemplating our own ideas.' This passage forms part of the argument against the existence of corporeal substance and follows the section in which Berkeley says 'try whether you can conceive it possible for a sound, a figure, or motion, or colour, to exist without the mind, or unperceived' (P22).

An initially attractive way of interpreting this argument is afforded by Luce, who says that it comes down to the claim that 'imagined existence is imagined perception' (Luce 2 p88). But the attractiveness of Luce's conception diminishes when one sees that he intends to be read as talking not about imagining or thinking of the existence of currently unperceived sensible objects, but solely of the existence of *imagined* objects; Berkeley's question in P23, says Luce, is 'In what sense do imagined trees and books exist?' (p86). Luce's reason for holding this is that since Berkeley's overall argument is directed against 'absolute existence', that is, existence without the mind, the argument must be 'that sensible existence is perceived existence, that imagined existence is perceived existence imagined, and that therefore all existence is relative to mind and absolute existence is an empty form of words' (ibid.). It is however clear that Berkeley is not talking about the existence of imagined objects, despite the support this interpretation appears to receive from C473, for in both of the published formulations what is at issue is the conceiving of there being real items currently unperceived – trees in the park, books in the closet, which are 'real things' not chimera or merely imagined items. At C473 Berkeley's remark about 'a larger sense of existence', contrasted to the sense in which existence is 'vulgarly restrained' to actual perception, is not intended to establish a category of intentional existence – nowhere else in the notebooks or, except in the two passages at issue, published writings does such a suggestion occur or gain support, even implicitly – but rather to take account of what is unquestionably true, namely that if one has an idea then even if it answers to nothing external, that is, is not an idea of sense, but merely the product of one's own imagination, it is nevertheless *there*, in one's mind, and in that sense exists. An *idea* of a purple three-headed man exists whenever it is entertained by someone, although no question of the existence of a purple three-headed man is at stake; and although for Berkeley such a man is himself an idea or collection of ideas, he has a uniform way of distinguishing between ideas of imagination and ideas of sense, which provides that only the latter count, under certain further constraints, as 'real things'.

Nevertheless there is also something right suggested by what Luce says, which comes out if one adjusts his account. This line of thought

4. Perceivability

is stated by Berkeley in P23, and it represents what is consistent with and defensible on his principles. It is that to think of a tree or book with no-one by to perceive it is to think of it as it is perceived when someone *is* by to perceive it. Now, this is in fact the case on *any* theory. Consider for example the currently received view which has it that a tree is a large collection of atoms, and that the sensible properties characteristically predicated of it – the green of the leaves, the grey or brown of the bark, its grainy texture, the perfume of its blossoms, and so on – are functions of the interactions between sense organs and the tree's intrinsic structure, so that in the absence of a relation between the former and latter, there are no colours or textures, and the rest, as there are perceived to be colours and textures when that relation obtains. So, when one thinks of the tree in the park, one thinks of it *as perceived*, with green leaves and grey bark; there is no other way of doing so. (This is not to claim that one cannot consider the tree under description of its atomic structure, or on a larger scale as a compound of organic molecules in certain functional arrangements; but that is to contemplate theory – or to think of small parts of trees viewed through microscopes – not, or not just, to think of a tree standing in a park.) No more than this is claimed by Berkeley. But the immediate implication of this fact is that there is no conceiving a sensible item which is not conceiving it as a perceived item, that is, of what it is or would be like as it appears to a perceiver; and hence the thought of some currently unperceived real thing is not the thought of something that exists in total independence of perception, but is the thought of something as it is to be met with in perception. And since that is so, to think of currently unperceived items is not to think of them existing 'without any relation to their being perceived' (P3); which is the claim that 'it is impossible for me to conceive in my thoughts any sensible thing or object distinct from the sensation or perception of it' (P5).

What has led commentators to think so ill of the argument is their taking it that Berkeley's claim is that no item can exist unperceived *because* to conceive or think of it is to perceive it and therefore it exists perceived. A first reading of the passages certainly gives the impression that this is no more than is meant by them. Were this so the argument would indeed be a bad one. Robinson places this construction on it, closely in line with the standard interpretation: '(Berkeley's) claim is that part of the intentional content by means of which objects are grasped in consciousness is *that they are perceived*. To imagine an object unperceived is to imagine it as not being an object of consciousness and this he supposes to involve a contradiction;

namely that the object is an object of consciousness (by dint of being imagined) and is not' (Robinson p73). What would make Berkeley's argument sound, Robinson says, would be the truth of the claim that we perceive things *as* perceived; but this Robinson denies (ibid. pp73-4). One thing that is surely right in this is that acts of perceptual awareness of things do not carry as an additional component awareness that the things are sensorily perceived *as* sensorily perceived, as though part of the content of such states were a reflexive act without which the perceiver could not take himself to be sensorily perceiving something. But this is not what is at issue in this argument, nor is it a feature of Berkeley's overall theory. The claim is different and more fundamental; it is that to conceive of an item which is not currently being perceived is to conceive of it as it would be perceived were a perceiver by, for it is a collection of sensible qualities which as such are wholly dependent for their existence on their having a relation to perception – as it turns out, on their being perceived, by God whether or not by any finite mind. This is to say objects are *conceived as sensorily perceived* when they are conceived, not (*sensorily*) *perceived as sensorily perceived* when they are so perceived. Accordingly the contradiction at issue does not reside in an assertion to the effect that an object exists unperceived while being perceived (conceived or imagined) by me, but rather it resides in the assertion that the object is conceived or imagined to exist as it would exist were it perceived, yet is wholly independent of any perception, that is, is not a sensible or perceptual object. The bottom line is, then, that what is not *conceivable*, in short, is an *unperceivable* object. And by the foregoing argument, a perceivable object is a perceived (by God) object. In *this* sense, any sensible object one conceives therefore exists.

From the formulation of the argument at 1D200 it is apparent that Berkeley thought he had found a short way with the claim that objects can be conceived as existing without relation to perception, that is, without dependence on mind, and that is to show *ad hominem* that a conceived object is, in virtue of being conceived, in the mind. Because the thrust of the argument is to establish that anything which exists is *ipso facto* mind-dependent – and this is simply another line of approach to EP – what the argument intends is consistent with what is elsewhere claimed. But as it stands the argument is too short a way to that destination, and this is what gives rise to its appearance of speciousness. It seems to be confined to saying something trivially true, namely that one cannot think about something without thinking about it; but what Berkeley means this to reveal, as P23 succeeds more than the other two formulations in showing, is something more than this, namely that any sensible thing thought of has to be thought of an as an object of sense perception and cannot be thought of otherwise, and therefore the object of thought is a thought-of object of perception, which shows that nothing sensible can be thought of independently of any reference to perception, which is to say, apart from dependence on mind.

5. Continuity

The perceivability considerations just discussed have as their terminus an interpretation of Berkeley which agrees with what has come to be considered the standard interpretation, namely that Berkeley's view is that God continuously perceives sensible objects and thus holds the entire order of nature in being, the regularly and coherently unfolding changes in which are accounted for by the 'wisdom and benevolence' of the divine will upon which everything is causally dependent (P30). That this is indeed what Berkeley holds would seem to be sufficiently testified by the foregoing perceivability considerations alone; but the standard view has been vigorously contested by Bennett, who claims that 'Berkeley does not regularly assume that objects exist when no human perceives them; he is not much interested in whether they do; and the continuity argument, which assumes that they do, is absent from the *Principles* and occurs in the *Dialogues* only in (a) two-sentence passage ... That passage is right out of line with everything else Berkeley says about the continuity of objects, and should be dismissed as a momentary aberration' (Bennett p171). This claim is supported at length and with ingenuity, and merits discussion, which in this section I give it. It is in my view wholly mistaken; showing how will serve to confirm the foregoing interpretation of Berkeley's views, and also to provide materials for an investigation, in the next section, of Berkeley's realism.

The two sentences Bennett mentions occur in the following passage at 3D230-1: '*Hylas*: Supposing you were annihilated, cannot you conceive it possible, that things perceivable by sense may still exist? *Philonous*: I can; but then it must be in another mind. When I deny sensible things an existence out of the mind, I do not mean any mind in particular, but all minds. Now it is plain they have an existence exterior to my mind, since I find them by experience to be independent of it. There is therefore some other mind wherein they exist, during the intervals between the times of my perceiving them: as likewise they did before my birth, and would do after my supposed annihilation.' The last two sentences are those Bennett has in mind. His two complaints about these sentences are that, first, they involve an equivocation on 'depend' which is fatal to this as to other arguments in Berkeley – I shall return to this point later – and secondly, as we have seen, that they are 'a momentary aberration' because Berkeley is in fact 'indifferent' to the continuity question (pp171-2ff).

Bennett's chief reason for making this claim about 'indifference' is that whereas Berkeley is keen to establish the *reality* of objects in terms of strength, orderliness, and coherence, resulting from their being caused in us by God (P33-4), he sharply distinguishes, Bennett claims, this question from that of their continuity when not perceived by finite minds (Bennett p173). The reality issue is always discussed in connection with the ideas one does have, 'thus positively divorcing the reality question from the continuity question' (ibid.). Moreover when Berkeley discusses continuity, as he does in P45-8, he appears, says Bennett, not particularly interested in rejecting the charge that 'things are every moment annihilated and created anew' depending upon whether one's eyes are shut or open (P45), for he first argues that the same can be charged of the materialist view, and only at last in P48 resists the intermittancy objection – but does so, Bennett observes, by saying 'we may not hence *conclude*' that the existence of things is intermittant; that 'there *may* be some other spirit' which perceives them when we do not; that 'it does not therefore *follow*' from the earlier stated principles that 'bodies are annihilated and created every moment, or exist not at all during the intervals between our perceptions of them' – the emphases are Bennett's, who, by drawing attention to 'may' and the other apparently noncomittal expressions, wishes us to see that Berkeley's attitude to the question is one of insouciance (Bennett pp174-5).

Turning to D, Bennett considers two passages other than the one cited above, and finds that neither of them give any support to the continuity thesis standardly attributed to Berkeley. One of these is the discussion of the creation at 3D250ff, which Bennett says proceeds entirely in terms of angels and phenomenalism, and is so far from supporting the continuity argument as actually to be in conflict with it (pp176-8), for if God, as Berkeley there says, 'knows all things from eternity', so that everything has always 'had a being in the Divine Intellect', in which therefore there is 'nothing new' and in which nothing 'begins to be' (3D253), then what Bennett calls the

5. Continuity   119

'idea-content' of God's mind is always the same, and hence 'cannot sense the present existence of the bookcase on which I have just turned my back; or, rather, God's present perceptions can secure this only if they also secure the present existence of the bookcase which I destroyed three years ago, and of the one which will someday be made for my grandson out of planks cut from a tree which has not yet been planted' (p177).

The other passage Bennett considers is at 2D211-12, where Philonous says 'To me it is evident ... that sensible things cannot exist otherwise than in a mind or spirit. Whence I conclude, not that they have no real existence, but that seeing they depend not on my thoughts, and have an existence distinct from being perceived by me, *there must be some other mind wherein they exist*'. Bennett acknowledges that this looks like a statement of the continuity thesis, but denies that it is; rather, he says, it is about the correct definition of 'real'. What Philonous is saying is that 'real' must not be taken to mean 'capable of existing out of all minds', but 'caused by God'; and thus, far from having to do with continuity, is simply a reassertion of the reality theme insisted upon in P (pp181-2).

Finally, Bennett offers an explanation of why Berkeley 'brushes off the mob's protests about continuity, and has no considered use for the continuity argument' (p188). It is because Berkeley 'is serious about idealism', in particular about its central principle which is that it is senseless or self-contradictory to hold that objects exist when no spirit whatsoever perceives them (ibid.). That is, Bennett takes it that EP makes Berkeley indifferent to the question of continuity, for it states that *esse* just is *percipi*, from which it follows, in Bennett's view, that what is not (currently) perceived does not (currently) exist.

It is possible for Bennett to offer this diagnosis of Berkeley's alleged indifference to continuity only because he takes certain questionable stances on allied matters. For one thing, although he rightly takes it that Berkeley is committed to the 'hard-line' version of EP and therefore does not have a form of phenomenalism available to account for what is perceivable, for the reason that EP and phenomenalism are inconsistent, he wrongly concludes from this that Berkeley has no account of perceivability. For another, he imputes to Berkeley the singular doctrine that real things as Berkeley defines them – the ideas in which they consist being orderly, coherent, and externally caused, and the connections between which are representable in terms of natural laws – have nothing to do with continuity, as though the conception of things which are real in virtue of possession of these characteristics is consistent with their being things which pop in and out of existence at hazard, or, more accurately, have an ephemeral existence which begins and ends with whatever individual state of awareness constitutes them. On both counts Bennett is detaching questions of perceivability, continuity and reality from each other as though they were three quite separate issues, and insisting not just that Berkeley is concerned with the last of them only, but that in doing so he is excluding the other two. This deeply implausible manouevre rests on a reading of P and D which neglects a considerable amount of material substantiating the continuity interpretation of Berkeley's views and connects it with his realism. The argument of the preceding section deals with perceivability as such; here I shall show that issues of perceivability, continuity and reality hang closely together, and that continuity considerations are central to a great deal of what Berkeley says. This is a matter of reading the texts correctly; when this is done the problem Bennett is concerned with vanishes.

There is first the question of the supposed absence, as Bennett has it, of continuity considerations from P. I count a total of forty-six sections, nearly a third of the whole, where it is extraordinarily difficult *not* to find that the continuity of things unperceived by finite minds is essentially at issue or presupposed. Bennett might dispute some of them, namely P3, 6 and 58-9, on the grounds that they constitute phenomenalist aberrations repudiated in D; but we may let them speak for themselves, as follows.

In P3 Berkeley talks of the table in his study which he might see were he there. On the perceivability argument given above, the table continues to exist although unperceived by a finite mind because it exists in God's mind and its perceivability with respect to finite minds rests on that fact. This in part is the force also of the remarks at P6, where Berkeley says 'all the choir of heaven and furniture of the earth, in a word, all those bodies which compose the mighty frame of the world ... so long as they are not perceived by me ... must either have no existence at all, or subsist in the mind of some eternal spirit'. The disjunction is ironic, the obvious intention being that no question can arise as to the dependence of 'the mighty frame of the world' on *my* perceiving it; and *so long* as it is not perceived by me or any finite spirit, it 'subsists' in the mind of 'some eternal spirit'. Since there is anything but evidence that Berkeley was converted to theism *after* writing P, 'some eternal spirit' is God; compare Bennett's emphasising 'may' in 'there may be some other spirit that perceives (things), though we do not' (P48) in an effort to make out that Berkeley is non-committal about God's conserving activity (Bennett

5. Continuity

p175). The phrase 'so long as', moreover, cannot be construed in any other way than as betokening continuity, and accordingly this and the preceding P3 to which it is related expressly assert the continuity view.

At P58-9 where Berkeley again talks of perceivability, in connection this time with what we would see if suitably placed to observe planetary motion relative to the sun, an appeal is made to the 'established rules of Nature', which are earlier accounted for in terms of the 'steadiness, order and coherence' of God's causal activity (P30) in producing those ideas not dependent on one's own finite will (P29). In both P58-9 and P29-32 the fact that the coherence and order of God's causal activity gives rise to connexions of ideas which can be represented nomologically enables us, Berkeley says, to make 'sure and well-grounded predictions' (P59), to establish plans and pursue them, to procure pleasure and avoid pain, and in general to 'regulate our actions for the benefit of life' (P31). Thus, for example, in accordance with 'the settled Laws of Nature' we can know that 'to sow in the seed-time is to reap in the harvest' (ibid.). It is difficult indeed to understand these remarks in a way which intelligibly connects them to an indifference to continuity. That these passages, and the entire discussion of questions in natural philosophy at P1O1-17, assume that the world exists in its fulness and continuously, independently of the perceptions of finite minds, is testified by a contrast Berkeley draws between the finitary viewpoint and an independently existing world to which that viewpoint has local access. At P81 Berkeley says 'And for me to pretend to determine by my own few, stinted, narrow inlets of perception, what ideas the inexhaustible power of the Supreme Spirit may imprint upon them, were certainly the utmost folly and presumption'. This asserts one part of the contrast; the other is set out in Berkeley's reply to the first objection (P34), which is that on his principles 'all that is real and substantial in Nature is banished out of the world: and instead thereof a chimerical scheme of ideas takes place.' Berkeley's reply is that 'by the principles premissed, we are not deprived of any one thing in Nature. Whatever we see, feel, hear or any wise conceive or understand, remains as secure as ever, and is as real as ever. There is a *rerum natura*, and the distinction between realities and chimaeras retains its full force'. Here it is asserted that whatever we can sense 'or in any wise conceive or understand' is as 'secure' and as real as common sense or materialist philosophy could desire. Bennett, as noted, argues that Berkeley detaches questions of continuity from question of reality, which latter are restricted to what is *currently* perceived; but in this passage, quite in contrast to Bennett's view, Berkeley asserts that 'the sun, moon, stars ... houses, rivers, mountains, trees, stones' (ibid.), whether sensibly perceived, conceived of, or otherwise understood, remain secure and real – so that, once again, it is simply implausible to think that Berkeley did *not* mean, in talking like this of the security and reality of the items in his list of physical bodies, that they continue to exist when unperceived by finite minds just as common sense views would have it. That at least part of the connotation of 'secure' is intended to be 'continuous' or 'enduring' ('real' takes care of 'independent' or 'objective') is not coherently deniable.

The same points can be made yet more forcefully in connection with P60-6 and 70-1. At P62, for example, Berkeley talks of God's 'producing of things in a constant, regular way, according to the Laws of Nature' and of the 'standing mechanical Laws of Nature', which implies not just uniformity but continuation, since what is under discussion in P60-6 are the reasons for there being 'that curious organisation of plants, and the admirable mechanism in the parts of animals' (P60), that is, an elaborate natural order. Berkeley argues in this connection that 'the reason why ideas are formed into machines, that is, artificial and regular combinations' is so that they can have a 'permanent and universal' use, to which end they are 'instituted by the Author of Nature' (P66). The word 'permanent' comes up again at P70-1 where Berkeley considers, in order to reject, the Occasionalist proposal that material things might serve as reminders to God to cause ideas in us at appropriate times, on the grounds that the 'orderly and constant manner' of our perceiving bespeaks 'constant and regular occasions' for their production; 'that is to say, that there are certain permanent and distinct parcels of matter' which God perceives and which prompt him to his causal duties (ibid.). To which Berkeley replies that everything required to explain the permanence and regularity of the world is furnished by the conception of a God 'infinitely wise, good and powerful' without further appeal to 'inert senseless matter' as providing the occasions for his activity (P72). In both these passages it is clear that the world constituted by God is in Berkeley's view both as objective and as permanent as common beliefs have it, for in the later passage he in effect says as much, while in the earlier he actually says as much.

Bennett quotes P90 in support of his contention that Berkeley's primary concern is with reality and that what he says about it sharply distinguishes it from the question of continuity. The section ends with the sentence 'Thus when I shut my eyes, the things I saw

5. Continuity

may still exist, but it must be in another mind.' This wording again gives Bennett cause to claim that Berkeley is non-committal about continuity and God (Bennett p176). But not only is this interpretation wholly unsupported by the above cited passages, it is equally unsupported by the sections which follow P90. At P91 Berkeley says of the mind-dependence principle: 'It were a mistake to think, that what is here said derogates in the least from the reality of things', for his disagreement with his predecessors is not over the question whether sensible things subsist in or are supported by a substance, but rather over whether that substance is material or spiritual. The concept of qualities subsisting in a substance may no more than *suggest* continuity, but the claim that taking the substance in question to be spiritual 'derogates not in the least from the reality of things' *more* than merely suggests this, since a conception of items considered real although impermanent and perishing is just such a derogation from ordinary views of what is real. Moreover 'the eternal mind of the Creator' is invoked here, and again at P93 where in contrast to the materialist view that 'a self-existent, unthinking substance (is) the root and origin of all beings' Berkeley asserts 'a providence, or inspection of a superior mind over the affairs of the world'.

Perhaps the strongest textual evidence for continuity and God's role in it, other than P48 itself, is afforded by P146-50, which Bennett does not consider. In these sections Berkeley (rather briefly) discusses God and our knowledge of him. He restates the argument that since the majority of our ideas are involuntary and hence not dependent on us, they are caused 'by some other spirit'; and Berkeley now cashes this expression by saying 'if we attentively consider the constant regularity, order and concatenation of natural things, the surprising magnificence, beauty, and perfection of the larger, and the exquisite contrivance of the smaller parts of the creation, together with the exact harmony and correspondence of the whole ... and at the same time attend to the meaning and import of the attributes, one, eternal, infinitely wise, good, and perfect, we shall clearly perceive that they belong to the aforementioned spirit, *who works all in all*, and *by whom all things consist*' (P146). His readers would be expected to recognise the quotations from 1 Corinthians xii. 6 and Colossians i. 17 respectively. All the earlier references to 'some other spirit' in P are accordingly by no means non-committal; and nor are the uses of the modal 'may' which in Bennett's view bespeak indifference to continuity, for one now finds Berkeley asserting, in line with the quotations from the Epistles just given, that it is God who 'uphold(s) all things by the Word of his Power' (P147), who produces the ideas 'which continually affect us' (P149), and who is therefore responsible for 'Nature' and its 'fixed and general laws' (P150), in which the 'slow and gradual methods' of plant growth and the rest (cf. P62) are an expression of God's 'working by the most simple and general rules, and after a steady and consistent manner', which explains the 'artificial contrivance of this mighty machine of Nature' – all which testifies, in short, to the fact that it is an *'all-wise Spirit* who fashions, regulates, and sustains the whole system of being' (P151). 'Upholding', 'sustaining', and the account Berkeley gives in general, are impossible to construe as having nothing to do with continuity, and that they are indeed specifically intended to cast God in the traditional role of conserver is confirmed by Berkeley in his first letter to Johnson (*Works* II pp280-1, sect. 3) with reference to what is argued in P: 'Those who have all along contended for a material world have yet acknowledged that *natura naturans* (to use the language of the Schoolmen) is God; and that the divine conservation of things is equipollent to, and in fact the same thing with, a continual repeated creation ... I am not therefore singular in this point itself, so much as in my way of proving it ... For aught I can see, it is no disparagement to the perfections of God to say that all things necessarily depend on Him as their Conserver as well as Creator, and that all nature would shrink to nothing, if not upheld and preserved in being by the same force that first created it' (ibid.).

In the light of these textual evidences it is clear that Bennett's view is quite magnificently wrong as an interpretation of Berkeley's attitude to continuity. It turns out not to be the case that continuity considerations appear only fleetingly and uncertainly until the single aberration of 3D230-1, where they are used as a supposed supplementary argument for God's existence, but, rather, that they are a sustained assumption of the entire theory. This is something to which other commentators, including Furlong in his well-known reply to Bennett, surprisingly fail to draw attention (Furlong in Martin and Armstrong *passim*). Moreover the foregoing considerations are drawn only from P, and further weight of evidence could be added from V and D, where the assumption's role is equally pervasive.

The continuity assumption explains a number of key elements in Berkeley's views, for example his reason for being committed to EP in its 'hard-line', non-phenomenalist form; how this connects with the perceivability issue; what he means by 'real' and in what his

5. Continuity

realism consists (see next section); and why he took it that his arguments conclusively rebut atheism as well as scepticism. They also therefore constitute a central part of Berkeley's level 3 account, to be discussed in Chapter Three below.

These considerations provide an answer to Bennett's question concerning why Berkeley sets out the 'continuity argument' for God's existence only once – at 3D230-1 – and does so 'without fanfare' as Bennett has it. The answer is that the continuity considerations are *not* an argument for God's existence separate from what Bennett calls the 'passivity argument' (Bennett pp165-6): there are not two different arguments, just one; and this is what one would expect, given the way Berkeley's conception of reality *includes* continuity, as the foregoing shows. Interestingly, the 'false imaginary glare' passage at 2D211-2 which Bennett says some commentators take as another statement of the continuity argument but which is in fact, Bennett says, about reality, shows that this is so. Berkeley's argument for God's existence is: objects are ideas; ideas are mind-dependent; any finite mind's ideas of real things – those constant, regular, etc. ideas – are involuntary, that is, are not caused by that finite mind itself; therefore there is an external cause of them; only spirit is causally efficacious; therefore the involuntary ideas in finite minds are caused by another spirit; the magnificence, harmony etc. etc. of the involuntary ideas perceived by finite minds testifies to that spirit's being infinitely wise, good, and powerful; therefore that spirit is God. This is a fuller and perhaps more information-preserving characterisation of the argument Bennett reports (p165); in his words it runs 'My ideas come into my mind without being caused to do so by any act of my will; the occurrence of any idea must be caused by an act of the will of some being in whose mind the idea occurs; therefore my ideas of sense occur in the mind of, and are caused by the acts of will of, some being other than myself.' (Here Bennett leaves out the second stage of the argument, which is in effect the traditional argument from design, without which Berkeley cannot get from the causal agency of *another* spirit to that spirit's being *God* – see Chapter Three Section 4 below.) Berkeley sums up the argument at 2D212 by saying 'I ... immediately and necessarily conclude the being of a God, because all sensible things must be perceived by him', for 'sensible things do really exist: and if they really exist, they are necessarily perceived by an infinite mind: therefore there is an infinite mind, or God'. What Berkeley says at 3D230-1 is in essentials the same: ideas do not depend (leaving aside for the moment what 'depend' means; see below) on any finite perceiver, therefore there is an 'omnipotent eternal Mind' which 'knows and comprehends' everything and 'exhibits' them to us 'according to such rules ... by us termed the *Laws of Nature*'. The recurrence of the Laws of Nature concept links this passage to P30 and the numerous other places where reality and continuity are at issue. What makes this passage particularly about *continuity* is that there is express reference to 'the intervals between the times of my perceiving (sensible things)' and their existence 'before my birth' and 'after my supposed annihilation'. The 'intervals' phrase recalls the 'so long as they are not perceived by me' of P6, and in general the passage accords with everything Berkeley elsewhere says about reality and God, so that to pick it out as a *special* passage, introducing another and different argument not elsewhere used, is again to rely on the exceedingly implausible, indeed incoherent, manoeuvre of treating questions about the continued existence of things as independent of questions about the reality of things, and moreover ascribing this incoherence to Berkeley. Once this is denied, for the foregoing reasons, the egregiousness Bennett imputes to 3D230-1 vanishes.

It has been pointed out that if Berkeley has and uses a continuity argument as such, then it is circular; for if the continuity of things is to be explained by appeal to God, then the continuity of things cannot in turn be used to prove God's existence (cf. Tipton 1, quoting Aschenbrenner, p322). This is indeed so. That there are real, continuing, independent (of finite minds) things in the world Berkeley from the outset takes for granted and nowhere seeks to prove. What he has to prove is that these things are mind-dependent; and it is for this reason that his overall argument is aimed at the twofold outcome of denying that matter exists and asserting that God perceives everything always.

These remarks raise another question, however, which is why or whether Berkeley is *entitled* to assume the real, continuing, independent (of finite minds) existence of things (Tipton pp327-8). A short way with the matter is afforded by Warnock, who says that Berkeley 'thinks that it would be merely absurd to question this', since he 'knows that any plain man would insist that the furniture in the unoccupied room actually does exist, not merely that it would exist if the room were occupied' (Warnock p115). Bennett's reading of P45-8 convinces him that Berkeley is by no means so anxious to square his account with the plain man's ontological prejudices (Bennett pp174-5), a view which might perhaps gain some credence from Berkeley's talk of 'opinions strangely prevailing among men'

(P4). But Berkeley altogether too often and insistently claims that nothing is taken away from the reality of things for Warnock's view to merit too quick a dismissal. Indeed, that Warnock is right is forcefully suggested by the fact that the contrary assumption, namely that it is not the case that there are real, continuing, independent things, constitutes the very *scepticism* Berkeley takes himself to be combating – as witness his characterisation of scepticism as the view that 'for aught we know, all we see, hear, and feel, may be only phantom and vain chimera' (P87); and again, his saying 'the supposition that all our knowledge & contemplation is confined barely to our own Ideas', that is, to merely subjective experience having no reference to a real, continuing, independent world, 'takes away all real Truth, & consequently brings in a Universal Scepticism' (C606). Together with Berkeley's insistent claims that his views accord with common sense and derogates nothing from the reality of things, these remarks show that it would be a deep misreading of his intentions to take it that he does not make and indeed rely upon the continuity assumption. And on any view other than a subjective idealist or solipsistic view, some such assumption, however explained by whatever level 3 theory, seems inevitable.

That Bennett is quite wrong about continuity does not however show that his analysis of Berkeley's use of 'depend' is mistaken. This is a matter of some moment, for Berkeley frequently talks of ideas 'depending' on or being 'independent' of minds, and his theory of reality turns on these usages, as does much else. Bennett's argument is that when Berkeley talks of ideas depending on minds he sometimes means that they are had by, that is are owned by, minds and sometimes that they are caused by minds (Bennett pp166-7). This ambiguity is, Bennett claims, fatal to the argument for God's existence because it proceeds, in his words, 'Some ideas are not dependent on (= caused by) any human mind; every idea is dependent on (= had by) some mind: [therefore] some ideas are dependent upon (= caused by) some non-human mind' (p167). The problem here is easily resolved, however, for the second occurrence of 'dependent', which Bennett construes as 'had by', admits of being interpreted as 'caused by' instead – and when it is so construed, it in fact better expresses Berkeley's aim in employing the argument. Indeed this is how the argument *has* to be interpreted, since it turns on Berkeley's thesis that every idea is caused, so if an idea is not caused by some finite mind it must be caused by some other mind, which is what the argument states – and it turns also on his view about the nature of spirit, particularly of infinite spirit, which is active, in sharp contrast to ideas, which are inert.

Bennett appears to accept that there are alternative renderings of the argument – he says of his own 'It does not matter whether this diagnosis is correct' (ibid.), and anyway himself gives a version of it wholly in causal terms (p165) – but insists nevertheless that in the course of Berkeley's work 'depend' is variously used, the ownership and causation uses being prominent among them (pp167-8). He lists eight occurrences of each; for the ownership use P6, 89, 91, 1D195, 200 (twice), 2D213, 3D261, and for the causation use P26, 29, 33, 106, 1D196 (twice), 2D214, and 3D235 (p168). He exploits the ambiguity chiefly in connection with the argument for God's existence – or as he has it *arguments* for God's existence – to show that it is invalid, but the consequences are far reaching, for if there is a muddle in Berkeley's view of the relation between ideas and minds then a great deal of the central portion of his theory is vitiated.

The difficulty here would be solved if it were to turn out that each of the 'ownership' uses in Bennett's list is in fact a causation use or analysable into such. Even in advance of going to the listed passages and inspecting them, one's expectation that this will be so is high, for the following reason. It is to be remembered that the terminus of the argument summarised at P1-7 is that there is only spiritual substance and ideas, which is to say that the only self-sufficient thing 'the conception of which does not need the conception of another thing' is mind, and that mind supports ideas by perceiving them; the relation of support which minds bears to ideas, or subsistence-in which ideas bear to mind, is perception. Perception is *wholly* causal: in the case of the infinite mind all, and in the case of finite minds some, ideas are caused by the mind in question; in the case of finite minds other ideas are *effects* of the infinite mind's causal activity. This is clearly stated in P25-6 and 28-30. The causal relation is dyadic; in all those cases where finite minds do not themselves produce the ideas they perceive, their perceiving is *passively receiving* ideas, as *effects* of God's causal activity. All talk of ideas' 'dependence on the mind' ultimately comes down therefore to talk of ideas either as caused by God or finite minds, or as effects of God's causal activity, and so all 'dependence' of ideas is ultimately causal dependence, as the thesis about substance demands. The 'ownership' uses of 'depend' are accordingly to be understood as, or reducible to, 'causation' uses when the theory is spelled out.

This analysis can be tested in the light of the passages which Bennett claims give evidence of a non-causal 'ownership' use of the term in question. In all of them the talk is of the unintelligibility of

6. Berkeley's realism

attributing to ideas existence without the mind or as subsisting apart from spirit, that is, unperceived. At P6 Berkeley asserts this, and at P89 contrasts spirit as active substance and ideas as inert dependent beings which cannot exist other than as perceived by spirit. The theme of P89 is continued at P91 where Berkeley points out that with respect to sensible qualities it is agreed on all hands that they do not exist independently of a substance or support. At 1D195 Berkeley employs the example of a tulip which exists independently of finite minds, but says 'that any idea should exist in an unthinking substance or exterior to all minds is a contradiction'. The two occurrences at 2D200 concern the tree or house Hylas thinks he can conceive existing unperceived, to which Philonous opposes the claim that nothing can be conceived of as existing 'independently and out of all minds whatsoever'. At 2D213 independence of mind is equated with 'existence without the mind', and at 3D261, near the end of D, Berkeley agrees that one could use the term 'matter' provided it is not understood to imply 'independency or subsistence distinct from being perceived by a mind'. In each case, then, dependence as ownership is connected to the question of the subsistence of ideas in the only substance there is, which supports them by perceiving them; and what that means is clearly stated at P25-6 and P28-30, namely that all ideas are the effects of the causal activity of spirit.

I conclude therefore that Bennett is as wrong on this score as he is about continuity. Demonstrating both these claims has been useful in serving to illustrate, among other things, the fact that Berkeley's theory has a remarkable degree of internal consistency. More importantly for present purposes, it shows also that his theory is tightly constructed, with relations of connectedness and mutual support everywhere apparent among his major theses. This is true of what he has to say about reality, continuity and perceivability also – something Bennett denies – and these conceptions jointly enter into the realism to which Berkeley is committed, and to a discussion of which I now turn.

6. Berkeley's realism

On pp19-20 above realism was characterised as the thesis that with respect to the items in some given class there are verification-transcendent facts of the matter about those items; that is, that such items exist, and have the character they do, independently of knowledge or experience of them. Thus there might, on this view, be entities not even in principle accessible to the capacities of any intelligent being to discover their existence. This, which I labelled 'absolute realism', is a very strong thesis. It is expressed by proposition (b′) on p20 above, which states that things exist independently of any acts or states of perceptual awareness of them, using 'perception' here in Berkeley's broadly inclusive sense to mean conceiving, imagining, and the rest, as well as sense-perception. As noted there, Berkeley rejects this conception, and holds instead that (b″) things exist independently of any *finite* perceivers' states of perceptual awareness of them. His realism is accordingly a qualified as opposed to an absolute realism. The reasons why are set out in the discussions of the last five sections. What those reasons ultimately hinge upon is EP. Absolute realism is ruled out by EP, for this thesis has it that the existence of anything other than a mind essentially consists in its being perceived by a mind, and hence there can be nothing which exists independently of any knowledge or experience of it. But (b″) does not therefore fail to be a version of realism. Rather, it is what has sometimes been called 'theistic' realism, for it has it that things may exist independently of the thought and experience of finite minds, their objectivity and independence relative to finite minds being explained by the fact that they exist in the mind of God. What is distinctive about, and indeed crucial to, any form of realism is the 'independence' thesis (see pp19-20 above), and this thesis is maintained by Berkeley with respect to the finitary viewpoint.

That Berkeley's position is realist in this sense is testified by the numerous passages quoted in the preceding two sections on the themes of perceivability, continuity and reality. As those passages show, objects are real for Berkeley in that they are independent of the wills of finite perceivers, and the ideas in which they consist are recognisably distinguishable from the imaginings and dreamings of finite minds by being regular, strong, and coherently linked with preceding and following trains of ideas, all which characteristics are lacked by 'chimerical' ideas or ideas of imagination. Moreover real ideas constitute a stable and enduring world just as common sense has it, whose existence is in no way contingent upon being perceived by finite minds. But there are yet other and more specific passages where realism is unequivocally asserted. One is at 2D211, and occurs during the panegyric on the magnificence of nature which Berkeley employs, along with the shorter one at 1D171, to resist the charges of scepticism and affront to common sense which P had provoked from his critics. In the panegyric Philonous invites Hylas to contemplate the 'pathless void' of the sky and its contents. One can

6. Berkeley's realism

see a 'negligent profusion' of stars with the naked eye; a telescope brings yet more of them into view, and although they appear small and close together, they are in fact 'immense orbs of light at various distances, far sunk in the abyss of space'. Imagination has to be called in aid to appreciate that these orbs are 'central fires' with 'innumerable worlds' revolving around them. And then Berkeley says 'But neither sense nor imagination are big enough to comprehend the boundless extent with all its glittering furniture. Though the labouring mind exert and strain each power to its utmost reach, there still stands out ungrasped a surplusage immeasurable'. He concludes with the questions 'What treatment then do those philosophers deserve, who would deprive these noble and delightful scenes of all reality? How should those principles be entertained, that lead us to think all the visible beauty of the creation a false imaginary glare?' This passage recalls, among others, P6 and P81, particularly the latter with its reference to 'my own few, stinted, narrow inlets of perception'. The 'false imaginary glare' question is designed to convey the fact that Berkeley's principles defend common sense proposition (a), namely that things are as they seem to us to be, and that the properties of colour and the rest – the secondary qualities – are not merely subjective, having no place in the objects themselves. But this defends (b″) also, as the rest of the passage shows, for if the colour and glitter of these 'noble and delightful scenes' are in things themselves and are not subjective to finite minds, then *a fortiori* neither are the things themselves – which those ideas constitute – subjective.

From the point of view of finite minds Berkeley's realism does what any realism does, characterised as any realism is by the independence thesis; namely, opposes to experience an objective realm part of which – indeed by far the greater part of which – transcends the capacities of perceivers to know how things stand in it, or even that such things exist. This transcendence may be irreducible in principle, not just in fact, for Berkeley's theory as for other realist theories. But Berkeley's realism concerns only levels 1 and 2, the levels of explanation at which what is at issue are, respectively, the contents of states of awareness and the world these constitute, which is to say the ordinary, everyday world of common sense. At level 3, that is, the metaphysical level at which an inclusive explanation of the levels 1 and 2 facts is to be found, matters are however otherwise as we shall see. Absolute realism is also a level 3 theory, asserting the existence of things independently of all thought and experience; it is a direct expression of what we take to be the case on the basis of level 2, and stands to level 2 as a generalisation of its dominating assumption about how things are. For Berkeley, by contrast, the level 3 explanation of the independence and objectivity of the world relative to finite perceivers is that the world is sustained by God's perception of it. This fact is taken by Berkeley to make only one difference to our ordinary view of the world, and it is not a difference which derogates one jot from the reality of the world as this is understood on the common sense view. Rather, the difference is that once men are recalled to the realisation that the magnificence, harmony, and so forth of nature is the immediate and present handiwork of God, they will return to their religious duty (cf. P92-3, 96, 147-56, 3D257). This exhortatory and pastoral consideration, although very significant for Berkeley, is however beside the present point, which is that Berkeley's substantive metaphysical claim to the effect that the universe is sustained by God's perception of it is what grounds and justifies his realism; and accordingly it is important to make out the nature of this view clearly.

It is interesting to approach this question by way of a parenthetical remark made by Dummett, taken together with a thesis for which he has been concerned to argue. Dummett, familiarly, questions the propriety of absolute realism as an assumption in various philosophical enquiries, particularly those constituting the philosophies of mathematics and language, asking instead whether an anti-realist understanding of the concepts central to those enquiries is not more correct. What is at stake is fundamentally a matter of metaphysics: 'The question is what it is that renders our judgments (thoughts, statements) true or false: in other words, what constitutes reality, or at least that reality of which we speak or about which we think. For a realist, our judgments are true or false in virtue of a reality that exists objectively and independently of our knowledge. For an idealist, we cannot so much as *conceive* of that which goes beyond our capacity to know it. More exactly this is the general anti-realist response, which need not assume an idealist guise ... Anti-realism takes an idealist form when it is held that reality is in some way constituted by our apprehension of it' (Dummett 3 p505). The reasons Dummett has for objecting to realism in respect of one or another class of statements are similar to those set out on pp18-20 above where anti-realist attitudes in the philosophy of language are sketched (cf. e.g. Dummett 1 *passim*); but his objections to realism do not automatically commit him to anti-realism. At one point, after talking about the shortcomings of realism in connection with various subject matters – mathematics, language, the past – Dummett remarks 'I personally have no unshakeable commitment to

6. Berkeley's realism

anti-realism in any of these cases, even the mathematical one. (Indeed, I once read a paper ... arguing for the existence of God on the grounds, among others, that anti-realism is ultimately incoherent but that realism is tenable only on a theistic basis. This is essentially Berkeley's argument for the existence of God, an argument usually caricatured and always sneered at)' (Dummett 2 pxxxix). The intriguing thought this expresses is not expanded upon, but what Dummett elsewhere says about truth, and in particular about the principles which govern our employment of the concept, suggests one direction in which the thought might be developed.

The two principles which govern our employment of the concept of truth are these. There is first the principle – Dummett calls it 'Principle C' – which states that 'if a statement is true, there must be something in virtue of which it is true' (Dummett 1 p89). This principle underlies the correspondence theory of truth, and it is regulative, in the sense that having chosen what concept of truth we are to apply to statements in some given class, we then settle what the nature of the reality is in virtue of which the statements in that class are true; which is to say that we do not *first* decide what there is in the domain over which the statements range, and *then* conclude, on that basis, what makes statements true, but the other way round. The degree to which we are committed to Principle C is revealed, Dummett says, by the dissatisfaction we feel in cases where it is apparently violated. An example is afforded by counterfactuals held true despite the absence of what could count as grounds for accepting that they are true. Dummett cites the example of theological claims about beings with free-will whom God might have created, but chose not to, because he knew how they would behave if created. The objection to this is that there is nothing in virtue of which the counterfactual could be true – nothing which *makes* it true – and what this comes down to is the claim that a counterfactual cannot be 'barely true', that is, cannot be true independently of some other statement or statements, not involving counterfactual claims, whose truth makes the counterfactual true when it is so (ibid. pp89-90). This leads to the interest in providing a satisfactory account of counterfactuals, for many statements are introduced by means of them, in particular those which predicate testable properties or measurable quantities of things. Tests and measurements are taken to reveal how things are in themselves, independently of those tests and measurements, which is what prompts us to take property and quantity-ascribing statements to be determinately true even when the relevant tests and measurements have not been or could not be carried out. It is this assumption which underwrites the adoption of a realist attitude to the statements in question, and in Dummett's view it shows how 'the notion of truth we take as governing our statements determines, *via* the Principle C, how we regard reality as constituted. We may, in fact, characterise realism concerning a given class of statements as the assumption that each statement of that class is determinately true or false' (ibid. p93). That is, taking it that statements in the given class are determinately either true of false, together with the principle that there are facts of the matter which *make* them true or false, constitutes a view of reality as something existing and having the character it has independently of our being able to establish which of these two truth-values attaches to a given statement about it, which is to say that the reality exists and has the determinate character it possesses independently of our knowledge of it.

Principle C presents no difficulties if the statements it governs are such that their truth-conditions are accessible to our investigations. The problem arises when, as just sketched, it is held to apply to statements whose truth-conditions are *not* accessible, which is in fact the case with the great majority of statements assertible in natural language. Such statements are sometimes called 'effectively undecidable' to contrast them with those effectively decidable statements characterised by possession of investigation-accessible truth conditions. What requires explanation is how we come to have, or come to think that we have, mastery of effectively undecidable statements, given that the inaccessibility of their truth-conditions means that neither in acquiring nor in manifesting mastery of them can the actual fulfilment of those truth-conditions *ex hypothesi* figure as a component. In Dummett's view, we come to think of our mastery of undecidable statements by means of a sometimes covert, sometimes explicit appeal to what he calls the 'observational model'. This model, as the label suggests, is derived from cases in which users of the language report observations; for example, if someone is able to tell which of two trees is taller than the other by looking at them, then he knows what it is for one tree to be taller than another and therefore what condition has to be satisfied for the truth of the statement 'this tree is taller than that one' (ibid. p95). Here the statement's truth-conditions are available to inspection and figure centrally in the utterer's displaying the fact that he understands that statement. In the case of undecidable statements this observational model is, Dummett suggests, *extended*, surreptitiously or otherwise, beyond its normal range of application; we 'try to convince ourselves that our understanding of what it is for undecidable sentences to be

6. Berkeley's realism 135

true consists in our grasp of what it would be *to be able to use* such sentences to give direct reports of observation' (ibid. p99). Such reports cannot of course be given, but we know what powers a 'superhuman observer' would require in order to be able to give them; and what we do, accordingly, is tacitly to assume that our understanding of the truth-conditions of undecidable statements consists in knowing how things would epistemically be with that superhuman observer. This line of thought reveals a second regulative principle governing our concept of truth, which is that 'if a statement is true, it must be in principle possible to know that it is true'. Dummett calls this 'Principle K' (ibid. p1OO). Principles C and K are intimately related, which can be shown by considering the question: if one could not *know* the truth of a given statement, how could there be anything which *makes* the statement true?' In Dummett's view 'even the most thorough-going realist must grant that we could hardly grasp what it is for a statement to be true if we had no conception whatever of how it might be known to be true' (ibid.). But so far as the appeal to a realistically-conceived concept of truth goes as an explanation of language-mastery, this covert appeal to the extended observational model leaves unexplained what it is in which an understanding of sentences consists. The motive for extending that model, namely Principle K, does not in fact succeed, says Dummett, in answering 'the question how we come to be able to assign to our sentences a meaning', since on the extended observational model the assignment of meaning to sentences 'is dependent upon a use to which we are unable to put them' (ibid.). Indeed Dummett says that such an account cannot be distinguished from one which states that 'we treat certain of our sentences as if their use resembled that of other sentences in certain respects in which it in fact does not', that is, we treat certain statements as if they were observational reports when in fact, since their truth-conditions transcend our capacities to gain access to them, they are very far from being such reports; and therefore we are committing ourselves to the unacceptable view 'that we systematically misunderstand our own language' (ibid. p101).

A consideration of the Principles C and K, and particularly the latter, suggest how Dummett's parenthetical remark about realism, God and Berkeley might be developed. It was noted above that the observational model derives from cases where the truth-conditions of statements are accessible to the investigative, or more generally epistemic, capacities of utterers of them, so that attributing to the utterer a grasp of those conditions is unproblematic. In such cases the truth-values of statements are determinate, as are the states of affairs which confer those truth-values on them. With respect to a domain for which an utterer has effective means for deciding every statement concerning it we can either characterise the domain as fully determinate and complete or, equivalently, we can describe the utterer as having exhaustive access to it. In such a case, not only are the facts which make the relevant statements true or false therefore fully in view, so that Principle C recognisably and unproblematically applies, but *ipso facto* Principle K also recognisably applies, for the utterer can, and indeed in this case does, *know* what makes them so. If we now take the extended observational method seriously and postulate an observer who has not just superhuman powers, since these may still be subject to finitary constraints, but *infinite* powers, as would be the case if there were a God possessing the standardly attributed divine properties, then we arrive at the conception of an ultimately priveleged observer with access to the truth-conditions of every possible statement, from the point of view of whom all statements are therefore determinate in truth-value, which is to say that he has reality displayed to him in its full determinateness and completeness (we suppose that at this level problems about vagueness vanish). An alternative way of putting this is to say that the infinitary viewpoint is the viewpoint of one who knows, of everything that can be said about the world, whether it is true or false, and for whom everything that can be said is determinately one or the other. If one were to take it that there is such an observer or knower, then the realist conception of truth ceases to be problematic; for even if finite beings cannot know whether certain statements or true or false, in virtue of not having access to what makes them so, nevertheless both principles apply, and there are facts of the matter in any given case which settle those statements' truth-value despite the transcendence of those facts relative to the capacities of finite beings to gain access to them, regardless of whether the limitations on their capacities are irreducible in practice or in principle. This indeed is Berkeley's view, although it does not proceed in terms of questions about truth as such; and it shows what Dummett's parenthetical remark might portend. For if it turns out that the anti-realist demand for verification-immanence as the key to explaining our conceptual and linguistic practices – and therefore, ultimately, the nature of the world – is incoherent, and that a transcendent conception of truth governed by Principles C and K (which is to say, realism) is in the end irresistible, then Berkeley's view becomes a potent option for explaining realism – indeed perhaps the only intelligible one, as

6. Berkeley's realism

Dummett's remarks imply.

These thoughts, however, have a twist in the tail; for if we reflect on them we find that the qualified realism in which they consist is *in the end not realism at all*, for what is central to realism is the independence thesis, and these views have it that the world does not exist independently of God's knowledge; the facts, even if they are all the facts, are verification-immanent for God. Moreover what is involved is not just a matter of God's *knowledge*, in the sense of his having access to the truth-conditions of everything that can be said about the universe – although this by itself is enough to show that 'theistic realism' is not in the end realism – for the theory to which Berkeley is committed and to which Dummett may be tempted to subscribe has it that the universe is dependent on God's causal or creative activity for its existence, and therefore rules out *any* form of independence thesis. From God's point of view, a realistic interpretation cannot therefore be given of what can be said or thought about the universe.

That this is so should not be surprising. It was implicit from the outset in the contrast between absolute realism and Berkeley's qualified – it should be labelled 'finitary' – realism, that nothing like the absolute conception could be sustained given on the one hand the independence condition crucial to it and, on the other, the role of God. And what holds good of Berkeley's view must hold good for Dummett's view too, if it is in any sense seriously Berkeleyan. The weight of Berkeley's theory therefore falls wholly on the question of God's existence and nature. If his argument for God's existence succeeds or can be made to succeed (and it does not have to establish the existence of a God *wholly* suitable for Berkeley's purposes, which is to say, one able to sustain the metaphysical role required by Berkeley's theory while still possessing the orthodox religious character Berkeley is anxious to attribute to him; for all that is required is a God apt for the metaphysical role) then the qualified realist view and much else in Berkeley succeeds likewise. If, conversely, it fails, then the result is a good deal more dramatic than is generally supposed. It is sometimes held that removing God from Berkeley's theory leaves a version of phenomenalism; but it should already be clear from what has been said in this and preceding sections that Berkeley's theory is far too tightly-knit for that, and far too dependent for its content and intelligibility on the fundamental metaphysical role it ascribes to God. I discuss these issues below (Chapter Three Section 4).

7. Matter

The doctrines discussed in the foregoing sections are taken by Berkeley to entail that there is no matter or corporeal substance, for they show that there is only spirit and its ideas, and hence the concept of matter is ruled out because it has no application. This is the terminus of the argument stated at P1-7, during the exposition of which there is no reference to matter but only – in the first sentence of P7, which is the conclusion of the argument – to spiritual substance. It is 'for the fuller proof of this point' (P7) that Berkeley employs a further array of arguments in P and D to proceed beyond the argument from exclusion and to claim that the concept of matter is not *just* excluded but, more strongly, is inherently empty or meaningless. Since for Berkeley adherence to the view that there is matter is responsible for scepticism and atheism (cf. e.g. P87, 92), the express denial of matter is what shows how and why both are to be rejected.

The greater part of Berkeley's argument against the concept of matter is directed at exhibiting its incoherence when considered either by itself or in the light of the view that all we are ever acquainted with in sense experience is ideas. The *a priori* argument by exclusion, just mentioned, which has it that there cannot be matter because all there can be is spirit and its ideas, is the *fundamental* consideration for Berkeley; but at P16-24, 67-84, and again at 2D215-26, the concept is exhaustively investigated in this broader way with a view to showing that in *whatever* light it is placed it nevertheless cannot be made intelligible.

Before discussing these considerations, however, it is necessary to look at a related matter, namely the argument, given at P19, 50, 101ff, 2D208ff, and 3D241-3, which Berkeley directs against the materialists' important claim that the concept of matter is a powerful *explanatory* concept and recommends itself as such. A full discussion of Berkeley's views in this connection should properly involve an examination of his philosophy of science, expressed in terms of the 'language model' of nature and his doctrine of signs (cf. Mirarchi in Turbayne pp247ff for comment and further references), but although Berkeley's views on science are exceedingly interesting and I think important, they can only be touched upon here.

At P50 Berkeley considers, in the form of a sixth objection to his principles, the view that 'there have been a great many things explained by matter and motion: take away these, and you destroy

7. Matter

the whole corpuscular philosophy, and undermine those mechanical principles which have been applied with so much success to account for the phenomena. In short, whatever advances have been made ... in the study of Nature, do all proceed on the supposition that corporeal substance or matter doth really exist'. This is a significant consideration, because it provides – it still provides – the most plausible ground for taking realism about a mind-independent physical world to be true (cf. Mackie pp66-7).

Berkeley has two replies. One is, in effect, that it is true that science has powerful explanatory utility, and as such is valuable, important, and greatly worth doing; but it does not depend on a commitment to there being matter, for its explanatory efficacy is wholly consistent with Berkeley's *im*materialist principles in terms of the doctrine of signs. The second reply is that something which an employment of the concept of matter does not and cannot explain is how our experience originates: 'how matter should operate on a spirit, or produce any idea in it, is what no philosopher will pretend to explain' (ibid.). This point Berkeley urges as P19 also. The replies are related, in that the second shows that the explanatory utility conceded (without admission of an entailment to materialism) in the first reply, is nevertheless limited to the observable phenomena of nature, since it cannot explain what on the materialist hypothesis crucially demands explanation, namely the relation of mind and matter, to a dualism of which that form of materialism is committed.

I shall take Berkeley's two replies in reverse order, beginning with the mind-matter issue.

The difficulty posed by dualism is a familiar one. If one accepts the Cartesian distinction, or something like it, between items to which exclusive predicates apply – for example, bodies have spatial location, are public, and are subject to mechanical laws, whereas minds are non-spatial, their workings are private to themselves, and they are not subject to mechanical laws – then it is wholly mysterious how they interact, more particularly if the interaction in question is taken to be causal, as would seem to be required. This is by no means a problem for Descartes and his followers alone; at *Essay* IV. iii. 28 Locke identifies this difficulty as one of the 'causes of ignorance' under discussion in that chapter, and concludes that the mystery of mind-body interaction in either direction cannot be explained otherwise than by attributing the fact that it occurs to 'the arbitrary determination of that all-wise Agent ... in a way wholly above our weak understandings to conceive', which directly echoes the solution (or 'solution') offered by Descartes.

II. *Esse est Percipi: Against Matter*

The problem for dualism remains unresolved in contemporary philosophy of mind. Efforts to make progress in this region of thought chiefly take the form of attempts to articulate instead a *monistic* conception adequate to the phenomena, typically by reducing mental to physical events or states, if not by asserting an identity between them then by specifying, say, functional correlations or by understanding the nature of what could count as psychophysical laws in terms of the logical form of action sentences (cf. Davidson pp105ff); or, conversely, by reducing physical to mental phenomena, as with versions of idealism. There are other theories; apart from epiphenomenalism and Malebranche's improbable attempt to retain Cartesian dualism on an Occasionalist basis, there is the 'neutral monism' of James and Russell, in which what counts as mental and as physical are both realisations of something which is neither; and Spinoza's not in fact dissimilar view, which has it that the mental and physical are two of the infinite modes of the one substance *deus sive natura*. (These constitute serious attempts to make sense of the issues, and a two-sentence sketch of them should not mask either that or the related fact that working out a philosophical account of them demands careful and detailed commitments in metaphysics and elsewhere.) In Berkeley's case, the outcome is obvious. Dualism is in his view incoherent; at P19 and 50 he rests content with an unelaborated reminder to his readers of the conceptual impasse which results from thinking in dualist terms, and concentrates attention instead on the question whether the concept of matter is, despite its explanatory impotence in *that* respect, nevertheless an intelligible one. A central feature of his view here is that causal efficacy is reserved to spirit alone (cf. P25, 50; I discuss this in Chapter Three below), from which it follows that matter could not in any case cause ideas in us; which is why the dualist conception has the character he ascribes to it.

It is difficult not to agree with Berkeley's rejection of dualism, and *ipso facto* equally difficult not to agree that the only plausible option is a form of monism, for we are to all appearances simply without the conceptual resources for specifying not just what would *explain* the relation between two so disjoint categories as the mental and physical, understood broadly in Cartesian terms, but where to begin looking for such an explanation. Moreover it has to be accounted a potentially fatal defect in any theory that, on the fundamental question of the ontology to which it is addressed, there should be an irreducible difference between inexplicably related categories of items in it. The failing with which Berkeley charges materialism in

7. Matter

this connection is accordingly a serious one, and it is hard to see what response is open to a materialist, at least of that persuasion, to give. A related charge can in fact be carried over to those non-dualist versions of materialism with which we are more familiar in contemporary philosophy, for here the problem is that what appears to be unexplained is the apparent difference (and in *other* respects the relation) between facts about physical entities and events, on the one hand, and consciousness or experience on the other (cf. e.g. Robinson, Searle, *passim*). Since on Berkeley's view the concept of matter is not only by no means explanatorily indispensable but, worse, *unintelligible*, he would deny the value of entering into a discussion of that aspect of the question; which dismissal of it is justified if his claims in these two respects can be made out.

Berkeley's first reply, concerning the explanatory power of the materialist hypothesis, rests on a detachment of natural philosophy from that hypothesis, which places on him the obligation to say what it is one is doing when one does science, and to what it is that one's scientific investigations are addressed. In the case of the materialist hypothesis those questions have ready and obvious answers, but the immaterialist, on the face of it, has some explaining to do. Berkeley sets about the task as follows. Natural philosophy or science consists in 'observing and reasoning upon the connexion of ideas', by doing which we 'discover the laws and methods of Nature' (3D243) and thus acquire an understanding of the world which enables us to act effectively in it (cf. P31). Berkeley describes what scientific knowledge consists in at P104-5: 'analogies, harmonies, and agreements are discovered in the works of Nature, and the particular effects explained, that is, reduced to general rules', which enable us to 'extend our prospect beyond what is present ... to make very probable conjectures, touching things that may have happened at very great distances of time and place, as well as to predict things to come' (P105). In the proceedings which constitute science – observation of phenomena, and explanation of them in terms of general rules – unexceptionable use is made of theoretical concepts; for example Berkeley says '*Force, gravity, attraction*, and terms of this sort are useful for reasonings and reckonings about motion and bodies in motion' (De M17, cf. P115), but they should not be understood to be referring terms picking out entities or properties of them existing independently of mind, but rather as theoretical fictions which are useful in making our observations and rules systematic (cf. P107-8).

The essential point is that science – which is 'knowledge both useful and entertaining' (3D243) – does not depend upon a commitment to materialism. At 3D208-9 and again at 3D242-3 Philonous argues, against Hylas' claim that materialism 'explains the phenomena', that since there is no explanation of how matter can affect mind, causally or otherwise, and thus produce in us the experience we have, the hypothesis in fact explains nothing; and at P50 and again at P104ff he further argues that descriptions of what goes on in nature are descriptions of regularities and connexions *between ideas*, no reference to corporeal substance being necessary or indeed involved.

What science therefore investigates is – at the metaphysical level – the ideas caused in regular, coherent, and uniform ways by God. Berkeley adopts the metaphor of nature as the 'language' of God in elucidating how science is constituted on that basis. The conception appears frequently in his work; at V147 he says 'the proper objects of vision constitute a universal language of the Author of nature', a point repeated at P44; and in its first edition version P108 says 'the steady, consistent methods of Nature, may not unfitly be stiled the *language* of its Author, whereby he discovers His *attributes* to our view, and directs us how to act for the convenience and felicity of life'. Thus science is the business of reading the book of nature (P109), and in line with this Berkeley has it that natural phenomena are 'signs rather than causes' (P108); in V visual ideas are 'signs' of the tactual ideas we would have if we did certain things (cf. P44), and at P108 and elsewhere that semiotic conception is generalised into an account of how from observations of phenomena we can arrive at general rules, make predictions on the basis of them, and formulate explanations. The same account is given in *Alciphron* (11.7). The doctrine of signs amounts to a philosophy of science – in the view of some commentators, one closely similar to that of the Positivists – which carries no commitment to there being matter, but which, rather, is explicitly designed to account for the utility of scientific explanation without it.

The force of this view derives not just from Berkeley's correlative argument, shortly to be investigated, that the concept of matter is under any description incoherent, but also, independently of that consideration, from the fact that it is just *true* that experience could be as it is without there being a material world existing independently of it. Berkeley appeals to this fact at P20 as a conclusive rejoinder to what is in effect a 'simplest hypothesis' argument in support of materialism (P19). With that thought the general conception of treating science as a systematisation of experience – as the business, in effect, of bringing experienced 'connexions of ideas' under rules – accords well. Berkeley's claim is that of the motives there are for postulating the existence of an experience-independent material realm, none cannot be explained on the immaterialist doctrine he opposes to it. Among these motives are the independence, objectivity, haecceity, and law-like behaviour of things; the constraints they place upon, or the resistance they offer to, our activities; their describability in terms of their publicly accessible measurable qualities; and so on. But Berkeley's claim is not just that his views are *equally* adequate to the phenomena; rather, he argues that they provide an intelligible and consistent account while the materialist view precisely fails to do likewise.

Before looking at Berkeley's charge of incoherence, however, it is necessary to be clear about what he took the concept of matter to be, and what he thought about the intimately related question of substance. Berkeley gives a definition of matter several times, representative formulations of which occur at P9 (cf. also P17), P67, and 2D216. At P9 the definition is attached to a report of the philosophers' view that primary qualities inhere 'in an unthinking substance which they call *matter*. By matter therefore we are to understand an inert, senseless substance, in which extension, figure and motion do actually subsist'. A slightly different formulation is given at P67: 'an inert, senseless, extended, solid, figured, moveable substance, existing without the mind, such as philosophers describe matter', and at 2D216 '*Philonous*: And doth not *matter*, in the common current acceptation of the word, signify an extended, solid, moveable, unthinking, inactive substance? *Hylas*: It doth.' These last two formulations *equate* substance and its properties, that is, make extension and the rest the essence of substance, as with Descartes (and perhaps, on one view, Locke).

There are three key components in Berkeley's definition. One is that matter is *inert* or *inactive*; the second is that it is *unthinking* or *senseless*, that is, without the capacity to have experience; and the third is that it is, or is what possesses, the primary or original qualities. The first two components are the ones of most concern to Berkeley; a little reflection shows that they are intimately connected, for only spirit is active, and the activity of spirit is willing and understanding (P27), which latter is to say, thinking. But Berkeley does not restrict his efforts to displaying the incoherence of the concept of material substance as he defines it himself, for at P67ff and again in 2D215ff he explores variations on the definition, that is, different proposals for making sense of the concept, all of which he gives grounds for rejecting.

The reason why Berkeley and his predecessors made use of a concept of substance, in some form, was that they inherited from

Scholastic thought the view that it is difficult if not impossible to conceive how qualities can exist, as Locke puts it, *sine re substante* (*Essay* II. xxiii. 2), the thought being that *something* must furnish a ground or support for qualities, which not only hang together in determinate ways – a fact itself in need of explanation, and traditionally given one in terms of substance – but which, yet more importantly, cannot be regarded as self-sufficient existents. Locke, who more than Malebranche is the major influence on Berkeley's thinking in this respect, pointed out that all our ordinary as well as philosophical ways of thinking and speaking carry a commitment to substance: in the case of individual substances, 'when we speak of any sort of substance, we say it is a thing *having* such or such qualities ... These, and the like fashions of speaking, intimate that the substance is always supposed something, besides the extension, figure, solidity, motion, thinking, or other observable ideas, though we know not what it is' (II. xxiii. 3). As the last seven words of this quotation show, Locke was at least uneasy about the adequacy of the concept of substance; he regards it as 'An obscure and relative idea' (ibid) and, earlier, remarks 'not imagining how these simple ideas can subsist by themselves, we accustom ourselves to suppose some *substratum* wherein they do subsist, and from which they do result; which therefore we call "substance"' (II. xxiii. 2). At II. xiii. 17-20 Locke goes further than this, almost committing himself to the view that talk of substance is frankly unintelligible – 'it has' he here says 'scarce one clear distinct signification'. But despite his unease he did not feel quite able to dispense with the concept; to Stillingfleet he wrote 'I conclude there is substance because we cannot conceive how qualities should subsist by themselves' (*Third Letter*).

Berkeley was well aware of Locke's doubts (cf. C89 'Material substance bantered by Locke') and he not only agreed with them but in one sense took them a great deal further. The respect in which he did so was to argue that the concept of *material* substance is wholly unintelligible, although he disagreed sharply with Locke's view that the concept of substance *as such* is in danger of unintelligibility, for in Berkeley's view spiritual substance is something of which we have a clear and secure *notion* (P142, 3D231).

In the early sections of P, as noted, Berkeley's rejection of the concept of material substance follows directly from the argument establishing that there is only spiritual substance: 'From what has been said, it follows, there is not any other substance than *spirit*, or that which perceives. But for the fuller proof of this point, let it be considered, the sensible qualities ... are ... ideas perceived by sense.

7. Matter

Now for an idea to exist in an unperceiving thing, is a manifest contradiction; for to have an idea is all one as to perceive; that therefore wherein ... qualities exist, must perceive; hence it is clear there can be no unthinking substance or *substratum* of those ideas' (P7). This is Berkeley's chief argument against matter; and granting EP and the need for a concept of substance in some form, it is valid. But, again as noted, it was his concern to show more than this, and therefore it is to the intrinsic vacuity of the competitor conception that his later arguments on this head are devoted.

At P9-15, however, the intention is to apply the consequences of the conclusion derived at P7, and here the argument proceeds in connection with the primary-secondary quality issue and abstraction. Our ideas of primary qualities, Berkeley says, are held by materialists to be resemblances of 'things which exist without the mind, in an unthinking substance which they call *matter*' (P9). But since these are *ideas*, and since 'nothing can be like an idea but an idea' (P8), it follows that 'neither they nor their archetypes can exist in an unperceiving substance' (P9). Moreover the primary-secondary quality distinction, understood in terms of a supposed difference between the way each kind of quality relates to mind, is specious because it rests on abstraction of one sort of quality from the other; but since one cannot conceive of extension or motion apart from colour and the other sensible qualities, it follows that the primary qualities must be where the secondary qualities are, namely in the mind. All these and their attendant considerations are familiar from the discussions of them above; the point to note about them in *this* connection is that they make use only of what has been argued in Pl-7 together with the Introduction's attack on abstraction. From P16 Berkeley broadens the scope of the attack 'to examine a little the received opinion', and it is these arguments which bring in an array of additional considerations.

It is necessary to remain with P9-15 for a moment, however, because they have given occasion for criticism of Berkeley by some, Bennett and Tipton among them, on the grounds that they show that Berkeley did not clearly distinguish, as he ought to have done, the primary-secondary quality distinction from the question of material substance (cf. e.g. Tipton p41). In the view of these commentators, Berkeley's attack is directed against the conception of an independent reality lying on the far side of the veil of perception and consisting in substance-inhering primary qualities; but in taking this as his target Berkeley is, they say, 'blurring' the distinction between reasons one might have for espousing a doctrine of substance and the quite other reasons one might have for distinguishing between primary and secondary qualities (cf. ibid.). This view is largely premissed on an interpretation of Locke which has it that, as the passage at *Essay* II xxiii. 3 quoted above seems unequivocally to state, that substance is 'something besides' the qualities which inhere in it. Now, it happens that there is a debate over the question whether this indeed was the view Locke held, or whether instead he took it that substance is not something other than its properties, or at least not separate from those constituting its real essence (cf. Ayers in Tipton 2 pp77ff). If the latter interpretation of Locke is right, then charges to the effect that Berkeley misunderstood Locke, and consequently misinterpreted him to the detriment of later understanding of Locke's work, are resistable (this is the same issue mentioned in section 2 above, in the same connection). Whatever the outcome of that debate, however, two things at least are clear about Berkeley's view. These are that, first, as his definition of material substance shows, he took it to be or at least to come down to a concept of an independently existing unthinking something whether or not the primary qualities subsist in it or constitute it, and secondly, and moreover, that if it is implied that there is a separation of substance from its accidents then this is precisely one of the things he finds objectionable, for the reason that, as he points out in P67, it is simply ridiculous to think of substance as something wholly detachable from its qualities, for just as qualities cannot be conceived apart from the substance which supports them, so likewise substance cannot be thought of as a support independently of what it supports. Hence to detach the concept of substance from that of accidents is in Berkeley's opinion to render it incomprehensible from the outset. In this respect at least, Berkeley's view of substance has points of contact with the Cartesian conception and the view Ayers ascribes to Locke.

All this apart, however, Berkeley does not limit discussion to material substance as he defines it himself, but considers various ways in which the concept of it might be articulated; in doing which he gives it what amounts to a fair run. Accordingly the dispute over whether Berkeley should or should not take questions of substance and the distinction of qualities together does not constitute the central issue, for his attack, as these last remarks suggest, proceeds on a broader front. What is chiefly at stake for Berkeley is the question whether any sense can be made of the concept of a non-spiritual, independently existing cause of our sensory experience, and it is to this that the following considerations apply.

7. Matter

At P16-17 Berkeley considers what sense can be attached to 'the two parts or branches which make the signification of the words material substance' (P17). 'Matter' signifies 'the idea of being in general', and 'substance' signifies 'the relative notion of ... supporting accidents' (ibid.). Neither, he says, makes any sense; for 'the general idea of being appeareth to me the most abstract and incomprehensible of all other' (ibid.), and the idea of 'support', which cannot be given its 'usual or literal sense, as when we say that pillars support a building', and on which therefore none other than a metaphorical sense can be bestowed, is in no better case (ibid and P16). Elsewhere it turns out that when it comes to 'support' as the relation in which *spiritual* substance stands to what it supports, namely ideas, there is in Berkeley's view no comparable difficulty; for spirits support ideas by perceiving them, a relation which he takes to be entirely perspicuous from the case of our own experience of being perceivers (3D233-4). This, familiarly, is the only intelligible way of thinking about substance and what it supports for Berkeley, and it provides not only part of his grounds for asserting that spiritual substance is all there can be, but also a way of rebutting Hylas' objection, known to commentators as the 'Parity Argument', at 3D232. There Hylas says 'You admit nevertheless that there is spiritual substance, although you have no idea of it; while you deny there can be such a thing as material substance, because you have no notion or idea of it. Is this fair dealing? To act consistently, you must either admit matter or reject spirit'. Philonous' reply is the one just given, strengthened by the claim that whereas the concept of matter is unintelligible, that of spirit is not, for even though one indeed has no *idea* of spirit, since spirit is not sensible, one has a *notion* of it, in Berkeley's technical sense of this term; and our notion of it is grounded on reflexion and reason. (The issues here involve the nature of spirit and our knowledge of it, discussed in Chapter Three below.)

Berkeley's denial of sense to the expression 'material substance' at P16-17 is persuasive, providing we grant two points. Granting first the propriety of Berkeley's strictures on abstraction, it cannot be held that the conception of 'being in general', or bare existence considered apart from particular and characterisable existences, has content. And granting, secondly, that matter is inert, it is impossibly difficult to know what is to be understood by 'support' or 'standing under' in the case of material substance, unless these expressions are to be thought of as surrogates for or synonyms of causal expressions like 'produce' or indeed 'cause' itself, which is just what is ruled out by the fact that matter is in Berkeley's view inert. The first of these two points seems to me unexceptionable. The second, however, is more problematic.

Berkeley's definition of material substance, as noted, states that it is inert, and does so because in his view the only active thing there can be is spirit. This he takes to follow from the argument of Pl-7, from his definition of spirit, and from the fact that the ideas in which sensible objects consist contain nothing of power or causal efficacy in them. The significance of these points for the inertness assumption can best be brought out by noting certain features of the background to them.

The concept of matter which many, at least, of Berkeley's predecessors employed appears on the face of it to have contained no inertness assumption, but, far from it, to have had it that matter is causally active. This applies both in the case of Descartes and in that of Locke and the corpuscularians, all of whom held that matter causes ideas in conscious beings by means of its property of *motion*. The inertness conception was specifically urged against these views by Malebranche, for the two related reasons that, first, on Cartesian dualist principles there turns out to be no account of how matter can interact with mind – the point we have met with already – and secondly, the only thing to which we have grounds for attributing activity is spirit, which accords with the doctrine of the Schoolmen that God is pure, in the sense of wholly impassive, activity, and he is spirit *par excellence* in whose nature finite spirits partake and which therefore are also active.

With these points Berkeley agreed, taking them further and giving additional arguments for them. At P18, for example, he considers whether, despite the arguments he has already advanced, it could be claimed that it is possible nevertheless that there might be matter; but concludes that it cannot, on the grounds that nothing can count as coming to know that there is matter either by sense or reason. Certainly not by sense, which is conversant only with ideas and not with a putative something lying behind or beyond them; and neither by reason, on the two grounds that, first, 'the very patrons of matter themselves do not pretend, that there is a necessary connexion betwixt [matter] and ideas' (ibid.), and secondly, we could have all the ideas we in fact have consistently with there being no externally existing material substance (ibid. and P20, cf. C476-7). The general point is well put at 2D223: 'That from a cause, effect, operation, sign, or other circumstance, there may reasonably be inferred the existence of a thing not immediately perceived, and that it were absurd for any man to argue against the existence of that thing, from

7. Matter

his having no direct and positive notion of it, I freely own. But where there is nothing of all this...where there is not so much as the most inadequate and faint idea pretended to ... my inference shall be, you mean nothing at all.' In short, where nothing *confers* sense, there can be none.

This agrees with and exploits Malebranche's point about the unknowability of matter, but it goes much further, for whereas Malebranche did not on this basis deny the intelligibility of the concept, and therefore the existence of matter itself, Berkeley for his part does so. It is the logical step. Again, at P19 Berkeley considers the Mackie-style suggestion to the effect that postulating the existence of matter, although it is otherwise quite unknown and unspecifiable, constitutes the simplest available hypothesis to explain the source and course of experience, and he rejects it for the reason, as noted above, that not even the materialists themselves can explain how matter is supposed to interact with mind – a difficulty which forms part of Malebranche's reason for the adjustments he made to Cartesian views. And finally Berkeley unreservedly accepts Malebranche's point about activity as essential to spirit – at one point indeed he was tempted to characterise God in Scholastic terms as *purus actus* (C701, 828), but not wishing God to be 'blind' agency, that is, without understanding, he rejected that as too limited a definition (C870, cf. 812).

Of these considerations, two might appear debatable. One, concerning the nature of spirit, I leave for later discussion. The other is that one might defend the 'simplest hypothesis' defence of the materialist conception by pointing out that Berkeley's objection applies to it only in its dualist form, and that contemporary materialism is monistic, and so avoids that difficulty. Berkeley's rejection of the 'simplest hypothesis' view can, however, be readily substantiated by pointing out that an hypothesis' being the best and simplest available is entirely consistent with its being false; which is enough to make it no option given Berkeley's other reasons for rejecting the materialist conception.

But Berkeley has yet further reasons for taking it that matter is by definition inert, even in the light of Descartes' views and those of Locke and the corpuscularians. This is that Descartes and these others did not in any case take it that matter is the *ultimate* causal agency in the realm of extension, for this role is reserved to God. Rather, material causality is secondary, qualified, and limited, deriving from the creative impetus given to the world, and thereafter sustained in it, by God's activity. Just this view indeed is put by

II. *Esse est Percipi: Against Matter*

Hylas, who argues for it shortly after agreeing with Philonous' definition of matter at 2D216, saying that there *is* a sense in which matter can be thought of as causally active, provided one takes this to be in 'a limited and inferior' way, and that is 'by that kind of action which belongs to matter, viz. *motion*' (2D217; cf. 2D215). Philonous' rejoinder is that motion is a sensible quality and therefore an idea, having as with all ideas nothing of causal power in it (ibid. and cf. P25); accordingly, it tells us nothing of the supposed causal efficacy of an unknown something lying beyond experience. More generally, since it is within God's competence to cause everything without intermediaries or instruments, the supposition of material causes considered as limited, secondary, or instrumental is redundant; and in any case our ordinary level 2 talk of cause in nature is based on successions and regularities in our ideas, which however are found upon a level 1 inspection of them to be discrete and particular, with neither necessary connexions between them nor anything of power or activity discernible in them; so that properly speaking what we ordinarily take to be a relation of cause and effect is in fact a relation of sign to thing signified (cf. e.g. P53, 65, 108, VV38), taught us by the overall course of our experience and reflecting, for our benefit, the orderly and systematic activities of the creator (P30-2).

Apart from the theological considerations in the foregoing, which will be discussed later, these arguments suggest that the second of the two points which required granting is as unexceptionable as the first. And the theological considerations can in fact be detached from some of the points Berkeley makes here, leaving fundamentally the claim that the concept of matter is unintelligible because it is the concept of something lying beyond the reach either of sense or reason, so that we have no grounds for asserting its existence; and if we try to form a conception of it in terms of 'support' and of 'bare existence' or 'being in general', then we are saying nothing which can be given content.

Berkeley does not however leave the question there, because the materialist's options for defending matter are not quite yet exhausted. These further options are discussed at P67ff and 2D218ff, where Berkeley tries to give the concept as much latitude as it will bear in his effort to show that, on any view of it, it is vacuous. He argues as follows.

For anyone persuaded by theological considerations, the Malebranchian view of matter as an *occasion*, prompting God to cause relevant ideas in us in relevant circumstances, offers one resource. Berkeley deals with it at P67 and 2D219. In Malebranche's view,

7. Matter   151

since matter is unknowable with respect to finite minds it can be conceived only as an inert unperceivable substance 'at the presence whereof God is pleased to excite ideas in us' (ibid.). Berkeley's objections are three, and they are together decisive. First, what is 'occasion' supposed to mean? It does not have a causal sense, for that is ruled out by matter's inertness; and it cannot be thought of as a sign accompanying or going before something perceivable, as a mark of the latter's being in the offing, for it is itself unperceivable (P69). But these are the only senses of the term which can be collected from its standard employment, Berkeley says, and accordingly 'This term is either used in no sense at all, or else in some sense very distant from its received signification' (ibid. and cf. C754). Secondly, if matter is perceived by God although not by us, so that the 'unperceivable' in the definition applies only to finite perceivers, then nevertheless it is an idea, and the question no longer concerns something independent of perception and spirit (P71, 2D20). If *this* is what is meant by matter, then Berkeley is content to accept that it exists. And thirdly, the conception of matter as a prompt for God is redundant, for God is competent to produce 'all the appearances of Nature' without aid of any sort (P72, 2D220). The first and third points are significant in that what Malebranche's view effectively comes down to is the thought that although little positive content can be assigned to the concept of matter, at the very least matter can be accorded a *role*, and that this is what makes sense of it. Berkeley's points constitute a rejection of that thought.

One feature of Malebranche's occasionalism which has interest is that it treats matter as something considered apart from what if any properties it might be thought to have. Earlier I noted Berkeley's remark that the attempt to conceive of substance without accidents is as absurd as attempting to conceive of accidents without substance; but he is prepared to consider for dialectical purposes the proposal suggested by but going well beyond Malebranche's thought, that nevertheless a wholly *negative* definition of matter might be given which succeeds in showing somehow that the concept of it has sense (P68, 80-1, 2D221-3). This is what Hylas does; after trying to defend matter variously as cause, occasion, and instrument as well as independent existent, he at last resorts to the strategy of saying 'by *matter* (I understand) neither substance nor accident, thinking nor extended being, neither cause, instrument nor occasion, but some thing entirely unknown, distinct from all these'. Philonous remarks 'It seems then you include in your present notion of matter, nothing but the general abstract idea of *entity*', and Hylas replies 'Nothing else, save only that I super-add to this general idea the negation of all those particular things, qualities, or ideas that I perceive, imagine, or in any wise apprehend' (2D221-2). This interesting exchange recapitulates P80-1, where Berkeley imagines his materialist opponent saying 'Whatever might be urged against *substance* or *occasion*, or any other positive or relative notion of matter, hath no place at all, so long as this *negative* definition of matter is adhered to', where the definition is as Hylas has given it. Something very like Kant's noumenon is at issue in this; for Kant too noumenal reality is specified negatively as being everything the phenomena are not (cf. e.g. the Fourth Paralogism). Berkeley's response is economical: 'I answer, you may, if so it shall seem good, use the word *matter* in the same sense, that other men use *nothing*, and so make these terms convertible in your style' (P80). The point is a substantive one, for all its economy, concerning once again the failure to give meaning to the idea of something it wholly transcends our capacities to know or say anything about, and consequently is as successful here as it is in the standard rejection of Kant's conception of noumenal reality.

What Berkeley takes the concept of matter ultimately to come down to, therefore, is either the self-contradictory notion of unperceived existence – which is contradictory because *esse est percipi* – or the empty concept of a noumenon. It is important to note that his rejection of matter is a level 3 issue; at level 2 talk of matter or material things can, in his view, go ahead in the usual way, provided nothing is taken to follow at level 3 as to the independent existence of an unknowable something which is the external source of experience. Berkeley's assertion of *the existence of sensible objects* and denial of *the existence of material objects* is therefore wholly a matter of metaphysics, that is, is wholly a matter of what *explanation* is ultimately to be given of sensory experience; and as such it leaves unchanged the level 2 conflation of the concepts of sensible and material objects enshrined in our discourse. Because his objection is to the technical philosophical conception of material substance invoked at level 3 to explain the source and course of experience, the 'opinion strangely prevailing among men' he resists at P4 is therefore the opinion that this level 3 account is *true*; and when it is recalled that it is precisely this philosophical conception of material substance which promotes scepticism (and atheism), by opening a gap between experience and an experience-independent realm, the reason for Berkeley's repeated and vigorous attacks on it become clear. In the preparatory studies in his notebooks Berkeley makes it plain that he took the issue to involve only a mistaken higher-order theory: 'I take not away

7. Matter

substances. I ought not to be accused of discarding Substance out of the reasonable World. I onely reject the Philosophic sense (which is in effect no sense) of the word substance. Ask a man never tainted with this jargon what he means by corporeal substance or the substance of body, He shall answer Bulk, Solidity & such like sensible qualitys. These I retain. The Philosophic nec quid nec quantum nec quale whereof I have no idea I discard. if a man may be said to discard that which never had any being was never so much imagined or conceived' (C517; cf. C22). And to emphasise that this applies only to the metaphysical level of explanation, leaving the mundane facts of experience as they are, he adds the *verso* claim, tying the discussion of matter to scepticism, 'NB I am more for reality than any other Philosopher, they made a thousands doubts & know not certainly but we may be deceived. I assert the direct Contrary' (C517a). And he concludes 'In short be not angry you lose nothing' (C518). The sentence at C517 'I ought not to be accused of discarding Substance out of the reasonable World' echoes almost word for word Stillingfleet's complaint to Locke over the latter's half-hearted attitude towards substance. Berkeley, by contrast, is unequivocal in his adherence to the concept; the difference between his account of it and the various accounts offered by his predecessors lies chiefly in the question of what is *meant* by it: 'I must not say the words thing, substance etc have been the cause of mistakes. But the not reflecting on their meaning' (C553).

The arguments *for* EP and, correlatively, *against* matter ultimately depend for their success on the metaphysical account which underpins them, a point which it has often been necessary to make in this and the foregoing sections. It is now time to examine that account, for by it stands or falls much of what Berkeley argues in connection with the topics so far discussed.

CHAPTER THREE
Esse est Percipere: The Nature of Substance

Berkeley's argument is intended to achieve its aims of refuting scepticism and atheism by showing that the only substance there can be is spirit. This conclusion is squarely based on the argument that, for sensible qualities, to be is to be perceived, which entails that sensible qualities are ideas and therefore that sensible objects are mind-dependent. This claim does not, given the doctrine of substance it rests on, call into question the reality and objectivity of sensible objects, but explains these characteristics of them in a way which is consistent with the thesis that they are wholly knowable. The competing supposition, namely that there is material substance, is shown to be unintelligible both on this basis and on the intrinsic incoherence of postulating the existence of something it transcends our capacities to know, a thesis derived from the austere empirical constraints Berkeley places on the sensefulness of experiential discourse. Berkeley therefore takes seriously the concept of substance, as did all his predecessors and contemporaries, and indeed his philosophical views turn precisely on the question of what content that concept has. His argument is that whereas no sense can be attached to the concept of material substance, and in particular that nothing can be understood by the relation of 'support' in which material substance putatively stands to its attributes, it is by contrast the case both that the concept of spirit or mind makes sense, and that its relation to what it supports can adequately be explained. For Berkeley, as for his predecessors and contemporaries, substance is the independent, self-sufficient ground of dependent existences, appeal to which constitutes a final explanation of what there is and why. Since this is so, it is of the first importance that the concept of substance should be perspicuous, intelligible, and wholly adequate to the role it is designed to play. Berkeley's claim is that the concept of mind satisfies, whereas that of matter fails to satisfy, these criteria.

In the light of this one's expectation is that Berkeley can give an account of spirit in general and God in particular which will

Esse est percipere: the nature of substance

satisfactorily complete the project of showing that mind is the only substance. All the more interest and urgency attaches to this in view of the plausibility, once they are properly understood, of many of the arguments discussed in preceding sections; which plausibility, however, rests largely on the promise that an explanation at the metaphysical level – that is, an account of spirit – will sustain it. But what Berkeley has to say on the topic of spirit, whether finite or infinite, is not only extraordinarily sketchy but deeply problematic. This gives rise to the chief cause for disquiet regarding Berkeley's doctrine, for his view of substance underwrites his overall theory, and failure to give an acceptable account of it threatens disaster for the whole. The task now is to investigate what Berkeley offers by way of such an account.

It is first necessary to comment on the reasons why so little is said about spirit in P and D, and to what extent the entries in C can help with an understanding of that little. To begin with it has to be recalled that P is Part I only of what was originally intended to be a work of two or probably more parts (See Chapter One, section 2 above), and the notebooks show that the projected Part II was to have been addressed specifically to the questions of spirit and morals. Berkeley confirms this in his letter to Johnson (*Works* II p282). Accordingly neither in P, nor – because clearly he then still planned to write a Part II – in D, does Berkeley devote much attention to spirit. He does however give it *some* attention in both places. In P, after considering the twelve objections discussed at P34-84, Berkeley proceeds 'in the next place to take a view of our tenets in their consequences' (P85). He says 'From the principles we have laid down, it follows, that human knowledge may naturally be reduced to two heads, that of *ideas*, and that of *spirits*'. He treats of these in order, ideas at P87-134, and spirit at P135-56 (P156 is the concluding section). Under the heading of *ideas* there occurs his highly interesting discussion of science and mathematics, which he may have intended to discuss more fully in a Part III (cf. C583). *Spirit*, by contrast, gets a mere sixteen sections, crammed into which are discussions of the nature of spirit, our knowledge of it, the immortality of the soul, the question of our knowledge of other minds, the nature and operations of God and our knowledge of both, an explanation of the workings of nature in terms of God's providence, a solution of the problem of evil, and an exhortation to religious duty. The fact that this hasty and wide-ranging sketch occurs in P at all, despite the projected treatment in a Part II, can to some extent be explained in terms of the conventions governing publication in parts. Like others of his time Berkeley intended to see what critical response he received to Part I before writing Part II, and accordingly Part I had to be a complete and self-sufficient work while, at the same time, not anticipating too much of the content of projected successor parts. The sketches of 'consequences' under the heading of *ideas* and *spirit* were therefore intended, as Johnson shows he understood them to be, merely as indications of how the lines of thought they contain would develop. The deeply unfavourable reception accorded by critics to Part I led Berkeley to try to promote its major theses in a different way before venturing Part II, which explains the appearance of D. Hume's decision to substitute the two *Enquiries* for the *Treatise* arose from similar motives.

By 1734, however, when Berkeley issued the second editions of P and D, it was clear to him that he would not produce further parts of P, and accordingly he dropped 'Part I' from the title page (but not, perhaps by mistake, from the other pages), and added the term 'notion' to tidy somewhat his account of our knowledge of spirit. In D he also added an extension to the 'Parity Argument', which therefore occurs in first edition form at 3D231-2, and in second edition form at 3D232-4. Otherwise his account of spirit remains as sketchy as it was in the first editions. This neglect of what is so obviously crucial a question, even when the opportunity arose in 1734 to repair that want by expanding the relevant discussions in P and D, cannot be explained away, as before, by intentions to produce further parts nor in terms of the conventions of staggered publication. Some commentators have concluded that the difficulties eventually came to seem just too great in Berkeley's estimation, even although he took his theory to be, in basic respects, on the right lines; and that he could not see his way clear to putting matters on a better footing (Tipton 1 pp260ff). Some go further and suggest that what he eventually became aware of was the fact that further detail in the relevant respects would involve inconsistency with the argument already developed. My own view is that Berkeley abandoned the project of adding to P for reasons which have to do with his reluctance to engage in philosophical theology as such; reasons for this view emerge in section 4 below.

There is an added complication. Berkeley's notebooks often illuminate the theses of the published works, as one would expect, particularly in connection with existence, matter, perceivability, and other central concerns. But the entries on spirit, marked 'S', are much less useful for an understanding of what is said in the published works than is the case with these other topics, a fact which

Esse est percipere: the nature of substance

many commentators rather surprisingly fail to notice. This is partly because the 'S' entries are a mixed bag, not all of them strictly relevant to the main issue. Some of the entries have to do with personal identity (cf. C194a, 650-2, 681, 857), some are bound up with the ultimately discarded powers theory (e.g. C155, 699 etc.), a few concern immortality (e.g. C814), and many concern the free-will question and, related to this, Locke's talk of 'uneasiness' as what 'in the train of our voluntary actions determines the will to any change of operation' (*Essay* II. xxi, 71), which view Berkeley held to be incompatible with freedom (cf. C145-6, 166, 357, 423, 598, 610-11, 613, 624, 625-31, 653, 707, 743, 833, 857, 879). Of these a number are specifically intended to have ethical purport, as is shown by the additional marginal sign 'Mo', and in any case it is obvious that this subject was aimed at the ethical discussions proposed for Part II. There is also a cluster of entries which show Berkeley entertaining a Humean 'bundle' theory of the mind (cf. C577-82). He takes this seriously for much longer than is generally recognised, and his thoughts about personal identity and time are related to it and indeed survive rejection of the bundle theory itself (these matters are discussed below). These and the remainder of the entries are more focally relevant to what appears in P and D. The majority of them concern will, understanding, and activity as defining of mind, and the absolute distinction between spirit and ideas. Between them these two topics get approximately fifty entries (representative references are given in the following discussion), and yet do much less than we might hope to advance understanding of the published theses, as I shall shortly show. A remarkable feature of the notebooks' 'S' entries is that all but half a dozen of them occur in the second notebook, and then with rapidly increasing frequency towards the end. The same is true of the 'G' entries, concerning God; of these there are a mere sixteen in all. It is difficult not to get the impression – indeed a strong impression – from reading the notebooks that, at the time he was writing them, the question of spirit was not as carefully thought through by Berkeley as were his other major theses, and that he began to pay closer attention to it at so late a stage that it is possible he had only the outline of a theory available when he began to write P. At the same time, however, what little he says in P and D is said with confidence, and therefore one ought perhaps not to read too much into the *distribution* of the entries in the notebooks. Commentators who take the view that Berkeley began writing P without a developed theory of spirit and God are inclined to argue that, since D shows no progress in that respect, it must have been when he drafted some of Part II on his Italian travels of 1715-6 that the real difficulties manifested themselves and led him to abandon the enterprise. If that is so, it is worth pointing out that there is nothing to Berkeley's discredit in this; the history of philosophy has relatively few figures in it who did not take their work as far as they themselves could go, leaving to others the task of making further progress. Something like the hope that this might happen is expressed by Berkeley in his correspondence with Johnson.

However the case may be, the doctrine of spirit is crucial and requires investigation, for on it the edifice of Berkeley's thought rests. I begin by looking at what Berkeley says about spirit itself, both finite (sections 1 and 2 below) and infinite (section 4), with a discussion of an importantly related matter, namely time, coming between (section 3).

1. Finite spirit

In summary characterisations of Berkeley's views he is said to hold that *esse est percipi aut percipere*, a neat alliterative formula which has the virtue of memorability. The slogan is not indeed inaccurate, but neither is it wholly accurate, for it lends an air of symmetry to Berkeley's view which is somewhat misleading. The reason is that the *esse* of mind is not as it turns out just *percipere*, but it is that and *cogitare* and *velle* also: 'by the word *spirit* we mean ... that which thinks, wills, and perceives' (P138). This more complex definition is foreshadowed at C429a where Berkeley says 'Existence is percipi or percipere' (C429) and then adds 'or velle i.e. agere' (C429a). Moreover the nature of our knowledge of spirit is entirely different from our knowledge of ideas. To understand this it is useful to note the respects in which Berkeley's view agrees with and differs from that of Locke, and the sense in which its ultimate source is Descartes.

At *Essay* IV. ix-xi Locke considers the question of 'our knowledge of existence' under three heads: first, knowledge of our own existence; secondly, of the existence of God; and thirdly, of the existence of other things (IV. ix. 2). He devotes a section each to the last two categories, and a paragraph to the first (IV. ix. 3), prefacing the whole by saying 'we have knowledge of our own existence by intuition; of the existence of God by demonstration; and of other things by sensation' (IV. ix. 2). With this Berkeley is almost wholly in agreement. Locke's paragraph on our knowledge of our own

1. Finite spirit 159

existence appears to come straight from Descartes: 'As for our own existence, we perceive it so plainly and so certainly that it neither needs or is capable of any proof. For nothing can be more evident to us than our own existence. I think, I reason, I feel pleasure and pain: can any of these be more evident to me than my own existence? If I doubt of all other things, that very doubt makes me perceive my own existence, and will not suffer me to doubt of that ... Experience, then, convinces us that we have an intuitive knowledge of our own existence, and an eternal infallible perception that we are. In every act of sensation, or thinking, we are conscious to ourselves of our own being; and, in this matter, come not short of the highest degree of certainty' (IV. ix. 3). With this also Berkeley agrees, and adopts the idiom of 'intuition' at 3D231. The agreement ceases there, however, for in this passage Locke is asserting that what the certain and immediate knowledge is of, is of one's *self*, the denotation of 'I'; but this does not square fully with Descartes' thesis, for elsewhere Locke shows that in his view what *underlies* the self, namely spiritual substance, is in as poor a case as material substance from the point of view of our epistemic capacities (cf. e.g. II. xxiii. 4-6, esp. 5). Locke therefore detaches questions of personhood from questions of substance, and his doing so enables him to construct an account of personal identity on the basis of another Cartesian view, namely that consciousness entails self-consciousness, which provides the ground of his argument that self-consciousness is the essence of personality, and that therefore identity of the person rests on identity of consciousness (cf. Allison in Tipton 2 pp105ff). This view also influenced Berkeley on identity and time, as will be seen later; but on the present issue Locke's separation of the self from spiritual substance constitutes Berkeley's central point of disagreement with him, because Berkeley takes it that the self of which we have direct intuitive knowledge just *is* the spirit: 'What I am myself, that which I denote by the term I, is the same with what is meant by *soul* or *spiritual substance*" (P139, cf. P2). And he therefore claims at P135 that 'with regard to [spirit] perhaps human knowledge is not so deficient as is vulgarly imagined', because we have direct contact with and knowledge of it. His argument is as follows.

Berkeley identifies the source of the view that we are ignorant of spirit as coming down to the claim that we have no *idea* of it, that is, that it is not an item of empirical awareness (P135). This is the thesis espoused by Malebranche. Berkeley agrees that this is the case, but argues that it does not follow from this fact that we have no knowledge of spirit; indeed our not having an *idea* of spirit is, he

III. Esse est Percipere: The Nature of Substance

argues, hardly surprising, since ideas are inert entities dependent for their existence on being perceived and therefore *toto caelo* different from spirit, which is active and the *esse* of which is to will, to think, to perceive. Accordingly 'that this *substance* which supports or perceives ideas should itself be an *idea* or like an *idea*, is evidently absurd' (ibid. and cf. P27). To the objection that 'if there is no idea signified by the terms *soul, spirit*, and *substance*, they are wholly insignificant or have no meaning in them' (P139), which follows directly from the ideational theory having it that the meaning of a word is the idea it stands for, Berkeley replies that we have a *notion* of it (P140, cf. P27, 89, 142, 3D233), and at the same time implies that the term's significance arises from the fact that it has a *use*: 'In a large sense we may be said to have an idea, or rather a notion of *spirit*, that is, we understand the meaning of the word, otherwise we could not affirm or deny any thing of it' (P140), which he exemplifies by remarking on our ability to speak of other minds (ibid. and P145). (A use theory of meaning for at least some words is suggested in the Introduction to P; see Chapter One, Section 2 above.) Philonous provides a summary of these claims at 3D231: 'I own I have properly no idea, either of God or any other spirit; for these being active, cannot be represented by things perfectly inert, as our ideas are. I do nevertheless know, that I who am a spirit or thinking substance, exist as certainly, as I know my ideas exist. Further I know what I mean by the terms *I* and *myself*; and I know this immediately, or intuitively, though I do not perceive it as I perceive a triangle, a colour, or a sound'. The thesis is, then, effectively Locke's with the difference that Locke's intuitively knowable self is identified by Berkeley with spirit, so that it is this of which we have knowledge, no distinction between an empirical or noumenal self being at issue. It is interesting to note that in C Berkeley was for a time attracted by the Lockean idea of personality and tempted to structure his account in terms of it (C14, 25), but abandoned that option during his repeated attempts to find a formulation of his conception of spirit (cf. C44, 154, 230, 286, 478, 576-81, 637, 712, etc., terminating with C848 where the thesis of the published writings is settled upon). One of his reasons for doing so is that the concept of personhood has theological implications and he did not wish to invite difficulties on that score, as C713 shows. Another is that Berkeley in the end chose for good reasons to reject the conception of substance as unknowable, and accordingly elected to go back beyond Locke to Descartes, for whom self-knowledge is intuitively direct, but is knowledge of *res cogitans*, not an empirical self distinguished from thinking substance as in Locke.

1. Finite spirit

So far, however, the account Berkeley gives of how one has knowledge of one's self *qua* spiritual substance is vague. Two other relevant remarks, one each from P and D, add the suggestion that we have access to ourselves by 'inward feeling or relexion' (P89) or by a 'reflex act' (3D232), which may echo the talk at C539 of 'Introversion, meditation, contemplation & all spiritual acts' which Berkeley in this entry is claiming cannot 'be exerted before we had ideas from without' and therefore suggests among other things introspection, which is the natural gloss both for 'reflex act' and in this context 'reflexion', the intended meaning of which is displayed by the equating disjunction with 'inward feeling'. Confirmation comes from *De Motu*: 'There are two supreme classes of things, body and soul. By the help of sense we know the extended thing ... but the sentient, percipient, thinking thing we know by a certain internal consciousness (*conscientia quadam interna*)' (DeM 21, cf. Avii. 5); which Berkeley takes to justify the broader claim he makes later, that 'reason and experience advise us that there is nothing active except mind or soul' (DeM 40). By 'experience' is not meant sense-experience, of course, for if it did then the spirit would be an idea which is just what Berkeley denies. Somehow, then, 'reflexion' or 'internal consciousness' has to be understood as a species of introspective awareness for which the spirit is not in any standard sense an object. At P27 Berkeley says 'Such is the nature of spirit or that which acts, that it cannot be of itself perceived, but only by the effects which it produceth', which suggests that the reflex act constitutes a recognition, in some sense, of what 'reason and experience' deliver.

The accessibility of the spiritual self in the way described tells us in Berkeley's view more than just *that* it is, but, as these quotations show, *what* it is. At P27 spirit is characterised as 'one, simple, undivided, active being: as it perceives ideas, it is called the *understanding*, and as it produces or otherwise operates about them, it is called the *will*'. The 'simple undivided' claim looks like a bald assertion, or an invitation to accept, without further justification, the long established thesis having it that what is substantial in the metaphysical sense must have none of the features of what Aristotle calls 'secondary being', one of which is compoundedness or analysability. The reason Berkeley has for saying this is, however, an unexceptionable one on his terms, the explanation coming at 3D231: 'The mind, spirit or soul, is that indivisible unextended thing, which thinks, acts, and perceives. I say *indivisible*, because unextended; and *unextended*, because extended, figured, moveable things, are ideas;

162   III. Esse est Percipere: The Nature of Substance

and that which perceives ideas, which thinks and wills, is plainly it self no idea, nor like an idea'. More important is the conception of spirit as *active*. The concepts of activity and the will are indeed fundamental to Berkeley's thesis because they provide him with his account of causality, which is central to the doctrine that spirit is the *only* substance; and therefore activity and will get an extensive discussion in C – but the discussion is extraordinarily tortuous and it is hard to see how the doctrine of the published works succeeds in emerging from it. Moreover that doctrine occasions, or at least threatens to occasion, difficulties for what Berkeley otherwise says, particularly in connection with perception, as we shall see.

Some of the windings of Berkeley's thought in the notebooks on will, activity, and the understanding are these. At the outset he asserts 'we cannot possibly conceive any active power but the Will' (C155). The remark is made in the context of a definition, rejected as the obelus accompanying it shows, of the soul as a complex idea (C154), together with certain remarks about freedom and desire (C156-62), also all rejected; and therefore occurs as part of a series of interim reflections on the consequences for morality of thinking of the soul in this way. The next mention is at C478a 'The soul is the will properly speaking & as it is distinct from its ideas', and here the soul appears to be exhaustively *identified* with the will. These early entries contain something of the view ultimately settled upon, but that Berkeley was not doing more than toying with the question as a corollary of other issues – in particular the question of freedom and whether spirit should properly be called an idea at all (C176a, 230, 478, 490, 523) – is shown by his saying at C579 'Consult, ransack your Understanding ... what mean you by the word mind', suggesting that serious discussion of the issue has at last begun. It is at this point (C576-82) that Berkeley first contemplates adopting something like Hume's bundle theory: 'Mind is a congeries of Perceptions. Take away Perceptions & you take away the Mind put the Perceptions & you put the Mind' (C580); 'Say you the Mind is not the Perception but the thing which perceives. I answer you are abused by the words that and thing these are vague empty words without a meaning' (C581). This view held its attraction at least until C708, but Berkeley quickly recalled the fact that the mind wills and the will is not an idea; which raised for him the question of how will and understanding are related. 'The Understanding seemeth not to differ from its perceptions or Ideas. Qu: what must one think of the Will & passions' (C587). After what appear to be vain attempts to make sense in different ways of the relation between understanding as a congeries of ideas and the will not as an idea (cf. e.g. C614-15a,

1. Finite spirit 163

643-5), and after indeed distancing will considerably from understanding – at C659 there occurs the remark 'I say nothing which is perceived or does perceive Wills' – Berkeley temporarily accepts that 'the substance of spirit we do not know it not being knowable, it being *purus actus*' (C701, cf. 828-9). Together these various thoughts amount to the view that will and understanding are two 'distinct' (C708, cf. 820) attributes of an unknown spiritual substance, or of will as the attribute of such a substance and understanding as a 'faculty' (cf. C848) standing in some unspecified relation to it. That this appears to be the view as late as C829 is extraordinary; the entry occurs a mere eight folio pages from the end of the notebooks, and yet is utterly opposed in character to the thesis found in P.

Nevertheless from much earlier, at C672a, a theme begins to emerge which eventually supercedes the view of understanding as a mere congeries of ideas, and this is that there is 'somewhat active in most perceptions i.e. such as ensue upon our Volitions, and as we can prevent & stop v.g. I turn my eyes towards the sun I open them all this is active' (cf. lD196). This account accords with C713, 777, 791 and many later entries, which is to say with those entries, beginning at C713, marking a shift away from the 'unknown substance' view of spirit. Here Berkeley talks of the 'concrete of the Will & understanding I must call Mind' (ibid.) which foreshadows the published view; at C777 and increasingly numerous later entries he reasserts, with less hesitation, the view that perception is 'not ... altogether Passive, there must be a disposition to act, there must be assent, which is active, nay what do I talk there must be actual Volition', which permits characterisation of mind or spirit as *essentially* active.

The closest approximation to the published view occurs at C848: 'I must not mention the Understanding as a Faculty or part of the Mind, I must include Understanding & Will etc in the word Spirit by which I mean all that is active. I must not say that the Understanding differs not from particular Ideas, nor the Will from particular Volitions.' It would give cause for satisfaction if this were the last word in the notebooks after a long and confused battle, on Berkeley's part, to win through to a position he could expound and defend in the published works; but there is an odd twist to the tale, which is that in two subsequent entries – C867 and 871 – Berkeley seems to be on the verge of dismissing both will and understanding as 'abstract ideas i.e. none at all' (C871), which is not merely a claim, consistent with many earlier ones, that they are not *ideas*, but rather that they are contentless terms of art having the status

Berkeley accords to 'matter' and 'absolute existence'. Nevertheless nothing is made of this, and it is C848 which comes closest to the doctrine finally settled upon.

The point to be drawn from this brief account of how Berkeley's thinking proceeded in the notebooks is that there is no question of one's discovering there a systematically developed view, but a series of experiments conducted with the aim of finding a fit between a suitable conception of mind and the rest of the central doctrines for which Berkeley wished to argue, one that moreover would square with theological and moral considerations he also hoped to develop, but which get nowhere in C nor reappear in P and D. This last point is exemplified by Berkeley's returning time and again to consider Locke's 'uneasiness' point and the question of free-will, a debate which bears no fruit. Earlier it was remarked that the notebook discussions of spirit are greatly less helpful to an understanding of the published views than is the case with other topics; here we see the reason why. The result is that Berkeley's account of finite spirit has to be judged solely on the little that appears in the published works, which makes the task of assessment, to which I now turn, more difficult.

It goes without saying that a complete assurance of one's own existence is attained whenever we contemplate it, as all of Descartes, Locke and Berkeley unexceptionably claim. The debate over the nature and status of the cogito shows that there is nevertheless something deeply puzzling about this truth, or at least the way it is known. Considerably *more* vexed a pair of questions still, however, concern what it is that is known to exist when one knows one exists, and what can legitimately be inferred from whatever answer is given to that first question. Berkeley's strategy is in effect to assert, without much argument but not entirely without justification, that what is in this way known to exist is spiritual substance, the definition given of which entails a ready answer to the second question. This places Berkeley's view much closer to Descartes' than to Locke's position. Locke's claim that what is known is the empirical self – understood as revealed to self-consciousness and therefore providing grounds for identity, and at the same time telling us nothing about the substance which underlies it, so that there is room to speculate whether the substance of the perceived self may not, after all, be *material* – is less ambiguous than the claims of Descartes and Berkeley, but at the same time is more vulnerable to criticism of the sort advanced by Hume. That criticism is to the effect that empirical self-awareness reveals nothing besides a collection or succession of

1. Finite spirit 165

ideas, which means in particular that no enduring principle existing independently of those ideas is detectable, showing how and why those ideas hang together in a less than adventitious way and which can therefore serve, among other things, as the self of folk psychology, which Locke effectively claims it does. In Descartes and Berkeley, by contrast, the fact that what is revealed to intuition or 'reflexion' is *spiritual substance* makes a much larger claim, for the conception of substance has the logical character of fulfilling a distinctive explanatory role which determines a richly-textured set of consequences. In the case of Berkeley these consequences are particularly far-reaching, since in effect they come down to the claim that once we see what spiritual substance *is*, we see that it is all there *can* be.

The claim that it is spiritual substance which is revealed to 'inward consciousness' or a special kind of direct introspective awareness of the results of reason and experience, is, however, at the very least in need of explanation. In the contemporary debate over personal identity there remains unresolved the question whether an even more modestly conceived species of empirical introspection reveals to oneself that one is a persisting, separately existing subject of experience, either directly or as a deduction from the contents of introspective states (cf. Parfitt pp223ff). Under the influence of Hume, such consensus as there is leans towards scepticism on this head. A different kind of argument, essentially Kant's, to the transcendental necessity of holding that there is a persisting ego which unifies experiences and makes them that ego's own – an argument which in effect has the aim of showing that the existence of a self is a necessary condition of there being experience at all – more closely fits the conception of substance as having the logical role which Berkeley and before him Descartes, as inheritors of a considerable tradition in this respect, require it to have (cf. Ayers in Vesey pp51ff). Like Descartes and unlike Kant, however, Berkeley takes it that it is the *substantial* self of which we are aware in introspection, and not, as noted, *empirically* aware, but by a species of intuition or reflexion which reveals the substantial self in both its character and its role.

One major difficulty with this is that it is not at the outset clear what it would *be* to attempt an act of non-empirical 'reflexion' in the hope of finding an indivisible, active self distinct from its experiences, memories, and the like. Empirical introspection is less problematic, but at the most what seems to be available on the basis of such introspection is the inconclusive result described by Hume, namely that in particular introspective acts all we have is the awareness of partially detached, partially associated collections or sequences of ideas, at least many of which have a temporally local character. If the mind is something apart from these ideas, explained by an ownership thesis which accounts for such facts as the perspective to which one is clearly always committed in experience, then the mind is, in acts of empirical introspection as such, peculiarly *transparent*, that is, not an object for itself – and therefore whatever conception we form of the mind or self (*however* explained, note, for *these* thoughts about selfhood are consistent with materialist views as well as with mentalist views) has to be a result of inference. Now, this is one of the reasons why Berkeley denies that the mind can be an idea, and why he suggests instead that what inward consciousness gives in the way of knowledge of mind is based on the effects of the mind's activity (cf. P27). Perhaps therefore 'reflexion' is simply an awareness of what is discovered by inference from the felt facts of mental activity. This appears unobjectionable. The fact that, on any view, knowledge of what one is has to be derived from something more than empirical introspection does nothing to suggest that it is unreasonable to suppose of oneself that one is a unitary subject of experience distinct from the particular experiences one enjoys; in line with the spirit but not the letter of Kant's views, some such supposition appears in any case to be inevitable if one is to make any sense of experience and particularly its perspectival character. Nor is it true that nothing follows from such a supposition as to the *nature* of the self or mind. At first blush, it may seem that far from answering any questions on that score, it is precisely what poses them; but in fact, once one has specified the *role* the conception plays, as Berkeley like Kant in effect does, a minimal characterisation of its nature is suggested which is not very dissimilar to the one Berkeley requires.

Berkeley's views on the character of mind have, it is true, a rather stipulative or legislative air. Their legislative character comes out clearly when it is recognised that he is anxious to describe mind in terms of what physical objects – that is, ideas – are *not*. Thus: objects are inert, extended, and the rest; mind is active, unextended, and the rest. Except in one respect it is not clear why a symmetrical opposition *should* subsist between substance and what it supports, unless there is a *logical* reason for it, that is, one explainable in terms of the criteria which have to be satisfied by things for them to fall into one or other of the classes of dependent and substantial being, so that we can recognise which is which. Such logical criteria may indeed be required, but nothing suggests why it should be necessary for them

1. Finite spirit

to be made out in terms of the sharp conceptual polarity Berkeley demands. The excepted respect has to do with causality; here it is crucial to Berkeley's case that ideas should be inert and mind active, since without this Aristotelian equation of causal and substantial priority his overall argument cannot work. But on *this* score Berkeley has a case, for it is hard to find an alternative source for our concept of agency than the one most familiar to ourselves – namely, our own personal capacity, however modest, for initiating and intervening in trains of events. (Familiarity does not always remove mystery; it remains puzzling *exactly* how my arm's rising differs from my raising my arm, although at both the explanatory and subjective levels the appeal to volition, however obscure, seems difficult to avoid. I comment on this below.)

In short, then, Berkeley's claim that we know ourselves to be *minds* as he defines them is more defensible than is generally allowed, for it could be argued that certain facts – for example, the internal unity or coherence of most stretches of experience, its being uniquely perspectival, and its displaying rich connections between current and remembered content – justify postulating a determinate self or subject, which in turn is most readily characterisable in terms of its being at least in part a conscious, thinking, and often active thing (an *agent*). Moreover these facts fit, on something like Kantian lines, what is required to explain why there is experience and why it has, at very least in part, an irreducibly subjective character. It does not follow, from these thoughts alone, that the *basis* of these facts – what it is that realises them and accordingly may be expected ultimately to explain them – has to be accounted for in terms of spiritual substance rather than, say, one or another version of materialism; but Berkeley has given grounds for taking the concept of material substance to be itself incoherent, and if those arguments work or can be made to work, then the case for mind as the fundamental reality is made. (Recent arguments to not dissimilar results may be found in Foster, Robinson, and Sprigge; see bibliography.)

So far, then, one might tentatively accept Berkeley's view. Nevertheless other difficulties remain. One is that the relation between mind and its ideas turns out to be a good deal less clear, given this account, than at the outset it appears to be. Another concerns the issue of time and identity, which Berkeley's theory of mind draws together in a highly problematic way. In the next two sections I deal with each of these problems.

2. The mind-idea relation

At P2 Berkeley states that the mind is 'a thing *entirely distinct* from [ideas], *wherein they exist* or, which is the same thing, *whereby they are perceived*' (my emphases). Three sections later he adds that it is not possible to conceive 'any sensible thing or object *distinct from* the sensation or perception of it', and in the same place asks, and answers, the question 'is it possible to separate, even in thought, my (ideas) from perception ? For my part, I might as easily divide a thing from itself' (P5). Reflection on these assertions suggests that in them Berkeley is committing himself to three principles which are together inconsistent, so that one or more of them requires to be dropped, the problem being that each of them individually plays a part in substantiating other theses in a way that would set these other theses at risk if it had to be abandoned. The three principles on the relation between minds and ideas are these (and I use Turbayne's labels for them, cf. Turbayne in Turbayne pp295ff). There is first the *Distinction Principle*, namely that minds and ideas are entirely distinct from one another (P2, 27, 80, 142). Secondly, there is the *Inherence Principle*, which is that ideas exist only in the mind (P2, 3 etc.). And thirdly there is the *Identity Principle*, which is that ideas are not distinct from perceivings of them (P5, 1D195ff). The second and third are consistent, but the first appears to be contradicted by the third, and its relation to the second at least requires explanation.

Most commentators argue that in view of the conflict between these principles, the one which ought to be dropped, since dropping it does least damage to the overall fabric of Berkeley's theory, is the Distinction Principle. An example is afforded by Pitcher, who argues that the Distinction Principle commits Berkeley to an act-object analysis of perception, whereas the Identity Principle commits him to an adverbial analysis, and since in Pitcher's view the act-object analysis has the consequence that ideas would have to be capable of existing unperceived in order for them to be *distinct* objects of acts of perception, it would be better for Berkeley to abandon the principle that entails it, and instead to commit himself fully to the Identity Principle, with its correlative adverbial analysis (Pitcher pp184ff, esp. p201). Turbayne usefully reports on the other commentators – a formidable array – who reach the same conclusion, if not always for exactly the same reasons (Turbayne ibid pp247-8). Their doing so controverts Berkeley's repeated and emphatic insistence that ideas

2. The mind-idea relation

and minds are entirely different kinds of thing (P2, 27, 89, 142, 3D234), the distinction between them being, as Luce points out, basic to the very plan of P: 'Human knowledge (reduces) to two heads, that of *ideas* and that of *spirits*' (P86 cf. Luce 2 p51). Moreover there is a powerful reason why Berkeley is so insistent about the principle, which is that if it is abandoned while the other two are allowed to stand, the result is that mind turns out just to be its ideas – which is to say that a version of the bundle theory applies. But ideas are inert, mind active; ideas are dependent entities, mind is substantial; if ideas and mind collapse into each other, the essential differences vanish, and with them almost all of what Berkeley wishes to say. The temptations of the bundle theory, as noted in the preceding section, were entertained and then rejected in C, and at 3D233ff, where Hylas charges Philonous' views with the consequence that they make the mind 'a system of floating ideas', Berkeley points out that mind cannot just be a collection of ideas for 'a colour cannot perceive a sound, nor a sound a colour ... therefore I am one individual principle, distinct from colour and sound; and, for the same reason, from all other sensible things and inert ideas' (3D234).

Equally, however, Berkeley is emphatic about the other two principles. Certainly it is impossible to see how the Inherence Principle can be abandoned, since it is simply a version of EP; and as to the Identity Principle, Berkeley's claim at P5 and the upshot of the discussion between Hylas and Philonous at 1D194-7 appears to be a firm commitment to its being inconceivable that a separation can be effected between the perceiving of ideas and those ideas themselves. Accordingly, and contrary to what is held by Pitcher and the other commentators Turbayne mentions, the difficulty appears to be one that must somehow be resolved, if it can be resolved at all, without abandoning any of the principles whose apparent mutual conflict gives rise to it.

An interesting and ingenious solution to the problem is offered by Turbayne (cf. Turbayne ibid. *passim*) who brings to Berkeley's assistance certain theses espoused by Plato and Aristotle. What he says is on the whole plausible, but it does not seem to me necessary to go so far afield in search of a solution. The reason is that the appearance of conflict among the principles disappears once one fully grasps what is intended by each. In particular, the labels 'Inherence' Principle and 'Identity' Principle are wholly misleading, for Berkeley was committed neither to the view that ideas *inhere* in minds as modes or attributes inhere in substance; nor to the view that ideas

170   III. *Esse est Percipere: The Nature of Substance*

are *identical* with perceivings of them, which one would anyway expect as a result both of the tenacity with which Berkeley adheres to the Distinction Principle and its importance to his overall theory. Matters are, rather, as follows.

The 'Inherence' Principle states that ideas exist only in the mind. The formula 'in the mind', familiarly by now, means 'with essential reference to perception', in the sense that the existence of an idea is wholly dependent upon its being perceived by some mind. The formula itself is innocuous. The definite article in it has an indefinite use, and the 'in' does not bespeak a container theory of mind; rather, as Berkeley himself asserts (P2) and all commentators acknowledge, the formula does duty for 'perceived by' or more generally 'dependent on' in the sense given to this phrase at pp127-9 above where Berkeley's use of 'depend' was defended against Bennett's charge of ambiguity. The sense in which ideas exist in the mind is however informatively characterised by *analogy* with certain kinds of containers whose contents have a specific relation to them – we could perhaps exemplify it by adapting Plato's obstetric example from the *Timaeus*, quoted by Turbayne (ibid. p304), which is of the relationship in which an embryo stands to a womb; it exists in it, and indeed is dependent for its existence on being in it, but is nevertheless distinct from it. *Inherence* by contrast is to be explained by such examples as, say, the relation of a wave to the sea, in which there can be no question of the wave being *distinct* from the sea through or over which it passes, but rather is a modification or 'mode' of the sea. This latter model, applied to the mind-idea relation, is what suggests adverbial analyses of perception, in terms of which it is strictly incorrect to say that the mind perceives a green colour patch, but rather that it perceives 'green-colour-patchly'. As noted, this option involves abandoning the Distinction Principle – and therefore conflates mind and ideas after the manner of the bundle theory – and it is the one Pitcher prefers. But the obstetric analogy shows that a clear sense can be attached to the notion of an inseparable dependence of something on some other thing from which nevertheless the first thing is distinct; which is exactly what is required in the case of Berkeley's 'Distinction' and 'Inherence' Principles.

These considerations explain the force of Berkeley's saying at P49 'qualities are in the mind only as they are perceived by it, that is, not by way of *mode* or *attribute*, but only by way of *idea*', and at 3D237 'It is ... evident there can be no substratum of ... qualities but spirit, in which they exist, not by way of mode or property, but as a thing

2. The mind-idea relation 171

perceived in that which perceives it'. In these passages Berkeley is deliberately distancing his own conception of the mind-idea relation from that of the Cartesians, for whom there is 'only so much difference between the soul and its ideas as there is between a piece of wax and the various shapes it can assume' (Descartes *Letters* p288). Berkeley takes the Cartesian view to have the unacceptable consequence that if one has ideas of red or blue, one's mind must therefore be red or blue (cf. P49). Pitcher remarks that this is a weak point, since it is not on the Cartesian view the *redness* which is a mode of consciousness but the *awareness* of red, and that Berkeley could have dismissed this as a resource for explaining what the Cartesian view comes down to only because it turns on a distinction between perceiving an idea and the idea perceived, which Berkeley cannot allow on the grounds that he is committed to the 'Identity' Principle, which rules that distinction out (Pitcher p196). This view of Pitcher's, however, rests on a mistake concerning the 'Identity' Principle which he shares with a number of other commentators, for the principle does not assert a relation of *identity* between 'perceiving an idea' and the 'idea perceived' at all.

What Berkeley meant by the 'Identity' Principle is explained by his theories of conceivability and abstraction (see Chapter One, section 2 above). Attention to what he says at P5 and again at 1D195ff shows that his claim is that ideas cannot be *conceived of as existing apart* from perceptual awareness of them, for the reason that their *esse* is *percipi* – in other words, that the independent existence of objects, in the sense in which this is demanded by absolute realism, is impossible. It is *not* the claim that a particular idea is to be identified with a particular perceiving of it, for the non-identity of states of awareness and their contents is a thesis already well entrenched as the view that, from the finitary viewpoint, ideas, at any rate those that constitute real things, are not dependent for their existence on any particular finite perceiving of them. What it means not to be able to 'conceive apart' any 'sensible thing or object distinct from the sensation or perception of it' (P5) is therefore far from a claim that the idea and the perception of it are numerically the same thing, but rather that an idea is always and essentially an *idea perceived*, and perception is always and essentially the *perception of ideas*. The impossibility of ideas being conceptually detached from perception of them, and vice versa, has the same anti-abstraction status as the impossibility of detaching any one sensible quality from any other sensible qualities and considering it as existing alone. This latter is not an assertion, obviously, of a relation of numerical

III. *Esse est Percipere: The Nature of Substance*

identity between all the sensible qualities, for that would be absurd; but rather it is an assertion of their non-abstractability one from the others, the term 'non-abstractability' not meaning or entailing 'identity', but just what it says. In exactly the same way, Berkeley is claiming that one cannot abstract ideas from perceivings of them – which can alternatively be put as the claim that there is no understanding what an idea *is* which does not essentially involve its being understood as an object of perception, *qua* 'content of state of sensory awareness'.

It will be recalled from Chapter One, section 2 above that Berkeley has small use for the concept of numerical identity, but is much more concerned with the broader category of items so related that they are non-abstractable from one another, that is, which are 'inconceivable apart'. On this view, the point he is making at P5 and 1D194ff is that ideas and perceivings of them are intimately correlative in precisely the non-abstractionist sense. Independently of Berkeley's commitments, it is quite clear that *distinct* items can indeed stand in this kind of relation to one another. Every process-product relation, for example, is of this kind; bread and the baking of it, a picture and the painting of it, are cases in point. A loaf of bread is distinct from the process of baking it, but there cannot be bread conceivable apart from its being or having been baked, nor is the relevant kind of baking conceivable apart from what is baked. From the finitary viewpoint, in Berkeley's theory, the relation which obtains between the sensory modalities and their peculiar objects is not a process-product relation in the case of *real* ideas, although it is so for ideas of imagination and for all God's ideas; but even in the case of finitely perceived real ideas the same internal conceptual relation of non-abstractability holds, with the Distinction Principle asserting that the idea perceived is *distinct from the particular finite mind perceiving it*, while not being, as the 'Identity' and 'Inherence' Principles demand, something that *exists apart from mind* in general. The failure on the part of some commentators to see this results from their attempting to treat Berkeley's views about how ideas are perceived apart from his views about what ideas *are*. Once the connection is made, the Distinction, 'Inherence' and 'Identity' Principles cease appearing to be in conflict among themselves but, instead, are recognisable as jointly determining the mind-idea relationship required by the conjunction of EP and Berkeley's realism.

The natural model for Berkeley's account of perception would therefore seem to be the act-object model, but although this comes a great deal closer than alternatives it does not properly apply, for one

2. The mind-idea relation

term of the relation is specified as an *act* whereas for Berkeley it is not always so. This is because finite minds are passive in perceiving real ideas, which are input from an independent external source. Their passivity is embedded in activity, however, in the sense that to receive an idea involves having, say, to turn one's eye or sniff at a rose (1D196). But although to this extent perception of real ideas involves activity, the content of a particular state of awareness is not produced by an act of will, as in the case of ideas of imagination, but is 'somewhat consequent' to eye-turnings and sniffings (ibid.), and therefore to be distinguished from them (1D197). Rather than an act-object model, therefore, something like a state-content model might in this case come closer to the mark, although the analogies such a model suggests are apt to be misleading – for example, hardware-software, C-fibres-pain – for in such analogies what is suggested is the realisation, in a functionalist sense, of content in a system, where the causal direction, or at least the relations of dependence which obtain between content and system, are different from the simple one-directional causal relationship in which, for Berkeley, passive reception of real ideas consists.

One reason why so many commentators dislike Berkeley's theory of perception, or more strictly his theory about the mind-idea relation since this concerns only part of what would enter into a theory of perception, is that the dominant tradition in thinking about perception has been, in the broad sense, Lockean, which is to say has involved specifying a relation between acts or states of certain kinds of awareness, on the one hand, and public, independently existing items of a quite different kind on the other. In its crudest formulation the problem concerns the question of how material objects affect suitably equipped beings and give rise to mental states in them, however these are ultimately to be explained, and how what mediates or sustains this interaction in some way represents the former to or in the latter. A formulation of one of the difficulties encountered in thinking of the relata and their relation in this way is aptly captured in the implications of Berkeley's 'Likeness Principle'. The broadly Lockean model constitutes a dualism of logical categories, a dualism, that is, of physical events and processes, and consciousness or experience; and as such makes for difficulties so vexed that the chief efforts to resolve them have taken the form of attempting to reduce, as noted earlier, one category to the other. Berkeley rather ingeniously offers a dualism in *one* logical category, mind and ideas, and so appears to have his cake and to eat it. Oddly enough the commentators' objections have been directed at the

174   III. Esse est Percipere: The Nature of Substance

relations in which Berkeley's minds and ideas have to stand, in order for the latter to be mental entities while being independent of (finite) perceivers' awareness of them, rather than to the metaphysical aspect of the theory, namely the ubiquitous, omnitemporal, and causal perceiving of God, which makes this view possible. Given that metaphysical basis, indeed, Berkeley's theory of the mind-idea relationship is defensible. Without it, it is very much harder to defend – for then, in particular, it becomes difficult to sustain the Distinction Principle, a corollary of the view that real ideas are independent of and external to finite perceivers; and without *that* view the overall theory is greatly weakened.

It is worth noting in conclusion that Pitcher's choice for Berkeley of an adverbial as against an act-object analysis of perception exposes two problems in his account of Berkeley. One is that his reason for taking the act-object analysis not to be an option for Berkeley is that it requires the objective relata in perception to be distinct from awareness of them, which Pitcher takes to be blocked by the 'Identity' Principle. Now, Pitcher could only misread the 'Identity' Principle, as he does, by forgetting the connected themes of passivity in perception, the independence of real ideas from the finitary viewpoint, and the argument for God's existence, all which show that the Distinciton Principle is essential and that the 'Identity' Principle is not about *identity*. And secondly, Pitcher seems to think that the adverbial and act-object analyses are the only available options, so that if one does not subscribe to the former, one must subscribe to the latter. For an understanding of Berkeley's position, neither will do.

3. Mind and time

Berkeley's theory of time is 'so odd', according to Tipton, that it constitutes one of the chief respects in which Berkeley's theory affronts common sense (Tipton 1 pp275-6). In Pitcher's view it is 'a total disaster' (Pitcher p209). There is an unconvincing attempt by Furlong to defend the theory (Furlong in Turbayne pp148ff), and an even less convincing effort by Luce to show that it needs no defence because it contains nothing surprising (Luce pp137-9). Luce nevertheless attempts a defence in a later work, but although he there calls attention to two suggestive entries in C which other commentators do not discuss, he does nothing to explain the serious inconsistencies which Berkeley's view on time appear to generate (Luce 3 pp178-81).

3. Mind and time

In his second letter to Johnson Berkeley reports that some of his earliest researches had concerned time (*Works* II p293), and this is confirmed by C, where all but one of the first sixteen entries deal with it. Those C entries on time not cancelled by an obelus show a remarkable degree of consistency in expressing, without difference or disagreement, the same view throughout, which Berkeley continued to hold in P and D (cf. P97-8, 1D190) and in the second letter to Johnson (*Works* II ibid.). The thesis uniformly expressed in all these places has two features. The first is that time is subjectively constituted by the succession of ideas in one's mind (cf. C4, 13, *Works* II p293), and the second is that because one cannot 'abstract the *existence* of a spirit from its *cogitation*', that is, since 'the soul always thinks' (P98), so that nothing counts as time elapsing while one is not thinking, as in sleep or death, it follows that there *is* no time when one is not conscious: 'No broken intervals of Death or Annihilation. Those intervals are nothing. Each person's time being measured to him by his own ideas' (C590). Both these features require explanation.

By the subjectivity of time Berkeley means that 'each man's time is private' (Tipton quoting Johnson p273), that is, that time for me is the succession of ideas in my mind, and time for you is the succession of ideas in your mind. At 1D190, where the discussion is about the relativity of motion, Berkeley has Hylas admit with Philonous the possibility that 'ideas should succeed one another twice as fast in your mind, as they do in mine', and that 'consequently the same body may to another seem to perform its motion over any space in half the time that it doth to you'. This is intended to demonstrate that motion is, because relative, a sensible quality on a par with colour or taste, but it rests on the view tht time is, from the point of view of any given finite mind, subjective to that mind and consists wholly in the succession of ideas it perceives. This captures something true about the phenomenology of time, namely that it appears to pass more quickly when one is enjoying oneself than when one is bored or suffering discomfort. But Berkeley does not connect this level 1 fact about perceived time with an account of objective time; rather, as he tells Johnson, perceived time simply *is* time: 'A succession of ideas I take to *constitute* Time, and not to be only the sensible measure thereof, as Mr Locke and others think' (*Works* II p293, Berkeley's emphasis), which is a direct restatement of C4 and 13, respectively 'Time train of ideas succeeding each other', 'Time a sensation, therefore onely in the mind'. His conception of time's subjectivity to the minds of finite perceivers is reinforced by the fact that in Berkeley's view there is no succession of ideas in God's mind, and hence no time for God, who occupies what is in effect an eternal present, 'the Now', τὸ νυν, of the Platonists. 'By the τὸ νυν I suppose to be implied that all things, past and to come, are actually present to the mind of God, and that there is in him no change, variation, or succession' (ibid.). Accordingly there is no level 3 account of time which will provide a framework for the particular subjective times of the finitary viewpoint, and therefore there is nothing which constitutes an objective or absolute time to which subjective times correspond. This however does not mean for Berkeley that nothing can count as way of indexing private times to one another, that is, that there is not in some sense *public* time, as we shall presently see.

The second feature of time, its gaplessness, follows from Berkeley's view of mind, which as noted above is that it is a willing, thinking thing. Because thought is essential to the mind, there is no question of the mind continuing to exist when it is not thinking. The series of entries C650-2 display the argument: 'Locke seems to be mistaken when he says thought is not essential to the mind (C650). Certainly the mind always & constantly thinks & we know this too In Sleep & trances the mind exists not there is no time no succession of Ideas (C651). To say the mind exists without thinking is a contradiction, nonsense, nothing' (C652). The commitments of these claims are sustained at P98: 'Time therefore being nothing, abstracted from the succession of ideas in our minds, it follows that the duration of any finite spirit must be estimated by the number of ideas or actions succeeding each other in that same spirit or mind. Hence it is a plain consequence that the soul always thinks.'

Before looking at the consequences of these claims for Berkeley's overall theory, it is instructive to note their motivation, which has broadly speaking two sources. One is Berkeley's disagreement with Newton over the nature of space and time, together with certain connections between the Newtonian view and the metaphysical conception of space and time as attributes of God, for example in Spinoza. The other is, once again, furnished by points of agreement and disagreement between Berkeley and Locke.

In his second letter to Berkeley, Johnson appeals to Newton's conception of space and time as *absolute*, something existing apart from and containing particular spaces and temporal sequences, which in Johnson's view suggests that they are best to be explained by their being thought of as properties of God. He quotes Newton in support: '*Deus – durat semper existendo semper et ubique, durationem et*

3. Mind and time 177

spacium, aeternitatem et infinitatem constituit' (quoted at *Works* II pp286-7). One of Berkeley's objections to this is that if space and time are attributes of God then God is spatially extended and temporally conditioned, which derogates from his divinity. Concerning space, for example, Berkeley says 'Hobbes and Spinoza make God extended, Locke also seems to do the same' (C825), and Hobbes and Spinoza are characterised as 'declared enemies of religion' in the preceding entry, where Berkeley's disagreement with them is strongly marked. As his response to Johnson shows, the same applies to God and time, for God is there described as occupying τὸ νυν, intended as a wholly atemporal point transcending distinctions of past and future and such finitary phenomena as change. The key to Berkeley's objections here is that time is an abstract idea (P97, 98): 'Whenever I attempt to frame a simple idea of *time*, abstracted from the succession of ideas in my mind, which flows uniformly, and is participated by all things, I am lost and embrangled in inextricable difficulties' (P98). Space, time and motion are all categorised together as abstract ideas, deployed in the Newtonian philosophy in terms of contrasts between '*absolute* and *relative*, *true* and *apparent*, *mathematical* and *vulgar*' (P110), to which distinctions Berkeley objects for the familiar reasons (P111-16, cf. DeM *passim*), asserting instead that all of space, time and motion are relative. If the Newtonian conception of time is taken seriously, then, in Berkeley's view, we fall foul of Zeno's paradoxes: 'That doctrine lays one under an absolute necessity of thinking, either that he passes away innumerable ages without a thought, or else that he is annihilated every moment of his life: both which seem equally absurd' (P98).

The points of agreement and disagreement between Berkeley and Locke turn on the fact that, like Berkeley, Locke held that the awareness of time is initially based on the subjective succession of ideas in one's mind (cf. *Essay* II. xiv. 12), but that this is insufficient to explain how the need for public time is satisfied. The 'simple idea of duration' once established, a public measure of time is constructed on the basis of the revolutions of sun and moon (ibid 19, cf. 32). This is a matter of convenience which leaves certain difficulties unresolved (ibid. 21ff), but it furnishes us not only with a standard sufficient for practical purposes, but, more, one that is adequate to the requirements of science; and it allows us to formulate our conception of eternity by extrapolation (ibid. 25). The upshot is that from the phenomenology of perceived successions we arrive, in effect by abstraction, at the concept of 'duration, [which] in itself, is to be considered as going on in one constant, equal, uniform course' (ibid.

III. Esse est Percipere: The Nature of Substance

21). Berkeley agrees with the phenomenological starting point; but since Locke's views go beyond a conception of standard or public time which the phenomenology of time might just sustain (in a way discussed in the next paragraphs), and arrives by abstraction at what looks like a doctrine of *absolute* time on the Newtonian model, his agreement with Locke quickly ceases.

Intriguingly, Berkeley does not leave the level 2 question of time unconsidered, but urges instead that there *is* a justified use for temporal concepts in ordinary talk and activity, which, when understood, shows that metaphysical questions about the *nature* of time are misplaced – a strategy both Tipton and Pitcher liken to the one adopted by Wittgenstein on the same head (cf. Tipton 1 pp284-5, Pitcher p211). At P97 Berkeley says: 'Time, place, and motion, taken in particular or concrete, are what everybody knows; but having passed through the hands of a metaphysician they become too abstract and fine, to be apprehended by men of ordinary sense. Bid your servant meet you at such a *time*, in such a *place*, and he shall never stay to deliberate on the meaning of those words: in conceiving that particular time ... he finds not the least difficulty. But if *time* be taken, exclusive of all those particular actions and ideas that diversify the day, merely for the continuation of existence, or duration in abstract, then it will perhaps gravel even a philosopher to comprehend it.' In a footnote to this passage Jessop aptly quotes St. Augustine's '*Quid est tempus? Si nemo me quaerat, scio; si quaerenti explicare velim, nescio*', which serves well to illustrate the point Berkeley is making. The parallel with Wittgenstein arises from remarks in the *Blue and Brown Books* to the effect that trouble arises when we try to provide a definition of the substantive 'time' (cf. ibid. pp6, 27), something Wittgenstein like Berkeley thinks it is simply an error to attempt, on the grounds, surely right, that it is mistaken to think of time as a *thing*, as something besides a certain way of constructing an ordering relative to a selected standard – for example, the apparent motion of the sun or the more sophisticated regularities ascribed to phenomena at the subatomic level in nature. Neither of these ways of giving a standard are merely arbitrary; they have at least a pragmatic justification, a suitability or propriety with respect to experience which is such that it is all too natural to think that these are in fact measurements *of* something. What is left, when one has resisted the temptation to think in these terms, is a conception of time as wholly conventional, an artefact, which suits because it is designed to suit ordinary experience. When different scales of things are at issue, say, at supra-experiential or sub-experiential levels of description invented

3. Mind and time   179

to explain natural phenomena, different standards of measurement have to be employed – light-years, for example – but there is no clear sense in which, from the phenomenological viewpoint, astrophysical time, say, can usefully be thought of as a large aggregate of conventional times – consider the astronaut for whom much 'less' time passes as he travels in space than for those left behind.

The concept of conventional time, considered as an ordering relative to selected standards, is enough to explain public time, for public time's being *public* does not entail that it is *objective*, that is, independent of any chosen means of constituting it. To this extent what Berkeley says at P97 presents no problem. It even disposes of those various objections commentators advance (cf. Pitcher's example of making an appointment at the dentist p211) on the grounds that Berkeley has to be presupposing time in saying that it passes more slowly for one person than for another. It may also therefore provide materials for rebutting the charge, laid by Tipton and Pitcher, that Berkeley's view of time is 'solipsistic' (Tipton 1 p278, Pitcher p208). The existence of a public measure enables one to make comparisons as to how fast or slow it seems to one that time has passed (as the common idiom has it), as against how it seems to someone else; it is perfectly intelligible both that there should be subjective variations in the perception of time passing and a conventionally instituted and hence non-objective public time which gives these intersubjective comparisons content.

The real difficulty here is that the idea of *succession* which underwrites both ways of talking is itself a temporal concept. Berkeley in fact takes not succession but 'diversity' to be the primitive concept at stake (C647), but diversity quickly turns out in the case of time to be succession (compare Berkeley's talk of the orderings which give rise to ideas of motion and extension at C406). The solitary man, on this view, might be expected to frame an idea of time as the result of noticing that his ideas of touch, taste, and smell cannot, like those of sight and hearing, come together in clusters, but always do so singly, and so notices that they are, as it would now clumsily but appropriately be put, stepwise arrayed (cf. 647 again). It is however hard to see how a conception of time results from, rather than underwrites, what it is to recognise the array as a successive ordering – at this fundamental level of explanation all that it seems possible to say is that it is deeply puzzling to know what could *count* as the required basis for temporal concepts which does not in its formulation presuppose those concepts for its very intelligibility. Berkeley indeed may be claiming no more than this; his saying at

III. Esse est Percipere: The Nature of Substance

C647 'diversity ... gives us the Idea of Time. or is Time it self' suggests that the concept of *time*, phenomenologically manifested as the diversity or succession of ideas, just *is* the primitive conception itself – but as such licenses no more than what it can be used to do at level 2 (make dental appointments, meet one's servant) given the appropriate circumstances. In this respect Berkeley's view has similarities to Kant's conception of time as a form of sensibility – in a sense, a primitive – which grounds the possibility of experience itself.

Pitcher's objections to Berkeley's view turn wholly on the unavailability of a concept of *objective* time in Berkeley's system, which Pitcher takes to be, as noted, 'disastrous'. These considerations show however that there is provision for *public* time in Berkeley, which is enough for level 2 purposes. What Berkeley denies is that there can be an answer to the question 'what *is* time?' at the metaphysical level, and with that denial one is inclined to sympathise.

The deeper difficulties in Berkeley's account lie elsewhere, with the second feature, namely with the *gaplessness* of time, and with the atemporality of God. The first difficulty relates to Berkeley's view of the mind and commits him to an at least unusual account of personal identity; the second relates to everything he has to say about the creation, continuity and reality.

In his second letter Johnson questions Berkeley's view that the soul always thinks, on the grounds that it makes the soul's existence intermittant, which apart from being an unintelligible conception in its own right introduces the difficulty that while we observe someone else asleep we have on this view to think of him as nonexistent as it were from *his* point of view, although manifestly otherwise from our own point of view (*Works* II pp288-9). Berkeley's reply is a simple reassertion of his doctrine, to which he rather unsatisfactorily adds 'But in these matters every man is to think for himself, and speak as he finds. One of my earliest enquiries was about Time, which led me into several paradoxes that I do not think fit or necessary to publish...we are confounded and perplexed about time' (ibid. p293). The suggestion is that the perplexities arise when time is considered abstractly, so that there is, literally, no more to be said than that it is subjectively constituted, and that we know what we mean in ordinary talk of it provided we do not ask what it is. But this appears to leave Johnson's point about intermittancy untouched; for Johnson is understandably concerned to argue that whatever the soul is, it must continue to be even if it is not for the time being thinking or conscious, and that this should provide grounds for thinking

3. Mind and time 181

univocally about someone's existence as well from his point of view as from that of a third party. He says: 'The existence of John asleep by me, without so much as a dream is not an abstract idea ... I think it is as easy to conceive of him as continuing to exist without thinking as without seeing' (ibid. p289).

Now, if attention is focussed strictly on the phenomenology of time, it seems to be true that there are no gaps – the experience of waking from sleep or an anaesthetic on what appears to be the instant of falling into unconsciousness is familiar enough, and one's discovery that the night has passed, or that the operation is over before it appears to have begun, can come as a surprise. But to say that the cessation of consciousness results in the mind's non-existence, as Berkeley has it at C651, goes far beyond the fact of there merely *seeming* to be no gaps (C590). It is indeed hard to credit Berkeley with this unacceptable view, and Luce makes an heroic effort to avoid doing so by arguing that Berkeley has ruled out intermittancy by the time he reached C791 with the comment there that 'While I exist or have any Idea I am eternally, constantly willing, my acquiescing in the present State is willing', which Luce takes to mean that the mind indulges in 'unconscious willing' (Luce 3 p180). Luce's ground for this claim is that Berkeley sometimes talks of *faculties*, which we possess even when we do not exercise them, as with the faculty of sight (ibid.); which in his view entitles Berkeley to think of willing as a faculty (Luce cites C614a, 777) and therefore of the mind as the 'continuously active ... seat of personal identity' (Luce ibid pp180-1). But this is unsatisfactory for the two reasons that, first, in P98 Berkeley unequivocally asserts that the soul *always* thinks – it is its *esse* to do so – which entails that it does not exist when it does not think, and secondly that Berkeley nowhere allows that there is unconscious thought or perception. Dispositions or currently unexercised capacities or faculties (like vision when one's eyes are shut), which he does allow, are not thoughts or perceptions; accordingly Luce's appeal to them to provide for personal identity is unconvincing as a reading of or remedy for Berkeley.

Berkeley, however, is committed to the immortality of finite spirits (cf. P141), and this together with his view about its nature show that what one is conscious of being is a *persisting* self, which follows from the fact that spirit is substance and consequently is what supports – sustains, upholds, which are temporal functions – what is dependent upon it. The claim at C651 – which is the only one suggesting intermittancy of the soul's existence – has accordingly to be overruled in the light of the published doctrine, that the soul is substantial, that is, *always* thinks (P98) and hence that there just *are no gaps*, which is what Berkeley claims at C590. As noted, this is indeed true from the phenomenological point of view; the 'gaps' one finds to have intermitted one's own conscious existence are always inferences from the fact that adjustments have often to be made between subjective and public time. But here indeed is a way of resolving Johnson's problem about the somnolent John. John asleep – as it might be snoring, twitching, muttering – is a succession of ideas for Johnson but not for John; neither of them experiences gaps from his own point of view, although time 'goes' very much faster for John (perhaps instantly) than for Johnson. It is in fact the limiting case of subjectively perceived differences – and once again it does not block the fact that there can be public time, the availability of which permits Johnson to tell John that he has been long asleep, and John to be surprised by that fact. John's being unconscious or unthinking is never a datum for John; it is a third-person attribution, which on inspection comes down to John's being from *Johnson's* point of view unresponsive, say, or oblivious to what Johnson perceives going on around them. Berkeley could, and perhaps should, have claimed that un – or sub – consciousness are abstract ideas arrived at on the basis of just such third-party observations.

It is incredible that time should pass for Johnson, observing John, but not for John, only if one is wedded to the thought that there is or has to be *objective* (not just public) time. But this is ruled out in Berkeley's view by the fact that there is no time at the metaphysical level, for God is atemporal. Now, if this is itself intelligible, it in fact makes the claim that there is time passing for Johnson but not for John a reasonable one. All the facts are present to God; it is 'now' true that Johnson from his point of view spends a long time stooping fondly over the sleeping John and that from John's point of view the ideas in which being bidden to rest consist are immediately succeeded by ideas of being told that he has slept for hours. Indeed it is only intelligible to suppose that one's own existence is gapless in the required way if at the metaphysical level there *is no time*; the kind of account which could explain this might look similar to an Absolute Idealist one in which the appearance of temporality is explained away in the telling of a fuller story about the character of what ultimately exists; or in terms of something like Bohm's by no means dissimilar model of the universe as an holistically conceived 'implicate order', constructed to explain among other things the apparent fact that at the quantum level there is superluminal transference of information between space-like extended systems (cf. Bohm *passim*). What such theories at least purport to offer is the prospect of making sense of time (and perhaps not that alone) as relative to a sharply constrained finitary viewpoint, and as figuring in a more inclusive description of what is the case *only* in that sense.

Berkeley does not undertake an account of this kind, and I do not propose to supply the lack here. Nevertheless the role he ascribes to God suggests that this is the direction an account, perhaps to be given in a Part II or III of P, might have gone. It also therefore shows what a resolution of difficulties about continuity and the creation might have to look like, as indeed Berkeley suggests they do (3D250ff), namely that they are to be understood as relative to the finitary viewpoint alone, and that from God's point of view their temporal character is comprehended in τὸ νυν. The 'paradoxes' to which Berkeley refers in his letter to Johnson, together with his reluctance to treat question of time in more detail, might have arisen from the conflict between Scripture – Genesis allocates six days to the creation, and talks of a thousand years as an evening gone in the sight of God – and the metaphysical conception of God which emerges from – or rather, is demanded by – Berkeley's theory. An attraction of the gaplessness view for Berkeley seems to have been its solution of problems about resurrection (P95), for on this view anyone's death, in any epoch, is immediately followed by the resurrection of *all* souls; but this neat solution to a doctrinal puzzle comes at the cost of controverting the manifestly temporal, indeed *historical*, character of the biblical divinity. If there is a reason for the extreme brevity of the treatment Berkeley gives to this important question, then, it probably lies here, for the foregoing suggests that what little he says is by no means as hopeless as the commentators have it, providing – as with so much of Berkeley's theory – that at the metaphysical level there is a suitably equipped divinity playing the role Berkeley accords to it. To this most important of all questions for Berkeley's theory I now turn.

4. *Infinite spirit*

Berkeley's arguments, as the body of the foregoing discussions shows, turn crucially on the claim that there is a God having a certain character and performing a central metaphysical task or set of tasks. One tradition among commentators has been to view Berkeley's appeal to the metaphysically explanatory role of God as an *ad hoc* manouevre designed to shore up an otherwise implausible theory, but this is a radically mistaken assessment, to which both of

184   III. Esse est Percipere: The Nature of Substance

Berkeley's editors, among others, have furnished correctives (cf. Jessop in Steinkraus p98, Luce 2 p68), with reminders that among his express aims is the project of defeating atheism and demonstrating the pervasive immanence of a deity in the world (see Chapter One, section 1 above). The apologetical task is explicit in *Alciphron* (cf. Aiv. 14), but is also unequivocally present in P and D where it emerges from the there more important metaphysical uses God has. It is present also in V, which Berkeley claims likewise 'affords to thinking men a new and unanswerable proof of the existence and immediate operation of God' (and similarly DeM). In tandem with these avowals is the evidence of the overall argument itself, which I have been concerned to show is tightly-knit and highly consistent, and moreover largely defensible if considerations about God, as their crucial metaphysical centrepiece, can themselves be sustained. Correlatively it has more than once been suggested that if the metaphysical centrepiece cannot be sustained – if Berkeley does not show that he is entitled to this foundation – then the theory as a whole is threatened, for there is no question of a version of phenomenalism remaining once God has been subtracted from the sum. If Berkeley is not justified in having it that there is a suitably propertied God, then either his overall theory collapses or an alternative account must be given at the metaphysical level which will in effect serve as his conception of God was intended to serve – which makes heavy demands of the required alternative.

As with finite spirit, what Berkeley has to say about God in P, D and the notebooks is surprisingly little. The two chief reasons for this are, once again, that he intended to dilate on the topic in a subsequent part of P, and that anyway he could trade to some extent upon there being a standard conception of God which he could expect his readers to share. A reservation on this second head is that Berkeley's method of appearing to adopt certain conceptions held by his readers, only to show later that they require revision or have more or different content, as is the case with Berkeley's treatment of tangibilia in V and P, raises questions about what a Part II of P might have had to say – for it is clear from the time issue in particular that Berkeley's natural theology sits a little awkwardly with revelation, which may indeed have been very high on the list of reasons why a Part II never appeared (Berkeley was scrupulous on the matter of giving theological offence, cf. C713, 715, 720).

Nevertheless Berkeley does give characterisations of God. At C845 he says he has a definition of God which is 'much clearer than that of Descartes and Spinoza', but he does not state it there; rather, he

4. Infinite spirit

gives sketches in several places, and deals with particular features of God in others. At C838 God is described as 'unextended incorporeal Spirit which is omniscient, omnipresent etc'; at P146 he is 'spirituality, omnipresence, providence, omniscience, infinite power and goodness'. These are orthodox and familiar descriptions. Interestingly, Berkeley offers a *demonstration* of God's attributes as specified at P146, on the basis of the 'constant regularity, order, and concatenation of natural things, the surprising magnificence, beauty, and perfection of the larger, and the exquisite contrivance of the smaller parts of creation, together with the exact harmony and correspondence of the whole', all which shows that God, if it is granted that he created these things and both sustains and governs them, as Berkeley has it, must be 'infinitely wise, good, and perfect', for only such an agent could, in Berkeley's view, be responsible for such a creation (cf. also 2D215). This is rather unconvincing, however, for it may be supposed that a description of the natural realm which proceeded in other terms – say, of the suffering, violence, hardship, indifference or apparent natural injustice in it, together with such features of consciousness as greed, cruelty, and hatred – might, granting the view that a God created and sustains it, issue in a contrasting view of what that God is like. Berkeley offers the briefest of explanations regarding natural evil (P151), and has not much more to say about moral evil (3D256ff and *Works* II p281). At P151 he claims that 'monsters, untimely births, fruits blasted in the blossom, rains falling in desert places, miseries incident to human life' are 'absolutely necessary [for nature to work] by the most simple and general rules, and after a steady and consistent manner', so that even natural evil 'argues the *wisdom* and *goodness* of God'. Hylas, on the second head, complains that if God is the cause of all things then he is ultimately responsible for 'murder, sacrilege, adultery, and the like heinous sins' (3D236), and Johnson does likewise (*Works* II p273). Berkeley's reply is that finite spirits have powers of will which, although limited, place what they do under their own direction (3D237, cf. *Works* II p281), and that this is the source of moral evil; and that in any case if finite agency is ignored, even on the materialist hypothesis moral evil would have ultimately to be attributed to God since matter, on that view, is in some sense God's instrument (ibid.). These comments represent familiar manouevres, usually supplemented by religious apologists with claims, in the case of moral evil, about the necessity of freedom for finite spirits, so that they can of their own choice take or not take God's ordained way and thereby merit the appropriate rewards or punishments. The notebooks show that Berkeley was concerned to argue for freedom, and the moral philosophy there promised for later Parts of P would presumably have developed this aspect of the matter. The fact that there is a problem of this kind at all, however, shows that the attempt to specify the character of God on the basis of what the world is like is at least rather fraught, for without a *good* argument to show that it is the outcome of a loving and benevolent plan that there should be grief, agony, horror, hunger, drudgery, and all the various wretchednesses to which the greater part of mankind, now as has always been the case, is subject, it is simply incredible to suppose that there could be such a plan or planner. In the absence of the required kind or argument, however, what is made implausible is not the conception of a deity competent to perform the metaphysical role assigned to it by Berkeley, but the conception of the personal, interested God of the Judaeo-Christian tradition. For the purposes of Berkeley's argument, it is strictly speaking neither here nor there whether the requisite deity is the God of that tradition, for what is alone required is a God more austerely conceived as the causal originator and sustainer of the universe. If this latter *metaphysical* God is available to Berkeley, his theory has its foundation; accordingly it is the intelligibility of God thus conceived which is at stake in the present discussion. Berkeley of course *wished* to identify the metaphysical with the personal and interested God, but his doing so is neither necessary for his theory nor justified. It is not necessary, for as just noted Berkeley's theory requires only a universal causal spirit; and it is not justified, for the following reasons.

Berkeley's argument for the existence of God, which is the main topic here and to which I shortly turn, is specifically an argument, as just shown, for the universal, causal, metaphysical God. He does however recognise that more has to be said to make it possible to identify this metaphysical God with the traditional God, and this is why he gives additional arguments, at P146 and elsewhere, to show that *apart* from the proof of the metaphysical God's existence, we can know something more of God than just that he causally, that is volitionally, perceives the world. That additional argument is in part the one reported from P146 above, about the evidence of nature, and in part one developed from his claims about how we have knowledge of other finite minds. On this latter head the claim is that 'we do not see a man, if by *man* is meant that which lives, moves, perceives, and thinks as we do: but only such a certain collection of ideas, as directs us to think there is a distinct principle of thought and motion like unto ourselves, accompanying and represented by it. And

4. Infinite spirit

after the same manner we see God ... every thing we see, hear, feel or any wise perceive by sense, being a sign or effect of the Power of God; as is our perceptions of those motions, which are produced by men' (P148). Berkeley concludes from these thoughts that although we do not have an idea but rather a notion of God, for the same reason as we have no idea but rather a notion of finite spirit (cf. P140, 3D232), nevertheless we know God 'certainly and immediately' (P147) as a result of being surrounded by and constantly presented with God's handiwork, viz. nature: 'we need only open our eyes to see the sovereign lord of all things with a more full and clear view, than we do any of our fellow creatures' (P148). It is to be noticed that Berkeley's other-minds argument is rather slender, based on the view that from certain ideas of form and behaviour can be inferred the presence of a 'distinct principle of thought', a view vulnerable to attack on the grounds of a sceptical appeal to automata and the like, and the general weakness of the argument from analogy (but cf. Strawson's attack on other-minds scepticism in *Individuals* and Sprigge on the argument from analogy, Sprigge pp2ff). Nevertheless his claim is that God is *more clearly* detected in nature than other finite minds, and that his characteristics of wisdom, benevolence and power are therefore inferrable from nature's order and harmony. These considerations are supplemented by the view that since God is an infinite *spirit* and we are finite *spirits*, there is a similarity between the nature of God and man, the difference being one of degree rather than kind – God is all the good things, in an infinite degree, that man is, and none of the bad; hence we know his nature by extrapolation from the case of finite spirit: 'my soul might be said to furnish me with ... [a] likeness of God, though indeed extremely inadequate. For all the notion I have of God, is obtained by reflecting on my own soul, heightening its powers, and removing its imperfections' (3D231-2, cf. C640-1). In this Berkeley is echoing Locke, who substituted this way of accounting for our knowledge of God's nature – 'we enlarge every one of these ideas of our own nature and capacities with the idea of infinity' – for the Cartesian claim that our knowledge of God's nature is *innate* (cf. *Essay* II. xxiii. 33-5).

Now, these arguments are wholly unconvincing. The most that could be detected in nature if Berkeley's argument for the metaphysical God is granted in advance is, circularly with respect to that argument, that nature *qua* ideas must subsist in spirit, for even if it is not permissable to suppose that one can always infer the nature of a cause from its effects, it is the case that what the world is like radically underdetermines what its supposed cause could be like, given that different lists of the world's features will, as noted above, give quite different results as to the character of what *makes* the world like that, some of which would be disagreeable to one of Berkeley's religious persuasion. Moreover, it is not even clear that we know enough about the universe to begin inferring much about the nature of its cause from it, as Berkeley's own comments about the 'surplusage immeasurable' suggest (2D211); all that appears available on this tack is at most the sparsely characterised metaphysical God, and not the traditional one. Again, the thought that God is the infinitely extrapolated sum of the good things about finite spirits seems to involve a species of abstraction not, it is true, proscribed by Berkeley, but no more defensible than the kinds he does proscribe; for it is not clear what it is to conceive infinite attributes of the kind in question – or indeed, on Berkeley's principles, infinities of any sort (cf. what Berkeley says about infinity in the mathematical case P120-3). In general there seems to be no reason why any of the human capacities should be exemplified in 'enlarged' form, still less in infinite form, anywhere or by anything; nor any reason why, if there is a God, he has to be even remotely like finite spirits. At 2D215 Berkeley says 'the Author [of my ideas] is wise, powerful, and good, beyond comprehension', which is an interesting incoherence. The weakness of the thought that if there is a God then he is like the good among us, only more so, is well illustrated by reflecting on what, as Xenophon pointed out, the God of the horses would be like if horses had one – an infinite horse, presumably. In short, Berkeley's desire to identify the metaphysical God required by his system with the traditional God required by his religious commitments is simply a result of those religious commitments, and is otherwise unsubstantiated.

The gap between the metaphysical and the traditional God, in short, is a very large one; Berkeley might have argued that it is bridged by faith, which would at least be no weaker a reason than the reasons he gives, and which would also at least be in accordance with the Pauline teachings on the subject.

All this is however independent, except in one crucial sense, of the main question in hand, which is whether Berkeley's conception of the metaphysical God will bear scrutiny. The excepted sense is that some of the considerations Berkeley advances to show that the independent external source of our ideas is both an *infinite* and a *single* spirit are closely allied to those he advances to show that this infinite single spirit is the traditional God. In assessing the second stage of his argument for God's existence, set out below, this double-duty to

4. Infinite spirit

which Berkeley submits his appeals to teleology has to be borne in mind: so far as the argument for God's existence goes, they apply strictly to the 'single and infinite' issue and *not* – for the foregoing reasons – to the issue of whether the metaphysical God (henceforth just 'God') is to be identified with the God of traditional Judaeo-Christian theology.

There are three related issues at stake in Berkeley's discussion of God: one concerns causality, the second concerns the sense in which certain of our ideas are independent of our will, and the third – trading upon what Berkeley has to say on these two heads – is the proof Berkeley gives of God's existence. I consider each in turn.

In the contemporary debate on causality Hume is taken to be the primary source for the view that causal efficiency in nature is not an empirical datum, that is, that the natural events we standardly interpret as causally connected have nothing discernible in them, over and above their bare occurrence, which is the power or efficacy by means of which the first putatively *produces* the second or *makes* the second happen. One billiard ball rolls towards and collides with a second, which thereupon moves away; but there is no third observable feature in this state of affairs, over and above what the first and second billiard balls do, Hume points out, which is the causal connection between them. In fact, however, the view that causal power or efficacy is not discoverable in nature was a commonplace among Berkeley's predecessors, for whom natural causes, consisting in the motions and impacts of bodies, were called 'secondary' precisely because matter itself was thought to be inert, and originally set in motion – and for many, Boyle among them, both set and sustained in motion – by God (cf. Boyle pp181ff and Jessop's note *Works* II p63). In Locke's view it is appropriate to locate causal power in bodies, not as a result of our detecting it there but as a result of inference, projection or analogy from our own felt capacity as agents, which affords us the 'clearest ideas of active power' we have (II. xxi. 4). *Essay* II xxi is indeed a chapter Berkeley studied with particular care, a fact to which the notebooks testify, for in the course of his discussion of causality Locke characterises will and understanding as powers, and discusses the concepts of freedom, necessity, and the determination of the will by 'uneasiness', which discussions supply a number of the notebook's recurring themes. The thesis Berkeley agrees with in Locke is that experience shows *spirit* to be the locus of agency, that is, that will or volition is the only causal power discoverable by empirical observation, and that no other such power is discoverable in the same way elsewhere; what he disagrees

III. *Esse est Percipere: The Nature of Substance*

with is Locke's claim that a projection or analogy from the agency of spirit to that of bodies is justifiable (cf. P28). At level 2, in Berkeley's view, we think and talk in terms of natural causes, which it is expedient and hence, for ordinary purposes, unexceptionable to do (P51); but since ideas are discrete and inert, and cannot therefore causally influence one another (P25), it is strictly speaking the case that the ideas of which we think in causal terms are in fact related not as cause to effect but as sign to thing signified (see above and P65), and that genuine causality is reserved to, and indeed is properly to be identified with, the agency of spirit alone (P105). This is a familiar Berkeleyan theme, and the passages just cited are representative of a large number more.

Essential to Berkeley's analysis are the two claims that causal efficacy is not detectable in natural events and that spirit alone is active. On the first head it is important to distinguish between the question of what facts are available to empirical inspection of sequences of events in nature, with the object of establishing whether causal efficacy is an experiential datum and if so in what cases, and the question of what goes into the application of a concept of causality once one has elected to formulate explanations of natural phenomena in terms of it. The enterprises are related in the sense that answers to the first may, if they turn out to be of an appropriate kind, settle what answers can be given to the second; but the second can proceed independently of the first on the *assumption* that some sequences of events are cases of consequence if the utility of doing so outweighs (as it does) the alternative of taking it that all sequences are mere conjunctions, which has a low if not a null explanatory value. Berkeley's doctrine of signs, however, adequately caters for the demand that an account should be given of the explanatory value of bringing some sequences of events under causal concepts, and in doing so leaves unaffected the matter of what should count as a proper specification of the conditions which have to be satisfied for a given event to count in a given case, or in given classes of cases, as a cause and hence as licensing a certain distinctive kind of explanation of its effect (cf. P30-2). From the practical viewpoint, where predictions and plans are at stake, it therefore makes no difference whether sequences of events are subsumed under concepts of causes or of signs, which is why answers to the second question may be given without its being necessary to wait upon particular answers to the first. From the *theoretical* standpoint, however, there is a large difference, since the upshot of an enquiry into why certain sequences display the uniformity they do may be expected to yield information

4. Infinite spirit 191

about the intrinsic nature of things, or at any rate to place informative constraints on what content can be given to theoretical models of them. In this sense the first question turns out to be the more important one, which explains why so much attention has been paid to it (cf. e.g. the discussions collected in Sosa). Berkeley's concern is to show that on this more fundamental matter the phenomenology of experience rules out a level 3 account in which causal efficacy is ascribed to things, but by contrast entails that such efficacy is the property of *spirit* for the reason that spirit alone is active, and moreover that the level 1 facts substantiate that claim and no other.

The first claim, that no causal power is directly observable in trains of events, seems quite simply to be true. Independently of a *theory* in terms of which events are to be interpreted as causally connected whenever the theory demands, awareness of bare successions of them does not display as a component the efficacy or power by means of which certain of them produce or make happen their successors, but rather appear to awareness to be related in no more than simply the way Hume describes. One feels a resistance to accepting that this is so because it is fundamental to our scheme of things that we should read-in our causal concepts, or at any rate our habits of interpretation and expectation, the better to make sense of what we encounter in experience; and accordingly it is hard to detach the phenomenology of the case from its standard interpretation. But even if we take these facts fully into account also, there are still no grounds for asserting that our interpretation constitutes more than a doctrine of signs, or that a doctrine of signs is inadequate to account for the habits of thought and expectation at issue. In the absence of directly observable causal power in events, the argument that the source of causal concepts has to be sought elsewhere is compelling – whether in a model or theory with particular explanatory ambitions, or among the Kantian categories, or in the kind of agency ascribed to free-willed conscious agents.

If it is true that activity and agency are capacities one feels oneself able to exercise, then the second component of Berkeley's claim has at least some initial plausibility. There is a familiar debate on this score, initiated by Hume's claim that we have no introspective awareness of power when we will something to happen (cf. *Treatise* Appendix). In more recent discussions, following Wittgenstein and Ryle, the issue debated concerns quite specific cases where the concept of will might be supposed to apply, for example, in marking what difference there is between my raising my arm and my arm's rising; one claim being that, as a matter of experiential fact, the first case is *not* distinguished from the second by the presence in it of what is observable to oneself as a volition or act of will (cf. Tipton 1 pp305ff). What is shown by considerations like these is that the notion of *will* or, still more, *the will*, is at least deeply puzzling, and much talk of it – often proceeding in terms of a discredited faculty psychology – appears to be simply implausible. But it is not clear that it is an empty notion, for there are cases where it is especially appropriate to invoke it, and such cases may be those where, for the agent, willing is something he is *actually* aware of doing. For example, the exhausted marathon runner completing his last few miles, or the visitor to Tibet of whom courtesy demands that he consume a raw mouse at a welcoming feast, may both be conscious of acting with a particular deliberation or effort – *forcing* themselves to act, as we say – and accordingly talk of will in these cases seems to have a quite readily graspable content. These are special examples, it is true, but if it can be shown that there are circumstances where, if willing is something conscious beings are able to do, we should expect to find it appropriate to say both that they are doing it and are aware of doing it, then it strengthens a reply we might give to the Humean claim that volition is not a datum of experience: first, by pointing out that it *is* so, in the cases – for example the ones just cited – which throw it into sharp relief; and that whenever it is not so, it is because we are used to it, or do not have to make a special effort in standard cases, and so on. Consider the ordinary enough proceeding of someone's writing a letter, manipulating a pen in order to form complex marks on a piece of paper. This is a deliberate activity of a highly specialised and elaborate kind which fulfils intentions of equal or even more refined elaboration; and the whole lies under conscious direction, with words being weighed, ideas expressed, and aims achieved – all which is inexplicable if it does not come, at least in part, under the description of volitional activity. The ordinary cases, however, do not have to run very deep to come under the description of willed or purposive activity, nor to count as cases in which the agent can recognise himself as willing what he does, for any example of someone's initiating or intervening in trains of events, however modest (making a pot of tea, perhaps), admits of the same account. In fact the distinction between events which are the outcome of volitional activity and mere occurrences is a sharp one, one that is applied whenever someone, say, reads in a newspaper that forensic scientists are seeking to determine whether or not a fire was the result of arson, or can recognise whether the cup he broke was

4. Infinite spirit

broken deliberately or accidentally (leaving aside the psychoanalytic view that 'accident' is simply *unconscious* volition, which takes matters to the other extreme). What these thoughts suggest is that it is far from incoherent to claim that we do more than *conceive* of ourselves as agents, but in fact *perceive* ourselves to be so. This claim may be further strengthened by noting that our perception of ourselves as agents in part turns on the very frustrations and limitations we discover in our capacity to initiate, or introduce changes in, courses of events, so that the range of our power as agents, as well as the nature of that power, turns out to be something in the end quite familiar. Nor does it derogate from the proper conception of ourselves as *agents* that our powers can on the whole only be exercised through the medium of instruments, which for some reason Tipton seems to think is the case (Tipton pp309-10), for this consideration only adds to the sense in which recognising limitations on our powers of agency constitutes a reason for taking it that we have them.

These brief remarks are not intended as a contribution to the debate on conceptions of the will and agency except as giving an outline defence of the view, adopted by Berkeley from his predecessors, that we recognise ourselves as agents – as active beings capable of starting and intervening in trains of events – in a way which contrasts with our failure to detect agency in trains of natural events themselves. So far, these premisses of Berkeley's argument for God's existence – for that is what they are – appear to be sustainable. The rest of the argument for God's existence is however another matter.

Descartes' argument for the existence of matter (sketched on p3 above), includes among its premisses the claim that some of our ideas are caused by something other than our own wills, that is, have a source independent of and external to us. The same thought plays an important role in Locke's account, at *Essay* IV. xl. 5, of why we are justified in taking it that there is an independent and external source of at least part of our experience: 'sometimes I cannot avoid ... having ... ideas produced in my mind ... if I turn my eyes at noon towards the sun, I cannot avoid the ideas which the light of the sun then produces in me ... therefore it must needs be some external cause, and the brisk acting of some objects without me, whose efficacy I cannot resist, that produces these ideas in my mind, whether I will or no'. And in a way which foreshadows both Berkeley and Hume, Locke goes on to remark that the ideas attributable to an independent, external source are distinguished from those of memory or imagination by their intrinsic character –

he means, although he does not list, such features as their vividness, steadiness and the like, which for Hume are the marks of 'impressions' as against 'ideas' as these terms are employed in his mental catalogue, and which for Berkeley are the marks of the real.

The independence considerations which persuaded Descartes and Locke are accepted also by Berkeley: 'whatever power I have over my own thoughts, I find the ideas actually perceived by sense have not a like dependance on my will. When in broad daylight I open my eyes, it is not in my power to choose whether I shall see or no, or to determine what particular objects shall present themselves to my view; and so likewise as to the hearing and other senses, the ideas imprinted on them are not creatures of my will' (P29). It is a short step from there to the conclusion that the ideas not produced by oneself are produced by some other spirit, for the reason that the only causal agency there can be is spirit (P26).

This is not quite all there is to the argument Berkeley gives, however, because the conclusion that there is another spiritual cause of the ideas I do not myself cause does not amount to the more substantial result Berkeley requires, which is that the other spiritual cause in question is a *single infinite* spirit which by itself causes *all* the ideas not caused by me. This more ambitious argument is given a variety of statements in the places it occurs, the main ones being C499, 838, P25-30, 90-3, 2D212-15 and 3D239-40. An inspection of these sources will show that the argument is rather more complex than one might expect, for Berkeley himself recognises that the conclusion he wishes to derive, namely that there is a single infinite spirit, apt for identification with the God of theology and the cause of all those ideas not caused by finite spirits, does not follow from the considerations about causality and independence *alone*.

It is appropriate to distinguish as (a) weaker and (b) stronger the two conclusions that, respectively, (a) ideas not causally dependent on my will are causally dependent on some other spiritual agency or agencies (the plural case is not ruled out for the weaker result) and (b) a single infinite spirit, apt for identification as a God, is the cause of all ideas not caused by finite spirits. The notebook entries C499 and 838 are early sketches of the argument to the stronger conclusion, and their occurrence marks the fact that, as we would expect, it is the stronger conclusion Berkeley is from the outset ambitious to derive. At C499 he says 'Those things that happen from without we are not the Cause of therefore there is some other cause of them i.e. there is a being that wills these perceptions in us', and at C838 'Every sensation of mine which happens in consequence of the

4. Infinite spirit

general, known laws of nature & from without i.e. independent of my Will demonstrates the Being of a God. i.e. of an unextended incorporeal spirit which is omniscient, omnipotent etc.' The second statement on the face of it goes further than the first, in that at C499 it is indefinitely 'a being' rather than, as in C838, God, although the being of C499 is clearly intended to be God. The second of these entries hints at how Berkeley proposes to get from the weaker conclusion to the stronger, which is by way of a claim to the effect that the scope and character of the ideas which constitute nature in all its breadth, intricacy, and order bespeaks a single infinite cause – and this is the line he takes in both P and D. But in P he first sets out to establish the weaker conclusion, and then, by supplementation, fleshes it out into the stronger conclusion.

In P the argument's major statement has all the appearance of being carefully handled. At P25 ideas *qua* things are shown to be causally inert, and therefore dependent on spirit (P26). Some of my ideas, those of the 'fancy', are causally dependent on me (P28) but matters are quite otherwise with my ideas of sense, and 'there is therefore some other will or spirit that produces them' (P29). This is the weaker conclusion. From the *character* of these independently caused ideas Berkeley then proceeds to infer the nature of their source: the ideas are 'more strong, lively, and distinct than those of the imagination; they have likewise a steadiness, order, and coherence, and are not excited at random, as those which are the effects of human wills often are, but in a regular train or series, the admirable connection whereof sufficiently testifies the wisdom of its Author' (P30); and to drive the point home Berkeley repeats the claim by saying that the 'constant uniform working' of the laws of nature 'evidently displays the goodness and wisdom of that governing spirit whose will constitutes' them (P32). In P30 and 32, therefore, the stronger conclusion is arrived at, with its purported justification.

Leaving aside the causal-dependence considerations, which are the basic premises for the argument either to the weaker or stronger conclusions, it is readily obvious that the argument from P29 onwards is highly and repeatedly question-begging. One immediately questionable feature of the weaker conclusion itself, as it is stated in P29, is that it is 'some other will or spirit' which is picked out as the cause of my self-uncaused ideas, whereas there is as yet no justification for thinking that *one* other spirit is responsible for the whole order of nature. The suggestion that this is so prepares the way for accepting, *via* the strength, order, and 'admirable connection' considerations, together with the question-begging reference to the limited capacities of 'human wills', that there exists the wise and benevolent 'Author' or 'governing spirit' of the stronger conclusion. In effect Berkeley has supplemented the causal dependence argument with the argument from design, or 'teleological' argument, which he accepts as valid: 'Divines and philosophers have proved beyond all controversy, from the beauty and usefulness of the several parts of the creation, that it was the workmanship of God' (2D212). But the argument from design, familiarly, does not work, and *a fortiori* does not license a derivation of the stronger conclusion from the weaker. One reason why it does not work is as follows.

It is true that from the finitary viewpoint nature appears ordered and regular, but it is not clear what is inferrable from this. For one thing, these characteristics are inductive ones to which no necessity attaches – nothing can guarantee, on the basis of what counts at any given point as having so far been the case in experience, that the regularities will continue to hold. For another, nature's *appearing* ordered and regular to finite awareness is consistent with its not being so, given that the point of view from which these are the appearances is *finite*, and that therefore the facts may be otherwise than it lies within the capacities of finite minds to grasp. This is a problem for any form of realism, whether absolute or, as in Berkeley's case, qualified. Again, it is observably the case that perceivers – whatever explanation may be given of this contingent but well-entrenched fact – have a propensity to *confer* order on what they perceive, as experiments with Rorsasch blots demonstrate; so that even if nature were in some degree irregular or anomalous, perception of it might consistently impose regularity and lawlikeness upon it. This consideration recalls Kant, for one example, who located the structure of experience in its interpretation rather than in the objective component of what gives rise to it. These and allied considerations show, in short, that the character of the world as it appears in experience underdetermines what can be inferred from it as to the source of that experience, which is to say that the world's appearing thus and so does not *uniquely* select an explanation of why it does so. Now, in Berkeley's case the explanatory options are, it is true, narrowed by the causal dependence argument, showing that nature as a system of ideas must have its source and subsistence in mind. But this – the weaker conclusion – does not entail that it is a *single* mind, nor does it rule out the possibility that if more minds than one are responsible, they may be finite minds. The notion of a world by committee appears to be conceptually far less appealing than

4. Infinite spirit

that of a single infinite spirit's being causally responsible for everything, which may be conceptually unappealing enough in its own right; but if this latter notion is at least intelligible, which it is, so must the former be.

The argument at P25-32, then, granting the causal dependence premises, yields only the weaker conclusion, and the weaker conclusion itself does not tell us more than that the source of experience is mind. Moreover the fact that the weaker conclusion leaves so much open makes for problems – *perhaps* not insuperable ones – when it is considered what, at the metaphysical level, is demanded of it in the way among other things of securing reality and continuity, cashing the counterfactuals required for an account of perceivability, and providing the atemporal framework which explains the competing subjective phenomenologies of temporal experience; in short, when it is considered what is demanded of it in the way of an *inclusive* explanation of why the levels 1 and 2 facts are as they are.

Certain of Berkeley's other statements of the argument are given varying formulations in their effort to secure the stronger conclusion. At P90-3 the weaker conclusion is derived in the same way as before, with Berkeley recapitulating his chief claims briefly; 'things perceived by sense ... have no existence distinct from being perceived, and can not therefore exist in any other substance than those unextended, indivisible substances, or spirits, which act, and think, and perceive them' (P91); 'The things perceived by sense may be termed *external*, with regard to their origin, in that they are not generated from within, by the mind itself, but imprinted by a spirit distinct from that which perceives them' (P90). The arguments which establish these two claims yield the weaker conclusion. Berkeley then obliquely sets out to turn it into the stronger conclusion at P92-3 by arguing that materialism has been a friend to atheism (P92) because it permits an undervaluation of spirit, making it 'divisible and subject to corruption as the body', and what is wrong with this is that it 'excludes all freedom, intelligence, and design from the formation of things, and instead thereof makes a self-existent, stupid, unthinking substance the root and origin of all beings', which denies 'a providence or inspection of a superior mind over the affairs of the world, attributing the whole series of events either to blind chance or fatal necessity, arising from the impulse of one body on another' (P93). In these remarks a great deal is being condensed into a short space, for Berkeley is simultaneously attacking the impiety of materialism – which in his view entails the

III. *Esse est Percipere: The Nature of Substance*

falsity of orthodox religious belief concerning the creation and divine government of the world, and subverts morality by denying freedom – and also, which is a quite different thing, he is attacking its intelligibility on the grounds that a 'stupid, unthinking substance' (this phraseology echoes Boyle's; cf. Boyle pp182-91) cannot account for the 'intelligence and design' in the universe, but substitutes for it the conception, wholly unacceptable in Berkeley's view given what he takes to be the order, regularity, and harmony in the universe, of 'blind chance or fatal necessity'. It is this question of intelligibility which has most bite, rather than the impiety claims – Newton and Boyle were, after all, both pious and materialist, without inconsistency – but a little reflection shows that what in effect the intelligibility issue comes down to is, once again, the teleological argument, which will not do. Moreover there is no reason to think that the weaker conclusion is inconsistent with chance and necessity, particularly if the mind (or minds) which constitutes the substance of the universe is impersonal, or whose volitions are blind or unselective in some way, none of which possibilities is ruled out by the bare conception of mental substance as such.

The most familiar, and perhaps definitive, statement of Berkeley's argument occurs as 2D212-15, or rather, it occurs there twice, in slightly different formulations – once at 2D212-13, and again, more briefly, at 2D214-15 after an interlude in which Philonous distances the argument from Malebranche's claim that all things are seen in God. Berkeley presents it with considerable forensic skill, beginning with a statement of the strong conclusion and setting out the premises dialetically in reverse order, so that the argument's statement at 2D212-13 *ends* with the weaker conclusion. At 2D214 the teleological considerations are briefly added. The argument as given here is indistinguishable in content from its P25-32 version, and therefore does not require reporting nor, since the criticisms are the same, separate discussion.

Only one refinement is added to the argument by Berkeley, and that occurs later, at 3D239-40. It is an important one, for it touches on the points made at the end of the last but one paragraph. After briefly setting out the argument Philonous says 'From the effects (i.e. ideas of sense) I see produced, I conclude there are actions; and because actions, volitions; and because there are volitions, there must be a will. Again, the things I perceive must have an existence, they or their archetypes, out of my mind; but being ideas, neither they nor their archetypes can exist otherwise than in an understanding: there is therefore an understanding. But will and

4. Infinite spirit 199

understanding constitute in the strictest sense a mind or spirit. The powerful cause therefore of my ideas is in strict propriety of speech a *spirit*' (3D240). This makes a better case than the teleological considerations for the claim that the spiritual source of ideas of sense is mind like our own minds, and it particularly well fits Berkeley's definition of mind as a 'concrete of Will and understanding' (cf. C713). Nevertheless these considerations are problematic, at least as regards what is implied by the claim that the mental source of ideas has *understanding* as well as will. The will aspect of the claim might, given Berkeley's commitments on activity and causality, be allowed to stand; but the rest needs discussion, for the following reason.

Perception for Berkeley is, familiarly by now, a catholic category, with sensory awareness, imagination, memory and conception all included in it. It can be either active or passive, which is shown by the fact that God's perceiving is wholly the former, and that finite spirits' perceiving is a mixture of both. There is no un- or subconscious mental activity in Berkeley's scheme, so all perceiving is conscious, and the implication (it is not explicitly stated anywhere) is that whatever a spirit perceives it is aware of doing so – 'understanding' implies a self-reflexive awareness of being conscious *of* something, and hence of being conscious, and hence of existing (cf. the preceding section). But although these are considerations which might be argued in respect of the kind of mental life we are familiar with – our own – there does not seem to be any obvious reason why the same should hold for the mental source of our ideas of sense, which for all we can guess might be an oblivious will or congeries of them, unaware of itself or themselves as producing those ideas. Now, Berkeley has two responses to this observation. One is to reassert the claim that if the mental source of things is *blind* will, then it is as unthinking and 'stupid' as matter, and the same risks to freedom and intelligence in the order of things results. This is essentially the teleological claim supplemented by a hint as to what is required for the foundations of morality, and remains no more than a psychologically rather than a logically compelling reason, on Berkeley's terms, for taking the mental substance of the universe to be aware of itself as having purposes. The other is to insist on the claim that perception must be conscious. This is greatly more plausible, for at least the reason that it is simply not open to claim of some S that S perceives x but is unconscious or unaware. But this does not yield the result Berkeley requires, however, because where S is, say, an animal like a rabbit or a shrew, it is difficult to attach sense to the thought that in perceiving x S *is aware of itself as doing so*,

III. Esse est Percipere: The Nature of Substance

although it is surely right that S is *aware*, since it is aware of x. Thus S's perceiving x logically involves S's being conscious or aware, but does not logically involve self-awareness. Nor, more to the point, does it necessarily involve deliberation, intention, or even comprehension. Berkeley takes it that perceiving qua conscious awareness *is* understanding in the sense of comprehending, that is, of having an intelligent grasp of what is perceived; but there is no reason to accept this. Were there such a reason, a combination of understanding and will would make it legitimate to pursue the claim that ideas of sense are *purposively* rather than just *volitionally* produced, but this, which is what Berkeley requires, has not been substantiated.

A resource here might appear to be the considerations advanced in Chapter Two, Section 4 above, where it was argued against Pitcher that God must *perceive* ideas as finite minds do, except that he does not perceive them sensorily. It is clear that Berkeley takes the provision about understanding to satisfy the requirement that in order to allow for realism from the finitary viewpoint, God must have present to himself all the facts about what actual and possible finite experience is like. But this thought is one employed to make sense chiefly of perceivability, and it cannot without circularity be in turn argued that facts about perceivability show that there is understanding of the required sort in the external source of our ideas of sense. In any case, as just remarked, that mental source may will ideas and even have a grasp of what it is to experience them finitely, without its being the main or even any part of its purpose, if it has one, that those ideas should be perceived in that way by finite minds. One of Berkeley's assumptions is that the external mental source of sensory ideas is *interested* in what it does respecting its effect on finite minds, an assumption in part sustained by the claim that the world and what happens in it is teleological in character. But that assumption is no better supported than that claim, and such marginal plausibility as it has (especially in the light of difficulties about evil and order) stems from no better a source that fideistic commitments on the topic of 'revelation'. In short, if the external mental source of sensory ideas required by Berkeley's theory perceives as well as wills those ideas, it remains that nothing follows either as to that source's being single and infinite, or to its being purposive and interested – still less, as Berkeley's theory demands, all of these things at once.

In sum, Berkeley's argument does not establish more than, at best, the weak conclusion, and the weak conclusion does not tell us whether the mental substance of the universe consists in one or more minds; nor whether that mind is, or those minds are, infinite; nor

4. Infinite spirit

whether the universe is caused purposively or otherwise. The conclusion of P1-6, namely 'there is not any other substance than *spirit*, or that which perceives' (P7), is not in itself, although it is intended ultimately to lead to, a claim to the effect that there is an egregious single consciousness apt for characterisation as God; adding the causal dependence considerations, in order to yield the weak conclusion that no finite mind causes its own sensory ideas, takes the case no further in that respect – although it is in other respects an extremely important step onwards from the claim at P7, for it blocks subjective idealism or solipsism and provides instead the major part of the grounds for Berkeley's theses about reality, continuity, and perceivability, and hence for a finitary realism consistent with the thesis about the ultimate nature of reality asserted at P7.

These last remarks indicate the directions in which one would have to look for an answer to the question that immediately and naturally arises here, as a consequence of seeing that Berkeley cannot on his principles arrive at the metaphysical God (still less, the traditional one) required by his theory. The question is: what remains of Berkeley's views in the light of his failure to establish that there is such a God? Efforts at a reply are, in a sense, afforded by the history of attempts, since Berkeley, to address the question of how to make out a level 3 theory, opposed to realism of the absolute and materialist kind, which can account for the levels 1 and 2 facts constituting the appearances any theory must save. In these general terms, what such a theory is aimed at explaining is the conception of the world's being in some fundamental sense *mental*, if the theory is idealist in character; or, at very least, of the world's being incapable of any description or explanation which does not make essential reference to the fact that it is *experienced*, with all that this implies for an analysis of what – if reference to experience of it is essentially ineliminable from an account of it – it can be. One reason for putting the pont in this mildly tendentious way is that 'immaterialism' and 'Berkeleyanism' are not coreferential terms; certainly all *idealist* approaches to metaphysics are immaterialist, but only that doctrine which is both immaterialist *and* whose level 3 theory turns on there being a purposive, interested, ubiquitously perceiving and causal God is Berkeleyan or like it. What these thoughts suggest is that Berkeley's failure to substantiate his metaphysical commitments in the relevant respects does not affect the connected theses in which EP and the denial of materialism consist, quite as directly and fatally, at any rate, as it affects his ambitions to defend against 'irreligion', and correlatively to provide the foundations for a morality associated with a God specified by the theological tradition to which Berkeley subscribed; for, most certainly, these last two aspects of his aims cannot be realised on the basis of his arguments, and accordingly must be dismissed. The major question therefore is: to what extent does EP and its untimately associated theses, including the rejection of materialism, survive given the weak conclusion alone as providing the metaphysical underpinning for them?

This is not a question which can be answered here, for although in my view it can indeed be shown that something like these theses are substantially defensible, and that the foregoing discussions have gone part of the way to demonstrating why – in some cases, a long way – nevertheless a more particular defence, and one which does not turn on Berkeley's theism, demands a full-length discussion to itself – and in particular it demands an approach somewhat different from, although related to, the one adopted by Berkeley; namely, an approach which starts from considerations about the nature of thought and talk, construed as having sense conferred upon them, when they are senseful, by evidentialist constraints not unlike those sketched in Chapter One, Section 3 above. (*One* way of doing this has famously been tried, by means of earlier versions of verificationism. What is being suggested here is the successor anti-realist conception of the relations in which experience stands to sense, along the lines mentioned; together with the results this has for metaphysics.) In Berkeley's case, his level 3 commitments make for sweeping and, were they successful, powerful economies in explaining the levels 1 and 2 facts, as Chapter Two above shows. The unavailability of that way with the issues makes the task of explaining those facts a much more complicated one, and it is this which prevents my attempting to give a detailed non-theistic reworking of Berkeley's central arguments here.

Nevertheless there is a point which merits comment in this connection, not least because it brings together the two matters of, first, the particular value of some of Berkeley's contributions to this debate, and secondly, the general value of exploring views such as or cognate to some of those he urges. This is the claim that the thesis Berkeley opposes – realism of the absolute and materialist kind – is, as he has it, unintelligible in principle. If there is reason to think this claim true, and if the reasons are, or are related to, those Berkeley gives for taking it to be true, then even if one does not think that Berkeley has succeeded in articulating the uniquely correct

4. Infinite spirit

alternative, it at least shows that he is in some way or in some respects on the right lines – and that would constitute, again at least, a partial vindication of what he sets out to do. In the next chapter, as a brief conclusion to these discussions, I set out reasons for thinking that Berkeley's views are entitled to such a vindication.

CHAPTER FOUR
Concluding Comments: Metaphysics and Realism

The project here, as set out at the end of the last chapter, is to show briefly and by way of conclusion that the task Berkeley set himself is at least on the right lines, even if his central metaphysical commitments are unavailable, and even if some of the detail of his views has therefore to be reworked in ways which do not depend upon them. To make out this claim I shall give reasons for taking it that the notion of an objective or absolute conception of the world, of the kind which Berkeley attacks because it involves a denial of EP and sets an independently existing material realm over against experience, is incoherent – and largely for reasons Berkeley gives. My task is made greatly easier by the fact that there is available a clear statement of a position which not only accepts and defends part of what Berkeley argues for, but nevertheless insists that the absolute realist view he attacks is sustainable. That statement is afforded by McGinn (McGinn chs. 6 and 7). The interest of McGinn's case is that the respects in which he fails to make it out are just on the whole those in which Berkeley's way with the issues is vindicated, and accordingly McGinn's view is tailormade for the task in hand.

McGinn's concern is to argue that perceptual experience contains irreducibly subjective elements which reflect the constitution of mind. He summarises his claims in the final chapter of his study as follows: 'I suggested that perception of secondary qualities and indexical thought counted as subjective modes of representation, in contrast to the objective character of primary quality perception and non-indexical thought. These two exemplifications of the subjective view were claimed to exhibit certain quasi-logical laws governing the internal relations between the ways in which the world is subjectively represented: these laws have their source in the constitution of the subject. I also said that the identification of these subjective features enjoys a certain kind of incorrigibility, and that they operate as a sort of grid laid over the world by the representing

Concluding comments: metaphysics and realism 205

mind. I then urged that these two kinds of subjective representation are ineliminable from any mind capable of perceptual and direct awareness of the world' (McGinn p157). A major part of McGinn's basis for these claims is his acceptance of what he variously calls 'the Berkeley point' or 'the inseparability thesis', namely that all perceptual experience of the world is experience both of primary and secondary qualities, and that there can be no such experience from which the secondary qualities are eliminated (ibid. pp80ff). The Berkeley point is the one made at P10, where Berkeley says 'I see evidently that it is not in my power to frame an idea of a body extended and moving, but I must withal give it some colour or other sensible quality which is acknowledged to exist in the mind. In short, extension, figure, and motion, abstracted from all other qualities, are inconceivable'. This McGinn accepts, and indeed says that is seems to him 'a necessary truth about perception' (ibid. p82); but because Berkeley took it to follow therefore that no sense can be made of 'an absolute and objective conception of things' (ibid. p80), McGinn restricts the inseparability thesis to *perception* alone, and claims that it does not apply to *conception*: 'My own view is that we should reject this inseparability thesis for conception but accept it for perception. To take this divided attitude is to commit oneself to a radical discontinuity between perception and conception: we cannot any longer regard conception as a kind of "faint copy" of perception; it is not explicable in terms of an imagined perceptual point of view, indeed it is not strictly a point of *view* at all' (ibid. pp80-1). Tying conception to perception in the way Berkeley does is one of the chief grounds substantiating idealism; detaching them, as McGinn says we should, leaves room for the claim that despite the ineliminably subjective character of experience, an 'absolute and objective' conception of the world remains available, which is precisely McGinn's motive for effecting that detachment. He says: 'Resisting idealism ... requires us to reject the inseparability thesis as applied to conception – on pain of making the mind-independent world literally unconceivable. (I suppose this could be seen as a partial vindication of Berkeley's argument for idealism ... in respect of its validity, not of its soundness)' (ibid. p115n9). And here therefore is the crux of the issue: *can* conception and perception be held apart in the way McGinn requires? The claim that they *should* be held apart to allow for an absolute and objective conception of the world demands that we specify a means of arriving at and applying concepts independently of experience, but which is such nevertheless that those concepts can be objectively descriptive of the world. How is this to be done?

Concluding Comments: Metaphysics and Realism

McGinn does not in fact give an answer to this question. He dismisses two ways in which an objective conception could be arrived at on the basis of sense experience but which prescinds from its subjective elements, one of which is a form of experience in which only primary qualities are perceived, and the other of which involves abstraction, specifically the abstraction of primary qualities presented in experience from the secondary qualities which accompany them (ibid. pp124-5). He rejects the first on the grounds, already noted, that secondary qualities are *necessary* features of experience and therefore that no experience can be of primary qualities alone; and he rejects the second for Berkeley's anti-abstractionist reasons (ibid. p125). He then says 'I do not have an alternative theory of how the concepts of the [absolute and objective conception] are come by', and suggest that a solution is to be looked for in the direction of 'the rationalists' idea of "pure intellection" – a means of mental representation which is non-sensory in character' (ibid. p111), adding 'it seems to me that a more rationalist epistemology is indicated ... the manufacture of concepts must be thought of as the province of more intellective faculties of mind' (ibid. p126). Beyond these two gestures no account is offered of how the concepts required by an absolute and objective description of the world are to be acquired. What he says more about, instead, is the motive for wishing to have such a conception: 'we *require* a conception of the genuinely explanatorily traits of an object ... we *wish to have* a unique and explanatory set of description of objects [sic] ... we *wish* a conception of physical objects as existentially independent of us – a conception that permits us to say "if no perceivers had existed, physical objects still would (or could) have" ' (p115, my italics). And we have these requirements and wishes, McGinn says, because 'to abandon the objective view is to abandon the idea of an observor-independent reality' (ibid. p127). In short, without a way of arriving at an objective conception we are left with something very like Berkeley's EP, and this McGinn is eager to avoid. He therefore commits himself to the view that 'Concepts suited to the objective conception are thus neither derived from, nor restricted in their application to, the contents of experience' (ibid.).

This commitment is, from Berkeley's and indeed from any point of view, unintelligible. In Chapter One, Section 3 above reasons were advanced for holding that conception *must* be empirically grounded, because concepts apply to the world over which experience ranges, and therefore both their source and the conditions of their applicability are and have to be constrained by the experiential facts if any content is to attach to the thought that they *do* apply to the world. This states an essential condition on concept formation and use which distances what can count as ways of thinking and talking sensefully *about the world* from what I earlier called 'Imagining' or fancying. In the light of these thoughts it is extraordinarily difficult to know how McGinn's alternative is to be given any content. It is not only that the concepts which putatively provide for *an objective description of the world* have, on McGinn's view, somehow to be derived from a source explicitly divorced from the ways we come to know anything about the world, or the ways we deal with the world, or ways the world affects us, which makes it hard if not impossible to see how conceptualisation and experience are to be detached from one another, but – more – it is manifestly obvious that the concepts we in fact have are anything *but* detached from experience, given their vulnerability to experiential pressure; their revisability in the face of experience shows how sensitive they are to it, a point surely familiar by now as a result, among other things, of the well-understood defeasibility of scientific theory. That marks the dependence in one direction; in the other, it is equally well understood that having experience *just is* to apply concepts – that is, to interpret, order, and organise input on the basis of a scheme of concepts whose possession by us is specific to that task. Considerations about the dependence in the first direction might alone be thought sufficient to show why rationalism so notoriously fails as a means of arriving at an understanding of the world; the deliverances of reason unconstrained by empirical tests are indistinguishable from consistent fairy tales, and nothing beyond the merely internal and hence vacuous standard of coherence for any theory of the world thus arrived at can give reason for taking it to be true – especially since on this view it is not truth to or of the world as it is encountered in experience which can be at issue, for then the concepts deployed would be attached to empirical conditions of derivation and applicability, and this is what McGinn is ruling out.

Nor, further, does it help matters to invoke the notion of an 'intellective faculty' which gives us, independently of experience, a grasp of the nature of the world as it is in itself; for what such a faculty could be, and how it grasps the nature of the world in itself, is utterly imperspicuous. Rationalists tempted to view that knowledge of what the world is intrinsically like – of what it is like in its true and ultimate nature, which many of them take to be *obscured* by the way it appears – rely less, on the whole, on a claim to the effect that we have a capacity for directly intuiting the metaphysical facts, than on one or other of two broad but not exclusive alternatives. One is the claim that excogitation from self-evident first principles will lead to a grasp of what the universe must be like. The other is innatism. (These options are not exclusive because one could, on this family of views, deduce – and hence in effect remember – what one innately but immemoriously knows, as Plato has it). No doubt these options for a rationalist epistemology are not exhaustive, but it would take ingenuity to devise another which is not as frankly incredible as these three. What McGinn can mean, therefore, by 'pure intellection ... a means of representation which is non-sensory in character' (ibid. p111), given that it is the *world* which is thus to be intellected and represented independently of experience of it, is wholly obscure. One can, indeed, make sense of pure intellection in the case of mathematical structures, say; there are many mathematical cases – one thinks of certain problems in topology, for example – in which what is being described does not readily, if at all, admit of being grasped other than through its purely formal properties. But the manipulation of formal structures is either not a representation of anything (consider what 'representation' *means*), or, if it describes what can be encountered in experience – knots, twisted strips of paper, Euler's bridges, say, for simpler examples of the topological case – there is a single and straightforward sense in which experience gives content to its *being* a description of the world, and which is *ipso facto* not available in any other way. That again illustrates the central difficulty with what McGinn gestures at: if the absolute and objective conception of the world is 'radically discontinuous' (cf. ibid. p112) with respect to experience of the world, what could substantiate the claim that the absolute and objective conception is a *description* of the world? This repeats, from a different direction, the fairy-tale charge.

Some of what McGinn says about the ineliminability of subjectivity from experience has an avowedly Kantian flavour (cf. ibid. pp106, 157). He does not however subscribe to Kant's chief claim, which is that *objectivity* is the result of the application of *a priori* concepts to experience, since this would, in the end, amount to denying that we can give content to the idea of an absolute and objective conception of the world in the full-blooded sense McGinn intends, for the two reasons that in Kant's view those concepts are, first, constitutional aspects of the forms of sensibility (space and time) and the understanding (the categories), and hence are subjective in McGinn's sense, because they are supplied by the mind; and secondly, are 'empty' unless they lie under empirical conditions of applicability. On neither count therefore can Kant's view of what makes for objectivity satisfy McGinn, which is doubtless why he eschews it without comment. But in the absence of this resource for explaining how we can possess *a priori* the concepts which make for an objective conception of the world, and given the inadequacies of rationalist views, it is not clear where else one should look for a way of giving substance to McGinn's proposal.

What these remarks strongly suggest is that there is no viable way of allowing Berkeley's inseparability thesis for perception while rejecting it for conception, and that consequently there is no way of attaching sense to McGinn's talk of 'an absolute and objective conception of the world' if the ineliminably and therefore necessarily subjective character of experience is admitted. But it does not follow from this that there is no account to be given of the world which does not accommodate and explain both the experiential facts and the theoretical needs they prompt, consistently with its being true that any conception of the world must be of the world as it is experienced; Berkeley indeed gives such an account, and one which retains its potential despite the unacceptability of a major part of its metaphysical underpinning. There is on this tack no urgency of the kind McGinn expresses in saying that we 'wish to have' or 'require' an objective conception – indeed, Berkeley would point out that in view of the sceptical problems such a conception generates, we rather do *not* wish to have it. More to the point, we do not need it, contrary to what McGinn suggests, even if we could make sense of it (for a succinct reminder of why we do not need it, see Bayle's argument, which Berkeley develops, as reported on p7 above). McGinn's suggestions in opposition to views, like Berkeley's, which tie an account of the world to questions of the conditions under which it is experienced, reflect an antecedent commitment to absolute realism, which is assumed and not defended in his discussion and which alone explains how it can even begin to seem plausible that there should be a description of the world which omits all reference to experience of it. But this, as the foregoing remarks show and as Berkeley was expressly concerned to argue, is an unintelligible view, and accordingly whatever account is given of the world must take under consideration some, at least, of what Berkeley argues in his attempt to work out the implications of recognising the unintelligibility of that view and the reasons why it is so.

There is much to be said on this topic, not least on the questions of objectivity, the nature of the deliverances of science, and the fundamental issue of what metaphysical consequences flow from

IV. Concluding Comments: Metaphysics and Realism

rejecting absolute realism, none of which can be gone into further here. (I deal with these and allied concerns in a forthcoming study.) The above brief remarks show, however, that what Berkeley had to say on *these* issues, discussed in Chapter One and Chapter Two sections 1-3 above, is much more pertinent to the question of getting them right than has generally been allowed, *because* of the extent to which he is right on the topic of the present chapter. And being in a position to say that in some important respects Berkeley's views are more right than has generally been allowed was, at the outset, specified as one of the aims for this investigation of Berkeley's thought.

Bibliography

The following is a list of works *cited* in the foregoing. It is not a bibliography of works consulted; an excellent one is given by Turbayne in Turbayne 1982 (see below).

Allison, H.E.	'Locke's theory of personal identity' in Tipton (2)
Armstrong, D.M.	'Introduction' *Berkeley's Philosophical Writings* London 1965
Aschenbrenner, K.	et. al. (edd.) *George Berkeley* Cambridge 1957
Ayer, A.J.	(1) 'Has Austin refuted the sense-datum theory?' *Synthèse* 1967
	(2) *The Central Questions of Philosophy* London 1973
Ayers, M.R.	(1) 'Substance, reality, and the great, dead philosophers' *American Philosophical Quarterly* 7 (1970)
	(3) 'The ideas of power and substance in Locke's philosophy' in Tipton (2)
	(4) 'Berkeley's immaterialism and Kant's transcendental idealism' in Vesey
Bennett, J.	*Locke, Berkeley, Hume: Central Themes* Oxford 1971
Bohm, D.	*Wholeness and the Implicate Order* London 1976
Boyle, R.	*Selected Philosophical Papers of Robert Boyle*, Stewart M.A. (ed.), Manchester 1979
Bracken, H.	*The Early Reception of Berkeley's Immaterialism 1710-33* The Hague 1965
Cummins, P.	'Hylas' parity argument' in Turbayne
Davidson, D.	*Actions and Events* Oxford (corrected ed.) 1982

Dicker, G.	'The concept of immediate perception in Berkeley's Immaterialism' in Turbayne
Dummett, M.A.E.	(1) 'What is a theory of meaning II' in Evans, G. and McDowell, J., *Truth and Meaning* Oxford 1976 (2) *Truth and Other Enigmas* London 1979 (3) *The Interpretation of Frege's Philosophy* London 1981
Foster, J.A.	*The Case for Idealism* London 1982
Frege, G.	*Philosophical Writings* tr. ed. Geach, P. and Black, M. 3rd ed. London 1980
Furlong, E.J.	(1) 'Berkeley and the tree in the quad' in Martin and Armstrong (2) 'On being "embrangled" by time' in Turbayne
Garber, D.	'Locke, Berkeley, and corpuscular scepticism', in Turbayne
Grayling, A.C.	(1) *An Introduction to Philosophical Logic* Hassocks 1982 (2) *The Refutation of Scepticism* London 1985
Kirwan, C.A.	*Logic and Argument* London 1978
Luce, A.A.	(1) *Berkeley and Malebranche* Oxford 1934 (2) *Berkeley's Immaterialism* London 1945 (3) *The Dialectic of Immaterialism* London 1963 (4) 'Another look at Berkeley's notebooks' *Hermathena* 1971
Martin, C.B. and Armstrong, D.M. (ed.)	*Locke and Berkeley* London 1968
Mackie, J.L.	*Problems from Locke* Oxford 1976
McCracken, C.J.	*Malebranche and British Philosophy* Oxford 1983
McGinn, C.	*The Subjective View* Oxford 1983
Mirarchi, L.A.	'Dynamical implications of Berkeley's doctrine of heterogeneity' in Turbayne
Moore, G.E.	'Is existence a predicate?' *Proceedings of the Aristotelian Society* supp. vol. 1936
Parfitt, D.	*Reasons and Persons* Oxford 1984

Bibliography

Park, D.	*Complementary Notions* The Hague 1972
Peacocke, C.	*Sense and Content* Oxford 1983
Pears, D.F.	'Is existence a predicate?' in Strawson (3)
Pitcher, G.	*Berkeley* London 1977
Popkin, R.H.	(1) 'Berkeley and Pyrrhonism' *Review of Metaphysics* 1953, reprinted in Burnyeat, M. *The Sceptical Tradition* California 1983. References are to this latter
	(2) 'The new realism of Bishop Berkeley' in Aschenbrenner
Quine, W.V.O.	(1) *From a Logical Point of View* Cambridge Mass. (2nd ed.) 1961
	(2) *Word and Object* Cambridge Mass. 1960
Robinson, H.	*Matter and Sense* Cambridge 1982
Russell, B.	*The Problems of Philosophy* 1912 (Oxford paperback reprint 1967 to which references are made)
Searle, R.	*Minds, Brains, and Science* London 1984
Sommers, F.	*The Logic of Natural Language* Oxford 1982
Sosa, E. (ed.)	*Causation and Conditionals* Oxford 1975
Sprigge, T.L.S.	*The Vindication of Absolute Idealism* Edinburgh 1983
Steinkraus, W.E. (ed.)	*New Studies in Berkeley's Philosophy* New York 1966
Strawson, P.F.	(1) *Introduction to Logical Theory* Oxford 1952
	(2) *The Bounds of Sense* London 1966
	(3) (ed.) *Philosophical Logic* Oxford 1967
	(4) 'Is exists a predicate?' in *Freedom and Resentment* London 1974
Stroud, B.	'Berkeley versus Locke on primary qualities' *Philosophy* 55 (1980)
Tipton, I.C.	(1) *Berkeley: The Philosophy of Immaterialism* London 1974
	(2) (ed.) *Locke on Human Understanding* Oxford 1977
Turbayne, C. (ed).	*Berkeley: Critical and Interpretative Essays* Manchester 1982
Vesey, G. (ed.)	*Idealism Past and Present* Cambridge 1982

Warnock, G.J.	(1) *Berkeley* London 1953 (enlarged ed. 1982) (2) (ed.) *The Philosophy of Perception* Oxford 1967
White, A.R.	*Modal Thinking* Oxford 1975
Wilson, M.D.	'Did Berkeley completely misunderstand the basis of the primary-secondary quality distinction in Locke?' in Turbayne
Wittgenstein, L.	*The Blue and Brown Books* Oxford (2nd ed.) 1964

Index

abstract ideas, 11-12, 15, 18, 27, 29-31, 35, 40, 41, 42-4, 57, 74, 75, 89, 91, 92, 145, 147, 171, 172, 177, 188, 206
act-object analysis, 172-3, 174
adverbial analysis, 172-3, 174
Allison, H.E., 159
Anselm, 82
anti-realism, 18-20, 32, 132, 202
Aristotle, 9, 40, 77, 82, 167, 169
Armstrong, D.M., 53, 54-5
Arnauld, 7
Aschenbrenner, K., 126
atheism, 12, 13-15, 49, 125, 138, 152, 154
Augustine, 82, 178
Ayer, A.J., 16, 60
Ayers, M.R., x, xiii, 9, 48, 93, 146, 165

Bacon, F., 43
Bayle, P., xi, 1, 2, 6-7, 15, 73, 209
Bennett, J., xii, 2, 31, 74, 95, 96, 97, 101, 117-29, 145, 170
Bohm, D., 182
Boyle, R., 1, 8-9, 10, 189, 198
Bracken, H., 5

causal dependence argument, 125, 192-9

causal theory of perception, 77-9, 80
causality, 23, 26, 44, 52, 74, 99, 121, 127-9, 147-8, 149, 151, 167, 173, 186, 189-91, 194-9
common sense, 17-22, 47, 109, 130
conceivability, 28-40, 112-13, Chapter Four passim
continuity, 14, 102, 117-29
corpuscularianism, xi, 8-11, 20, 26, 148, 149
counterfactuals, *see* Subjunctive conditionals
Cummins, P., 71-2, 80

Davidson, D., 140
Democritus, 8
Descartes, R., xi, 2-3, 9, 139, 143, 148, 149, 158, 159, 160, 164, 165, 171, 184, 187, 193-4
Dicker, G., 62, 65
distinction principle, 168-74
dualism, 9, 109, 139-41, 173-4
Dummett, M.A.E., 132-7

empiricism, 4, 28, 32, 40
esse est percipi, passim, *see esp.* Chapter Two
esse est percipi, passim, *see esp.* Chapter Two

215

216 Index

evil, 185-6
existence, see Chapters Two & Three, passim

Fardell, M-A., 5-6, 7
features, 40-2
finite spirit, passim, see esp. 151-67
Foster, J.A., 107-8, 167
Foucher, S., 6
Frege, G., 35-6
Furlong, E.J., 174

Galileo, G., 8
Garber, D., 11
God, passim, see esp. 184-203
Grayling, A.C., 43, 104, 109
Grice, H.P., 79

Hobbes, T., 9
Hume, D., xiii, 23, 28, 40, 51, 87, 88, 89, 92, 156, 157, 162, 165, 189, 191, 192, 193-4

idealism (and see Immaterialism), 17, 96, 119, 205
ideas, passim, see esp. 50-81, 168-74
identity, 25-6, 34-6, 86, 95
identity principle, 168-74
imaginability, 32-4, 37-8
immaterialism, x, xi, 142-3, 201
infinite spirit, see God
infinity, 188
inherence principle, 168-74

James, W., 140
Jessop, T.E., xiii, 51, 178, 184, 189
Johnson, S., 13, 14, 45, 99, 103, 124, 155, 156, 158, 175, 176-7, 180, 181, 182, 183, 185

Kant, I., xiii, 39-40, 87-8, 89, 92, 152, 165, 166, 167, 180, 191, 208-9
Kirwan, C., 36-9

Laws of Nature, 23, 52, 74, 103, 121-4, 126, 141-2
Leibnitz, G., 35
levels 1, 2, 3, passim, see esp. 22-46
likeness principle, 80, 173
Locke, J., xi, xiii, 1, 2, 8, 9-12, 20, 25, 27, 28, 30-1, 34-5, 40, 43, 50, 52, 56, 74, 76, 79-80, 90, 94, 139, 143, 144, 146, 148, 149, 153, 157, 158-9, 160, 164, 165, 173, 175, 176, 177, 178, 187, 189-90, 193-4
Luce, A.A., ix, xii, xiii, xiv, 3, 48, 81, 95, 96, 114, 169, 174, 181, 184

Mackie, J., 56, 79, 139, 149
Malebranche, xi, 1, 2, 3-6, 10, 52, 99, 100, 140, 144, 149, 150-1, 159, 198
Marc-Wogau, C., 95
materialism, passim
matter, passim, see esp. 2, 4, 13, 15, 138-53
McCracken, C.J., 5
McGinn, C., 57, 73, 204-10
meaning (and see Sensefulness, Conceivability), 11, 19, 27-8, 42-4, 54, 91
Meinong, A., 82
Mill, J.S., 106
mind, passim, see Causality, Dualism, Substance
Mirarchi, L.A., 138
Moore, G.E., 83-4, 91

Index

New Principle, passim, *see esp.* Chapter Two
Newton, I., 1, 8, 176-77, 198
nominalism, 18
notions, 36, 50, 147, 160, 187, Chapter Three passim

Parfitt, D., 165
parity argument, 147, 156
Peacock, C., 57, 64
Pears, D.F., 84, 85, 91
perceivability, 94-117
perception, passim, *see esp.* 10, 15-17, 25-7, Chapter Two passim, 168-74
personal identity, 159, *and see* Time
phenomenalism, x, 16, 27, 60, 96, 97, 118, 124
phenomenology of experience, *see* Levels 1, 2, 3
physical objects, passim, *see esp.* Chapter Two
Pitcher, G., xii, 17, 22, 24-6, 34, 35, 63, 67-9, 71, 78-9, 102-3, 108, 109-13, 168, 169, 171, 174, 178, 179, 180
Plato, 18, 169, 170, 176, 208
Popkin, R., 3, 5
Positivists, 40
possibility, 36-40
'powers' theory, 96-101, 111-12, 157
primary qualities, *see* Sensible qualities
Pyrrho, 6-7, 73
Pyrrhonism, 4, 6-7

Quine, W.V.O., 85, 86

rationalism, 205-9
realism, 18-22, 37, 55, 56, 110, 129-37, 172, Chapter Four passim
reality, passim, *see esp.* 15-17, 61, 94, 102, 119-20, 130, 131, Chapter Four passim
Robinson, H., 115-16, 141, 167
Russell, B., 16, 35, 71-2, 82, 140
Ryle, G., 191

Salt, R., 3
scepticism, 3-6, 6-7, 10-11, 12, 14-17, 48-9, 125, 138, 152, 154
schoolmen, 28, 144, 148, 149
science, 141-3
Searle, R., 141
secondary qualities, *see* Sensible qualities
selfhood, *see* Finite spirit
sense-data, 16, 59
sensefulness, 27-40, 72
sensible qualities, passim, *see esp.* 2-12, 50-81
Sextus Empiricus, 8
signs, 75, 138, 141-3, 190-1
solipsism, 17
solitary man, 43-4, 179
Sommers, F., 40-2
Sosa, E., 191
Spinoza, B., 2, 93, 140, 176, 184
spirit, *see* Finite spirit, Infinite spirit, Substance
Sprigge, T.L.S., 167, 187
Steinkraus, W.E., 213
Stillingfleet, 9, 153
Strawson, P.F., 39-40, 84, 85, 187
Stroud, B., 74, 76
subjunctive conditionals, 103-6, 133-4
substance, xi, 2, 4, 9, 13, 15, 40, 48-9, 93, 97, 145-6, 147, 148,

153, Chapter Three passim
suggestion, 62, 63-4

Taylor, R., 3
teleological argument, 125, 194-9
time, 45, 174-83
Tipton, I.C., xii, 2, 9, 17, 22, 62, 65-6, 71, 72, 113, 126, 145, 156, 174, 175, 178, 179, 192, 193
tree argument, 113-17
truth, 19, 56-7, 132-7
Turbayne, C., 168, 169, 170

Vesey, G., 213
vision, 23-4, 24-5, 28-9, 63, 77-8
volition, 191, *and see* Will

Warnock, G.J., xii, 16, 70-1, 78, 126-7
White, A.R., 106
will, passim, *see esp.* 158-67
Wilson, M., 74
Wittgenstein, L., 27, 178, 191

Xenophon, 188

Zeno, 6, 7, 73, 177